Active Analysis

Active Analysis combines two of Maria Knebel's most important books, *On Active Analysis of the Play and the Role* and *The Word in the Actor's Creative Work*, in a single edition conceived and edited by one of Knebel's most famous students, the renowned theatre and film director, Anatoli Vassiliev.

This is the first English translation of an important and authoritative fragment of the great Stanislavski jigsaw. A landmark publication.

This book is an indispensable resource for professional directors, student directors, actors and researchers interested in Stanislavski, directing, rehearsal methods and theatre studies more generally.

Maria Knebel was an actor, director, teacher, author of five books and pioneer of 'active analysis'. She is, arguably, one of the most influential theatre pedagogues in 20th-century Russian theatre. Knebel was a student of Michael Chekhov, Nemirovich-Danchenko, and Stanislavski with whom she collaborated closely during his final years at the Opera-Dramatic Studio. She was instrumental in promoting and disseminating their acting and directing methodologies through her own teaching and directing practice.

Anatoli Vassiliev is one of Europe's leading theatre directors, theatre innovators and pedagogues. He trained at GITIS (the Russian State Academy of Theatre Arts) under Maria Knebel and Andrei Popov. In 1987 Vassiliev founded his own theatre company School of Dramatic Art in Moscow, a creative experimental laboratory, which he ran until 2006. He has directed many internationally acclaimed productions both with his own company and with others, including the Comédie Française and L'Odéon in Paris, TNS in Strasbourg, and the Hellenic Festival in Epidaurus. He has taught all over the world, including at GITIS and VGIK in Moscow, the Grotowski Institute in Wroclaw, ENSATT in Lyon, Isola della Pedagogia in Venice, and the Royal National Theatre and the Stanislavski Centre for Contemporary Practice at Rose Bruford College in London.

Irina Brown, originally from St Petersburg, has lived and worked in Britain since 1978. She is a theatre and opera director, dramaturge, translator and theatre pedagogue. A former Artistic Director of the Tron Theatre, Glasgow, she has directed for the Royal National Theatre, the Royal Opera House in London's West End and internationally. She is Programme Director of the MA/MFA in Contemporary Directing Practice and Curator of the Stanislavski Centre at Rose Bruford College of Theatre and Performance, London.

D1438441

"Maria Knebel's contribution to contemporary actor training is invaluable and to date, somewhat under-estimated. This much anticipated book – thoughtfully edited by Vassiliev and sensitively translated by Irina Brown – brings crystal-clear understanding of Stanislavsky's innovative 'active analysis' into sharp focus and easy implementation."

Bella Merlin, actor and professor at the
University of California, Riverside, USA

Active Analysis

Maria Knebel

Text compiled and edited by Anatoli Vassiliev

Translated by Irina Brown

With the support of
Anatoli Vassiliev's Foundation for the Development of Dramatic Arts

Фонд развития искусства драматического театра Анатолия Васильева

Routledge
Taylor & Francis Group

LONDON AND NEW YORK

Maria Knebel

Maria Knebel was born in Moscow in 1898. She joined Michael Chekhov's Studio at the age of 19. From 1921 she continued her training at the Second Studio of the Moscow Art Theatre, where she remained a member of the acting company until 1949. She made the transition from acting to directing in 1935, at a time when women were rarely entrusted with such a job. While continuing to act at Moscow Art Theatre, she began directing at the newly formed theatre studio named after Yermolova. In 1936 Stanislavski invited her to join him as an Assistant Pedagogue in his research into theatre training at the Opera-Dramatic Studio. There Knebel taught the Mastery of the Word ('stage speech'), experimenting together with Stanislavski with etudes and improvisations, as he perfected his method of 'physical actions' and 'active analysis'. It was a formative pedagogical experience for Knebel. In 1940 she went on to teach acting at the Shchepkin Theatre Institute. In 1948 she joined the GITIS Directing Department, where she taught directing, later becoming the Chair of the Department until her death in 1985. In the 1950s she was Artistic Director of the Central Children's Theatre in Moscow, opening doors into the profession to a whole new generation of actors, directors and playwrights.

In 1954, in her book *The Word in the Actor's Creative Work*, Maria Knebel set out to summarise the entirety of Stanislavski's work, including his latter-day discoveries. That book was quickly followed by another, *On Active Analysis of the Play and the Role*, which instantly became the indispensable textbook for generations of Russian theatre practitioners, a key reference point that illuminated the Stanislavski system. Aided by her many recollections of the classes and conversations with the founding father of the Moscow Art Theatre, she endeavoured to provide a theoretical perspective on acting itself, in which a continuous creative search leads to an organic unity of mind and body.

Book One was published under its original title *On Active Analysis of the Play and the Role* by Iskusstvo Publishing House, Moscow in 1959. A second edition came out in 1961, which added several new chapters. This book is based on the second edition.

Book Two was published in Moscow in 1970 by Iskusstvo/VTO (the All-Russia Theatre Society) under its original title of *The Word in the Actor's Creative Work*, edited by Nikolai Gorchakov. It was based on Maria Knebel's notes from her third-year Directing course of lectures on 'Verbal Action in the Stanislavski System', GITIS, 1954.

The Russian text, compiled, edited and verified by Anatoli Vassiliev, is based on these original editions.

Cover image: From the personal archive of Natalia Alekseievna Zvereva, theatre pedagogue and director, and Maria Knebel's close collaborator. Photographed from the original by theatre photographer Aleksander Ivanishin.

First published 2021
by Routledge
4 Park Square, Milton Park, Abingdon, Oxon OX14 4RN

and by Routledge
605 Third Avenue, New York, NY 10158

Routledge is an imprint of the Taylor & Francis Group, an informa business

British Library Cataloguing-in-Publication Data
A catalogue record for this book is available from the British Library

Library of Congress Cataloging-in-Publication Data
A catalog record for this book has been requested

ISBN: 978-0-415-49852-4 (hbk)
ISBN: 978-0-415-49853-1 (pbk)
ISBN: 978-0-203-12520-5 (ebk)

DOI: 10.4324/9780203125205

Typeset in Bembo
by Apex CoVantage, LLC

Contents

Translator's note

In translating this book I drew inspiration from Jean Benedetti's approach to his translation of Stanislavski. Maria Knebel often quotes from Stanislavski's books published in English under the title *An Actor's Work*. Jean Benedetti's learned and vivid translation of *An Actor's Work* became an indispensable source and training ground for me. However, in a number of places small sections of his translation had to be adapted so that Knebel's comments would relate directly to the original text.

I would like to express my deep gratitude to Anatoli Vassiliev for entrusting me with the translation of this volume, and for his time, patience and generosity in sharing with me his knowledge, insight and experience regarding the issues discussed in the book.

I would also like to acknowledge the unstinting support of Inna Schorr and Stone Nest, as well as the indispensable contribution made by my colleagues and friends Robert Price and Kristin Corbet-Milward, who kindly reviewed my translation and offered invaluable feedback both in terms of language and subject matter.

Notes on the text

Stanislavski, Konstantin Sergeievich (17 January 1863–7 August 1938): as Knebel points out in her foreword, some material used in her books is based on her own private notes as an eyewitness and participant in the process of Stanislavski's discoveries. In the original Russian, she mostly uses Stanislavski's surname when she quotes from the official sources, but when she recalls her own personal experience, she uses his first name and patronymic, 'Konstantin Sergeievich'. This gives it a warm and 'distinctive' sense of their relationship, and conjures up the immediacy both of the encounter and the text that follows. However, to make it easier for the English-speaking reader, I have mostly referred to him as 'Stanislavski', keeping his first name and patronymic in just a few particular instances.

Michael Chekhov: I have used the Anglicised version of Michael Chekhov's name throughout the book because of its familiarity to English-speaking readers. However, in the chapter 'I am Mikhail Chekhov's Student', I have reverted to his Russian name and patronymic 'Mikhail Aleksandrovich' or just 'Mikhail' since the story in that chapter takes place long before his emigration in 1928 first to Germany, then to Britain and later to the USA where he made his name as 'Michael Chekhov'.

Square brackets: used throughout the book to indicate those passages and dialogues based on Knebel's personal record of Stanislavski's classes or their private meetings.

Pronouns: although in the original Russian text 'an actor' or 'a director' always uses a masculine pronoun, I have made a decision to use 'they' wherever possible in acknowledgement of present-day sensibilities.

Footnotes: can be found at the bottom of the page to assist the reader in their understanding of specific Russian references or particulars of terminology.

Endnotes: have been used for bibliographical references.

Appendices: Knebel uses examples from a number of popular Soviet plays that were part of the repertoire at the time. Although the reader may not be familiar with these, Knebel always provides clear context to support the reader's understanding of the material.

Literary texts: a number of literary examples are used in translations referenced in the endnotes. I have translated the rest as literally as possible (including Griboyedov's *Woe from Wit* and Pushkin's *Gypsies*) so that Knebel's analysis and references can be readily understood.

Beginnings

Reader! Don't bother reading this introduction, go straight to *Active Analysis*, turn over these futile couple of pages ... No, wait, hear me out. It was so long ago, so very long ago it was: the year 1968 in the Soviet Union, just like in your country, was a turning point. Our country was finished with 'the Thaw', and 'the Stagnation' was coming, a period that we looked back on with nostalgia during Perestroika. So, it was then, in 1968, that I took entrance exams to get into GITIS,[1] but instead of Anatoly Efros's course – he had just been shown the door for his production of *Three Sisters* – I applied to study under Andrei Popov, an actor – playful, gentle, remarkable – just as he was in everyday life. That is when the Chair of the Directing Department, Maria Osipovna Knebel, assessed me, an entrant, in my Directing oral. 'Why do you want to be in theatre?', 'What's theatre to you?'. 'It's my whole life', I showed off, and, shamefaced, noted to myself – a direct hit to her heart.

At the end of this book you will find a chapter on Michael Chekhov from Knebel's book *My Whole Life*. It is a sublime piece of writing about theatre, particularly the pages about his Russian period, a magical piece! I embarked on studying the art of directing under Andrei Popov. Our year was a large group of students, freethinking, hard to manage. So they split us, by then a close-knit fellowship, into two halves – for the sake of keeping us in order, and I, anticipating disaster and mentally protesting, took my place on a school-bench in the little old woman's class.[2] I detested everything about her now, most of all those who surrounded her: my new teachers, her undergraduates and final-year students, the syllabus, pedantry and nothing but. I dreamt of the freedom they stripped me of. I wanted to drop out of GITIS, and I remember how, once, I walked down the stairs past the bust of Lenin and tried to pluck up the courage to open the door into the poplar park outside and return to the sea, the sea I had left behind to become a theatre apprentice! I was always late, dressed to

---

1 GITIS, an abbreviation for the State Institute of Theatre Arts (now the Russian Institute of Theatre Arts) in Moscow (trans. note).
2 Reference to Knebel (trans. note).

DOI: 10.4324/9780203125205-1

shock, and at one point even sported a metal chain as a trouser-belt; I walked around in a torn leather jacket, and was outraged by having to do those absurd improvisations: you're a migratory bird, and you – a domestic one. I had no wish to be a goose! Nor did I want to be a crocodile, nor to pick wee flowers in a wee meadow, or impersonate a happy horse, or the torments of a cheated husband – all that after the freewheeling compositions with Andrei Popov, indulged by him …

Having started at the top of the class, I was turning into a pariah, while the grey mediocrity scrambled up to the top – there were some among us with no talent, but I had never thought of myself as one of them. I leap-frogged to the bottom of the class, and by the end of my second year my expulsion from GITIS was on the agenda at the departmental meeting. 'What do you think you're wearing?!', said Maria Knebel, hurting my feelings. I wore a black silk scarf over my torn leather. 'You look like a hair-dresser! No dress sense!' So what? I dreamt of love-making on the stage, built a bed, covered it with a dark blue velvet, and my classmates, a boy and a girl, barefoot (which was far too much for the Soviet sensibility!), their heels tightly nestling against each other, cried and laughed, and loved each other with their palms, and parted for ever with their backs. It was a near 'fail', but Maria Knebel fought for me at the departmental meeting against the wrath of the Communist puritans and the spite of the truly salacious prudes. I started my third year.

An introduction should be brief, but the story of my student life was a long one, and my teacher and master tested my obedience. We began our third year with etudes based on Chekhov's *Ivanov*. I loved Chekhov at the time, particularly his *Ivanov*, the sufferings of a Moscow Hamlet, his suicide – well suited to my fits of hypochondria. Etudes, as taught by Knebel, demanded artistic concentration as well as some kind of – not yet clear to me – scientific and professional approach, taking me back to happy times at the University and the Chemistry Department, as everything began to form up a precise, legitimate and grammatically correct pattern while being simultaneously liberated for an improvisation. It is hard to remember now whether I succeeded as an actor in my etudes, most likely not, not yet; it took me a year to be able to be organic onstage. For me a real revelation about theatre was the moment when I suddenly discovered that I was onstage doing nothing, and that turned out to be the genuine action.

As a student director I instantly fell in love with etudes in my very first year under Popov, but it was under Maria Knebel that I mastered the science of how to be in command of and apply the technique. All of a sudden the essence of the art of theatre, how that essence manifested itself, and who was its truth-bearer, became clear to me – the director – through my own experience as an actor; the secrets of directing were revealed to me through the art of acting. During the year of my protest I had been full of sarcasm and spite. I had a slim little book by M.O. Knebel entitled *The Word in the Actor's Creative*

Work. I crossed out 'K' and wrote 'M' instead, turning it into M.O. Mebel,[3] and I quipped, 'Knebel – for the people' as in 'Mebel (furniture) – for the people'. On the front page, forging her handwriting, I inscribed: 'Tolya, be a good boy. Your teacher.' Signed: M.O. Mebel. Now, trying to heal my wounded vanity, I became extra diligent in my etudes, but, reader, the best was yet to come! When I objected to and fought against the Department's attacks by using 'the rural theme', setting up a peasant-cart onstage, creating foliage shadows, or imitating the wind and the clatter of hooves, I had been just a little boy of theatre. I was growing up now.

In the February of my third year I was at Knebel's, reading her my adaptation of Dostoyevsky's *The Possessed*, five hours on the trot. Knebel listened, not a sign of boredom or exhaustion on her face. I wanted to do *The Possessed* with my fellow-students, but my personal story took a different turn, away from the gloomy and terrifying account of Russian life. The play chosen for our etudes was *Tales of the Old Arbat* by a Soviet playwright Alexei Arbuzov, whose work I knew well and really loved. For my entrance exam, I developed an explication for his play *My Poor Marat*. Delighted, I started working privately on scenes from *The Tales*, when out of the blue Knebel appointed me the Head Student of our year, entrusting me to direct the comedy with my fellow-students. It was not something anyone could have expected. This was the first time ever that the Course Master-Director had pulled out of directing a production on the Directing Department syllabus, and offered it to a student-director. For almost a year I was virtually in charge of both pedagogy and directing.

Reader, what else, what else? A postcard from Knebel to Oleg Yefremov[4] with a reference for me, my joining the Moscow Art Theatre as a trainee director, the success of *The Solo for a Clock with Chimes*, then, with gratitude, a bouquet of roses for Maria Knebel's birthday on May 19th, dress-runs of *Vassa Zheleznova* and *The Grown-Up Daughter of a Young Man* just for Maria Knebel in an otherwise empty auditorium. No, do not bother to read my introduction, reader, instead go straight to the two fundamental texts of Russian theatre, two manifestos on the art of psychological theatre. On the skill of acting the way you speak, and the skill of speaking the way you act! If my experience has not convinced you, let my mentor convince you herself. Let her teach you to be organic, teach you silence, ethics and action – that's where theatre begins.

With gratitude to my teacher, with gratitude to everyone who has been part of making this book available to the English-speaking reader. I am happy that my mentor's teachings are in your hands now. Read, reader. Study, student.

Anatoli Vassiliev

---

3 *Mebel* means 'furniture' in Russian: from German *Möbel* (trans. note).
4 Oleg Yefremov was Artistic Director of the Moscow Art Theatre from 1970 to 2000 (trans. note).

About Maria Knebel

It seems that Providence played a hand in her destiny. It is not surprising that when questioned by an inquisitive student whether the Creator existed, Professor Maria Knebel waved her away with an ironic 'Don't you doubt it'.

Her father, a native of a small Galician shtetl, came from a large poverty-stricken Jewish family. Having learnt Russian as a grown man, he became a great connoisseur of Russian art and a torch-bearer for enlightenment.

His life, reminiscent of a Hollywood movie, reveals Maria's own journey in a wondrous light, with her impact on the history of theatre becoming more and more acknowledged. No wonder – she initiated a radical change in the thinking of a whole generation of theatre directors.

In the 1860s Maria's father left his parental home as a teenager with a small bundle over his shoulder and made his way to Vienna in search of his fortune. He cleaned boots, starved and studied: at a secondary school, then a medical school, then at the Institute of Commerce. He spent all his free time visiting museums, having caught the fine arts bug.

And then … wait for this! On their graduation day, all his fellow-students drew lots: where to go and look for work? On one of the many pieces of paper there was a name of an exotic country – Russia. That was the one picked by Joseph Knebel. His friends' raucous laughter was stifled by his determination to follow his lot. He brushed aside all the arguments that his intention was sheer madness, and left for Moscow with not a penny in his pocket.

Countless events occurred between the day he joined a German bookshop as a sales assistant and the emergence of the 'Joseph Knebel Publishing House'. His encounter with the art collector Pavel Tretyakov[1] was the one to define his fate.

Maria Knebel's father found himself in a curious land at a rare point in its history when it resolutely progressed. Russia never moves at an even trot. She either gallops away, or stumbles and falls, then struggles back to her feet and hurtles forth again. Taking the world by surprise – it is what she does best.

---

1 Pavel Tretyakov (1832–1898), a Russian merchant and textile manufacturer. He bequeathed his art collection to the city of Moscow. This collection served as the core of the Tretyakov Gallery, the largest collection of Russian fine art in the world (ed. note).

DOI: 10.4324/9780203125205-2

Who in the West could have imagined that theatre regeneration was to come out of Moscow? At the time, having finally rejected slavery,[2] the country was determined to make up for lost opportunities.

Once the merchant class realised the benefits of disseminating knowledge, they got down to business on a characteristically grand scale. They opened museums and galleries. Not just any old gallery or museum but exemplary ones. Encyclopaedias, reference books and dictionaries were being published. Societies for the support of artists, charitable foundations and grants were established, invitations were issued to European singers to come over. Muscovites grew as proud of their Symphony Orchestra as they once had been of their market stalls. The chair of the Assembly for promoting the development of national music was a factory-owner, the Governor's cousin, Konstantin Alekseev, who performed in amateur circles under the name of Stanislavski. He set up the Society of Art and Literature. Savva Mamontov, the amateur actor's relative, built railways creating a network that connected the furthermost 'bear-infested' corners of the country. In his house he brought together new artistic talents. Mamontov discovered Mussorgsky and Rimsky-Korsakov, nurtured Chaliapin, and built an exhibition pavilion for Vrubel's paintings.

Without merchant-patrons of the arts, Moscow would have been like Florence without the Medici. Tretyakov presented the city with the Gallery of Russian Art, one of the Shchukin brothers collected paintings by the Impressionists and exhibited them for free, the other brother opened the Museum of Antiquities. There was a new Theatre Museum. Book publishing flourished.

Joseph Knebel by now had mastered Russian (by the end of his life he spoke fourteen languages), and was caught up in the whirlwind of Moscow life. He, a foreigner, saw more clearly than some native Russians what a unique moment it was. Being an admirer of icon paintings as well as Russian modernists' experimentations, he was puzzled: why were they not known to the outside world?

Knebel's admiration and confusion led him to Tretyakov with a proposal to publish reproductions of the paintings from the Tretyakov collection. When asked, 'What capital do you have at your disposal?', the young enthusiast replied honestly: 'Not a kopek'. But if he got the permission to have the paintings photographed, he would persuade photographers to do it on credit, and the printing-house to give him paper and print albums on credit, too. He had no doubt that his enterprise would succeed, and offered Tretyakov all the profit from it.

'How much are you going to keep for yourself?', the money-man roared with laughter.

'Nothing. But I'd like to keep all the profits from the second edition.'

Tretyakov decided that the person in front of him was either extremely talented, or completely mad – most likely mad. Since he risked nothing personally, he mulled it over and agreed to have his collection photographed. Knebel's fate was set.

---

2 This refers to the emancipation of the serfs in 1861 (ed. note).

Soon in every respectable household – as they used to call it then – there were albums, monographs, children's books, books on the history of architecture and the history of costume, all of them published by Knebel. The books took pride of place among owners' possessions – they were works of art in themselves. The typeface, illustrations, the interleafing between the pages, all spoke of the publisher's supreme taste and his awareness of his high educational mission.

Joseph (later baptised as 'Osip') Knebel's apartment, in the same building as his publishing house and the bookshop, soon turned into a favourite meeting place for writers, philosophers and painters.

The list of people Masha[3] Knebel met at her parent's house reads like an encyclopaedia of Russian artistic life. To pick but one, her guide into the world of art was Igor Grabar,[4] a friend of her father's. Together with Masha, her sister and her brother he staged *tableaux vivants* based on different paintings. Her memories of Levitan, Roerich, Benois and Dobuzhinsky,[5] or of sitting on Leo Tolstoy's lap while he told her a fairy-tale, helped Maria Knebel, the actress, director and pedagogue, to survive the trying times she was destined to live in.

Dostoyevsky says in *The Brothers Karamazov*: 'Nothing is better, or stronger, or healthier, or more beneficial for one's life than a wonderful memory of some kind, especially if it comes from childhood, from the parental home. ... If a person brings a multitude of such memories with him into his life, then he is saved for as long as he lives.'

Maria Knebel was saved, having just started to live.

She worshipped her father. She inherited from him many qualities to be proud of: his zest for life, fortitude, tenacity in pursuing goals, seasoned with a healthy dose of risk-taking, a mixture of idealism and a sober pragmatism. What is more, she inherited his educational mission (so in tune with the Russian sense of the messianic role of art).

Most probably that is why Maria Knebel came into her own in pedagogy, a discipline that requires a clear sense of one's mission.

The second half of her long life was, for the most part, devoted to pedagogy and the great tasks closely connected with it, which Knebel took upon herself. Surprisingly, she succeeded in accomplishing them despite the fact that the prevailing historical circumstances, all that Russian tumult, were not conducive to such things.

It is easy to identify these tasks among Knebel's multifaceted interests.

The first task. To save for posterity the character and discoveries of Michael Chekhov,[6] whose Studio she joined as a nineteen-year-old girl. It was thanks

---

3 Masha is short for Maria (trans. note).

4 Igor Grabar (1871–1960), painter, restorer and art historian. A member of the artistic fellowship World of Art. Before World War I, Grabar wrote a number of monographs on Russian painters for the Joseph Knebel Publishing House. His book on Repin was published in 1937 (ed. note).

5 Russian Symbolists and stage-designers, part of the World of Art movement (ed. note).

6 Michael Chekhov (1891–1955), the son of Anton Chekhov's elder brother Alexander. At sixteen he joined the Suvorin Theatre, St Petersburg, at nineteen became an actor at the Maly Theatre,

to him that she realised: 'A teacher's creative personality is a powerful formative force.'

Unlike most of his colleagues, Chekhov was not as concerned with the
result as with getting the grasp of internal and external acting techniques. He
believed the actor had to master them until they developed into *new capacities
of his soul.*

There is a well-known Stanislavski quote that his system must be studied by
observing Misha[7] Chekhov, whose acting expresses it fully. But like any true
disciple, Chekhov searched for his own answers to the secrets of his craft. At
the point when, due to his mental illness,[8] Chekhov was not able to perform
in public, he craved contact with young people at his own Studio. Chekhov's
classes made Knebel, still a schoolgirl at the time, give up her ambition of devot-
ing her life to mathematics and instead hurled her in the direction of theatre.

Her father was not at all thrilled with such an unexpected turnaround. But
despite bringing his children up very strictly, he never stood in the way of their
true passion. It was clear that Maria was spellbound by the sacred mysteries that
took place at the Chekhov Studio.

In her memoir, *My Whole Life*, she conjures up, with enviable powers of
observation, the atmosphere of the Studio, Chekhov's anguish and spiritual
search, his way of rehearsing. In the book she presents Chekhov's disagree-
ments with Stanislavski as an error of judgement that led this astonishing actor
to his inner crisis and emigration. (What was that about? She must have done
it in response to the demands of the time.)

For some reason the actor's escape from the country is branded as a mistake
in her book. And yet it is well known that the warrant for his arrest had been
issued already. Chekhov would have met the same fate as Meyerhold and the
many others who were murdered by the Bolsheviks.

Now it seems that the zeal with which Knebel went about making sure that
Michael Chekhov's creative legacy saw the light of day, in his native land, may
have been provoked by her desire to overcome her own fear of the powers that
had cast him out.

Maria considered it her life's duty to bring her teacher back to Russia, if only
in print. She said that she could not – must not – die until that was accomplished. 'I must' were two words Knebel used constantly.

A lot of her efforts went into persuading the oafs in high authority that the
publication of her teacher's books was essential, but she always came up against
the same obstacle: 'Chekhov? the follower of Steiner's ideas? Out of the question! Not now, not ever!'

Moscow, at twenty joined the Moscow Art Theatre. An actor of genius: many of the roles he played
left an indelible mark on the history of Russian theatre. In 1928 he emigrated to Germany, and then
to the USA in 1938 (ed. note).

7　Misha is short for Mikhail (Michael) (trans. note).

8　See more at the end of the book in an excerpt from Maria Knebel's memoirs *My Whole Life* (ed.
note).

Maria even started to frequent gatherings of some Marxist philosophers in the hope of finding a loophole in the impenetrable wall of their materialistic ideology through which she could smuggle in Chekhov's anthroposophy.

It had been much easier for Joseph Knebel, poor as he was, to talk to the millionaire Tretyakov. But had her father been alive, he would have been proud of his daughter. She did get what she had been fighting for, and lived long enough to see the publication of the first volume of Michael Chekhov's works – though not long enough to see the second volume come out. She never learnt that the censors, who also denounced Knebel's introduction as a political error typical of the idealist philosophy, banned its publication.

Maybe it was for the best that she had never learnt that, and left this world with a sense of having fulfilled her duty to her teacher. Which she did indeed.

Knebel's other task was to disseminate the method of active analysis that was passed to her directly by Stanislavski.

She got into the Moscow Art Theatre (MAT)[9] via its Second Studio where creative independence and initiative were nurtured and encouraged. Maria often repeated the motto she fell in love with at the time: 'No one can be taught; everyone can be self-taught.'

It was there that she first got interested in directing. But she never seriously considered doing it. Nevertheless, it seems quite auspicious that as a young Studio member Knebel first appeared on the MAT stage as a daughter of Dr Stockmann played by Stanislavski.[10]

And then …? From then on she lived under the spell of the MAT creator's charismatic personality, unwaveringly loyal to him. Meyerhold once came to see Knebel in Dostoyevsky's *Uncle's Dream* and paid her a visit backstage: There isn't much else you can do here at the MAT! Such a physical and comedic role comes once in a blue moon, doesn't it? Come and join my company. No future for you here.' According to Maria, she never even gave it another thought.

Still the temptation must have been great. In the 1920s avant-garde theatre reached the crest of the revolutionary wave. At the same time the Moscow Art Theatre – the theatre of the Russian intelligentsia – was desperately floundering about, looking for a way to survive. It was not clear whether they could make it to the shore, navigating to safety through the stormy events of those damned days that carried artistically inclined youth further and further to the left …

The young actress managed to hold back from changing sides thanks to the ethics and aesthetics of the Moscow Art Theatre being close to the tastes cultivated at her father's house, and to everything she had absorbed at the Michael Chekhov Studio. As for Meyerhold, his words proved to be prophetic.

Maria's lot at the MAT was not a happy one. Increasingly lavished with government honours the MAT turned into a showcase establishment for spectacles. After the demise of the theatre's founding fathers, Knebel's position went from bad to worse.

9 MAT – abbreviation for the Moscow Art Theatre ('MXT' in Russian) (trans. note).
10 Doctor Stockmann – a character in Ibsen's play *An Enemy of the People* (trans. note).

But she never wavered from being a true disciple. She lived for the Art Theatre that had once been the standard of fine acting. She lived for Stanislavski, with his experiments and eccentricities who to his dying day sought 'the blue bird' of truth.

The Soviet image of Stanislavski as a sort of all-knowing theatrical Stalin is a sham. Communists, while smothering the culture with sanctimonious deviousness, canonised the director so that they could use him in their fight against dissent. It seems that in the very idea of 'the system' they saw something absolute that would allow them to induce order into the most disorderly of all things – creativity.

Stanislavski invited Maria to teach at his Studio, when he was no longer able to and, by all accounts, did not want to go anywhere near the MAT. At death's door, he felt an urgent need to pass on to those he trusted the new working method he had discovered. He suggested that Knebel should do as he himself was doing: 'teach and learn'.

She became the Master's right-hand person in the sessions he conducted at his house. Away from the hustle and bustle of the theatre, from its practical preoccupations, Stanislavski concentrated on his theoretical work. As a director, he always found it hard to realise his fresh ideas under the 'standard operating conditions'. Now he was in a rush to share his latest research, anticipating that it could take theatre to a qualitatively different level.

Maria was asked to focus on the issues of 'artistic recitation' and 'verbal action' – part and parcel of the innovative approach to making productions based on text-analysis done *in action*.

It took Knebel years to interpret that discovery and find ways and means of realising it in the process of rehearsals. Her books convey the essence of that experiment in such depth that they have become handbooks for anyone practising theatre.

They require a thoughtful reading. There is no point in giving a quick summary of the method that liberates actors from inertia and expands their potential – no one can do it better than Knebel. Let's just say that its foundation is the salutary spirit of improvisation that had so enchanted Maria at the Studio of her first teacher, Michael Chekhov.

Knebel's third task – bringing Stanislavski's teachings together with the theoretical legacy of the other MAT's founder, Vladimir Nemirovich-Danchenko[11] – turned out to be the most complex of all and the hardest issue to resolve. Conscious of this as she was, she never ceased trying to find a solution. She succeeded in going down that road as far as it was possible, for as long as she could justify it.

11 Vladimir Nemirovich-Danchenko (1858–1943), writer, stage director, co-founder and joint Artistic Director of the Moscow Arts Theatre (together with Stanislavski). The whole of that theatre's history is marked by a complex personal relationship between the two directors. Less known in the West than Stanislavski, Nemirovich-Danchenko left behind vital literary works as well as his own theatrical theoretical legacy (ed. note).

Her determination is easily explained by the fact that she was one of the few *mkhatovets*[12] who managed to stay on good and creative terms with both leaders of the MAT who had been in a relationship of 'hostile friendship' for many years. She stayed above the violent skirmishes between the internal cliques at the theatre. The secret to her apparent impartiality could be found in the gift that later assured her pedagogical success: her ability to read people.

When asked about Stanislavski, her answer was succinct: 'A genius.'

When speaking of Nemirovich-Danchenko, her third mentor, she chose her words more carefully to express the magnitude and tragedy of his personality.

'The second plane', 'inner monologue', 'the nature of the character's attention and mentality' – these concepts were an integral part of the MAT's artistic endeavours instilled by Nemirovich-Danchenko into the actors' consciousness at every rehearsal.

Knebel could not rest easy, knowing that Nemirovich-Danchenko's practical experience and theoretical research were underrated, under-researched. She was convinced that his legacy must be used in educating the younger generations. She went out of her way to make sure that her students got a vivid sense of the rehearsals that she had taken part in. The direct outcome of this was her book *Nemirovich-Danchenko's School of Directing*, the best book ever written about this major theatrical figure.

The intervening period between Maria Knebel's times and today allows us to separate the essential from the secondary; sing praises to this, question that. But the turmoil of feelings that made up each passing day can easily go unnoticed. The incidental retreats into the shadows, while the essential reveals itself in a blinding light that destroys all semitones and nuances.

And yet, when we hear that one day Maria's father led her up to a mirror and asked her to have a closer look at herself before deciding if it was feasible to dream of the stage with looks like hers; or when we sense in her admiration for Michael Chekhov the young girl's heart beating faster – it is as if we are lifted by a warm wave and pulled into the depths of time, away from our cold rationality. There, in the past, we sense the hot flow of days.

It would be a pity if someone reading Knebel's books were to imagine her as an academic and dispassionate mentor. Such a woman could never have enthralled hundreds of students.

She was infectiously charismatic in spite of being, to a conventional eye, plain; she was audacious, damn clever, wickedly mischievous and funny. Quick shrewd eyes, a reassuring smile, instantaneous responses. Someone compared her to a little mouse, but oh no … She was more like a little monkey, poking fun at those who imagined they knew and understood her better than she did herself.

Looking at the grey-haired Knebel, it was easy to imagine her as Charlotta in *The Cherry Orchard*, a role she once played. So much in her appeared

---

12 A Russian name for the company-members of the Moscow Art Theatre, MAT, or 'MXT' in Russian, pronounced 'M-Kh-a-T', hence 'mkhatovets' (trans. note).

contradictory: her fortitude despite being ill-suited to everyday life, her keen curiosity about everything despite being very private herself, her readiness to face vicissitudes of life despite her child-like helplessness. Her many students, as they fought for the right to get a taxi for their professor from GITIS[13] to Studentcheskaya Street where she lived, or to see her to her door, could have exclaimed like an estate owner in a Chekhov play, 'Enchantress, I'm simply in love'.

She was infected with the bug of playfulness. In her youth she loved to act old women. She loved character-acting, its acute characterisation and outrageous physicality (think back on those Michael Chekhov lessons, and Meyerhold's invitation to join his company).

Her father on seeing her onstage for the first time said, 'If at twenty you play old women, when are you going to be young? I think, it is rather sad.'

He did not get a chance to witness the phenomenon of Maria's life: as years went by she grew younger. She even grew prettier. Perhaps by being in constant contact with the young, she was charged by their energy. Or perhaps it was because in the critical moments of her life she, just like her father, demonstrated singular will-power and remained true to her principles: she did not pursue material rewards, nor did she engage in frenzied battles with her adversaries, aware that the worst part of being the winner was to inherit the vices of the loser.

Her irregular features were further transformed by the inner light radiated only by those few lucky chosen ones who have found the purpose and meaning of their life on earth.

One of her colleagues at GITIS, whose relationship with her was far from perfect, christened her Mother Teresa of the Directing Faculty.

The opening sentence of her book *The Poetry of Pedagogy* – with the title that itself expressed the very essence of what she had lived for – says: 'Pedagogy requires a person to have qualities akin to those of a mother.'

She had no surviving children. One child died in infancy, the other at birth. That's all we know about the tragedy that had clearly left its mark. Not given to confidences, Maria kept private things private. Only a few isolated remarks, usually humorous in nature, might reveal to those close to her that her life as a woman had been a rich and complex one.

She chuckled and cut short a mutual friend of ours who tried to confide in her, 'It all sounds very familiar – I've had three husbands after all.'

She also preferred to keep her theatrical trials and tribulations to herself. If she had to speak of them, she did so reluctantly, with no drama. That's good breeding for you! Less focus on yourself, on your own feelings, more – on others. Her memoirs are full of tenderness for the people she writes about. The rest of it is left at the periphery of her consciousness – no, not even her

---

13 GITIS, an abbreviation for the State Institute of Theatre Arts (now the Russian Institute of Theatre Arts) in Moscow, largest and oldest independent theatre arts school in Russia. Maria Knebel began her work at the Directing Department there in 1948 (ed. note).

consciousness, but her narrative. She neither could nor wanted to talk about 'the rest of it', at most in passing, through hints. Her book *My Whole Life* is – in reality – only a part of it, a minuscule part of what she had been through.

We can only assume that the chapter on the MAT's rehearsals of the play about the Leader of the Proletariat, Lenin, would have been shorter, had her book been published after the Rottweiler-style censorship and the power that instigated it had ceased to exist. And yet, personally Maria owed a lot to the play's protagonist. After the Revolution, when her father was stripped of everything he had created through his hard work and talent, the Leader did not destroy him. Instead he asked Joseph Knebel to take charge of organising the national printing business. That saved him from famine or execution.

It is pretty certain that Maria Knebel's account of the lawlessness and humiliations suffered by artists would have been more detailed and fearless had they not all lived in 'the most liberal country in the world'.

The problem was not that she and her second husband were coerced into sharing their apartment first with one large family, then with two – until all they had left was a single room with just a thin plywood partition separating it from the entrance hall; nor was it that Knebel, while working at the country's premier theatre, had to earn extra cash in order to survive and feed her family, working as a guide at the Tretyakov Gallery where her father's ascent had begun; nor that she had to sell her prized possession – her father's albums of reproductions: unassuming in her everyday life, Maria Knebel stoically endured all these hardships, with quiet dignity and no bitterness, without calling anyone to account.

She stood by those with whom she shared time and space. When her communal flat neighbours were being dragged off to the labour camps one after another, Knebel looked after their families, helping them in every way she could.

But the plague spared no one. Soon after, Maria's much loved brother Nikolai was arrested in front of her, her mother and her sister.

Everything was leading to her being arrested next. Nemirovich-Danchenko made a vow that as long as he was at the theatre, Maria would continue to work alongside him. But her colleagues kept their distance, whenever possible avoiding coming face to face with her in the passageways of the theatre, or backstage.

These are all well-established realities of life under Stalin. As they say, worse things happened. Her brother was lucky. He did make it back from the place that very few returned from. The point of this is: what strength of character it took her to not lose heart, to go on making theatre and develop the methodology of acting!

A pushy student once asked her point-blank, 'How can we hold out against the insanity of the world? How can we go on living?' Knebel answered, 'Self-improvement.' 'But what about you? You, having seen what you have seen, experienced first-hand all that, God forbid, anyone else will have to – where do you get your strength from? What keeps you going?' – 'Self-improvement', she responded with a smile.

To draw her students into this life-saving process is the goal of Knebel's pedagogy.

She followed her own teacher's tenet. Once, during spectacular jubilee celebrations for his seventieth birthday, Stanislavski, when asked 'What constitutes earthly happiness?', tore off a piece of paper from a flower wrapper and scribbled a powerful statement with his weakened hand: 'Cognition. Art and work, getting to the essence ...'

Her interest in what goes on inside us, in the mysteries of the creative sense of self and the ways to attain it, nudged Knebel towards directing.

At the time, there was a deep-rooted belief that directing was not a woman's profession. Maria found the only genuine way to overcome that prejudice: she made use of the advantages she had without trying to imitate the characteristics of a male director, employing her adaptability, flexibility, solicitude and gentleness in working with volatile actors.

She realised that she had an ability to 'fuse' with an actor, to penetrate deep into their soul, and sense what they were going through while creating the character. And the actor was eager to accept her help, sensing her care and feeling empathy for their anguish and struggle.

'A midwife that helps to deliver the production', one of the early comparisons Stanislavski had found to help define the director's function. This could have been said of Knebel when she first started directing.

She never became an outstanding stage director. But her knowledge of painting and sculpture, of all the different fine arts genres, and her impeccable taste allowed her to master the craft of staging (in as much as it interested her). Maria was invited to join the Yermolov Studio,[14] while her old classmate, Nikolai Khmelev,[15] the best actor of the new MAT generation with a studio of his own, suggested they should form a new theatre together.

There is no better place than a theatre studio for a director in the making!

There is no inertia or scepticism there. Time spent at a studio[16] is brief but highly beneficial, the time when the *studijtsy*'s[17] hunger to grasp the secrets of their profession is stronger than their awareness of the relative nature of what they desire; when soloists are still happy to sing in the chorus; when the theatre studio, in trying to make sense of life, starts to inhabit it as it searches for its identity amidst the general hustle and bustle.

At the Studio, where there was no fear of making mistakes or of failing, Maria Knebel could put to the test the method of active analysis. This method

---

14 The Yermolov Studio, formed in 1925 and named after a great Russian actress from the Maly Theatre in Moscow, merged with Nikolai Khmelev's Studio in 1937. Khmelev became the Head of the new Studio, which was later to become the Yermolov Theatre (ed. note).

15 Nikolai Khmelev (1901–1945). An actor and director at the Moscow Art Theatre (ed. note).

16 In Russia 'studio' refers to a relatively open theatrical infrastructure, something between a laboratory and a workshop. Under the leadership of an actor or a director young people are brought together in a studio for educational and experimental work (ed. note).

17 *Studijtsy* – members of a studio theatre (trans. note).

requires a particular rehearsal set-up: it is necessary to turn the person's gaze towards their inner self, to awaken the dormant improvisational nature in every actor.

That's where Maria started to rehearse using etudes,[18] and became a confirmed believer in the method. From then on, come what may, she never abandoned it. She did not imitate her mentors; she came up with new exercises, looked for new approaches, and did everything she could to make actors fall in love with that little-known way of rehearsing.

It worked because of the close attention she paid to each student's individuality. A pedagogue by nature, she would always make adjustments according to the unique artistic and intrinsic characteristics of each person she taught. She was up-front about the difficulties that actors would encounter when applying the method especially by those accustomed to working in the old way. That set her apart from the opportunists who forced 'the system' on everyone, the way Peter the Great forced propagation of potatoes.

Her father, Joseph Knebel, had once taken his little Maria to see Surikov's *Boyarynya Morozova.*[19] For a long time the little girl peered at the woman who had chosen exile over apostasy. Fighting for her right to cross herself with two fingers rather than three, the Boyarynya proudly thrusts them up. 'What is she fighting for?' – 'For her faith.' Maria did not possess the Boyarynya's stately bearing, feverish eyes or affecting gestures. Tiny, funny, impractical in everyday life, and seemingly helpless … And yet! She was as firm in her convictions, and in her likes and dislikes – she never, no matter what, let go of the essence, the fundamental principles of the school she came from. Throughout the years of adversity, she upheld her faith – that which cannot be taken away from someone without taking their life. She became the Master in her own right.

Misfortunes ambushed the Yermolov Studio. Two of its directors, Tereshkovich and Azarin, unexpectedly died. Here is what Knebel wrote about it later in her life:

> Khmelev and I talked all through the night. The two Studios had to be merged. That was the only way out. We were connected in so many ways, had shared so many thoughts and experiences. But the deaths of the two directors were not to be the last of the many catastrophes of that tragic 1937 – one after another we were losing our actors. That night we talked of it all. And of the particular kind of unity, both human and creative, that was required in the face of what was going on; we talked about each other, and of our innermost beliefs …

18 The meaning of the term 'etude' as used in theatre was developed in detail in Maria Knebel's practice and writings. See chapter 'Etude rehearsals' (ed. note).
19 A famous painting by Vasily Surikov at the Tretyakov Gallery in Moscow. See Fig. A1 at the end of the book (ed. note).

There is no explicit mention that the night-time conversation took place at the height of Stalin's persecutions. That year's tragic losses might explain the bitter state of affairs at the Studio. But if we read the text carefully, then everything – from 'losing our actors' to 'our innermost beliefs' – each word, each sentence reveals the true meaning of what was said.

Under Khmelev's wing Knebel put on productions that compelled even her foes, as well as misogynists, to acknowledge Maria's skill as a director. It was the training-ground for new exciting actors, with the whole of Moscow flocking to see her production of Shakespeare's *As You Like It*. Celebrating *joie de vivre* in those dark times was a thing worthy of admiration. Not everyone would have had the courage to rise above the turmoil of those days.

The production, incandescent with tragedy and comedy, came to life through improvisations. As a result, the actors' work had a lightness of touch, and its exquisite style combined the natural and the fantastical. The best qualities of a genuine art theatre could be discerned within it. The show was not just a one-off success story but the laying of the path that made it possible to progress.

Knebel was aware that for the *studijtsy* it was important to know what lay ahead. But neither Stanislavski, nor – later on – Nemirovich-Danchenko, took kindly to their assistant's work elsewhere. For her, too, the MAT was home. How could she disregard its interests? And once the war broke out, with the theatre evacuated to Saratov, there was no longer any question – her place was at the MAT.

Knebel could not imagine herself without the Moscow Art Theatre. On top of that, it was far from easy working with her adored Khmelev. Despite being attached to Maria, the actor was jealous of her relationship with the *studijtsy*. With his heightened vulnerability and mistrust, it was not easy to sustain the now legendary high-minded relationship that they now had.

Khmelev used to 'quarrel silently' with anyone who expressed an opinion he did not share. Great actor though he was, he was also, as is often the case, ego-centric and liked to be the centre of attention. His egocentricity was so pro-nounced that once a friend remarked when they visited the Louvre together, 'Nikolai, are we here to look at you, or at the *Mona Lisa*?'

Even Khmelev's sudden death was touched with a sinister theatricality: he was in full costume and make-up for the part of Ivan the Terrible when death caught up with him during the run-through of the play *Hard Times*.[20]

1949. No Stanislavski, no Nemirovich-Danchenko, no Khmelev. And this is the country that had defeated fascism beyond its boundaries, but failed to do so on its own soil.

Shielded by the rallying cry to combat 'rootless cosmopolitans', the system-atic persecutions of intelligentsia, particularly those of Jewish extraction, had got under way. Knebel never admitted this motive to be part of the plot which led to her expulsion from the MAT, but the reverberations of it were there. She pretended not to hear them, embarrassed for those who danced to its tune.

---

20 The 2nd Part of Alexei Tolstoy's (1883–1945) play *Ivan the Terrible*, written in 1943 (ed. note).

Maria was a Christian, yet the anti-Semitic campaign was targeting not the Jewish faith but the citizens' ethnic origins.

At the Committee for the Arts, Knebel was sheepishly informed that the new Head of Theatre wished to work only with his own disciples.

The Arts Theatre was the oxygen she had been breathing since her youth. Now Knebel found herself in a vacuum. Job offers that followed from other places were withdrawn as soon as she filled in an application form.[21]

1949. No Stanislavski, no Nemirovich-Danchenko, no Khmelev.

Yet she was exceptionally lucky with people. Who knows what would have happened to Knebel, had she not had Alexei Popov[22] on her side? A man of conscience, and one of the most distinctive figures of the Russian theatre in the Soviet period.

A talented actor, passionate about directing, he, like Meyerhold, went away to the provinces to spread the ideals of the Moscow Art Theatre. On his return he staged several productions at the MAT that proved him to be a spirited director, an inspiration to the actors. His interest in theory and questions of methodology brought him and Knebel closer together.

Since the moment they first met to collaborate on the show that ended up being fatal for Khmelev, their mutual respect had grown into a friendship that no vicissitudes of life could ever unsettle.

These knights of the theatre were destined to live in an age far removed from chivalry. The deplorable times made them clutch firmly at each other. Popov was distressed that he had no way of helping Knebel who found herself cast out from the MAT. She, in turn, was at a loss how best to soften the blow to Popov when he was forced out of the Red Army Theatre.[23] Both were in a bad way, but for both their situation turned out to have been a blessing in disguise.

Popov had long been asking Maria to join him at the Directing Department at GITIS. At the time the Department had become the main haven for those who after years of hardships found themselves washed ashore there. What started as a tolerable way out of a tough predicament, turned into a source of joy for them, and into a unique success story for the Russian theatre.

Under Popov – and later Knebel – the Department developed a unique school of directing. Is there another one like it in the world? This is a rhetorical question. It is only now that many are beginning to realise that the process of director-training defines the future of theatre.

---

21 In the Soviet Union all passports and many other official documents, as well as application forms, contained the question on 'Nationality' that implied the ethnic origin of Soviet citizens rather than their citizenship status (ed. note).

22 Alexei Popov (1891–1961), actor, director and pedagogue, Knebel's close collaborator at the GITIS Directing Department. He was Artistic Director of the Soviet Army Theatre (1935–1960) (ed. note).

23 The Central Academic Theatre of the Russian Army is the largest theatre in Moscow. It was established in 1929 as the Red Army Theatre, and renamed the Soviet Army Theatre in 1951. It always specialised in war-themed productions (trans. note).

Under Popov and Knebel, something quite unprecedented was taking place. They created a research centre, where they explored and developed ideas never before realised in theatre. They developed a programme for cultivating directors. Nurturing them, rather than just training and educating them.

The meaning and purpose of the programme was to mould the director's *personality*. The method of active analysis (Knebel managed to infect Popov with it) was offered to student-directors as a tool to be used if they wanted to do creative work rather than just 'blocking' actors onstage.

Directing is a young profession. A hundred and fifty years ago it did not matter who put on the show. The public went to see the star performer, and had no interest in who might have coached them for the performance. Impossible to imagine then that the director's name could become a draw, sometimes bigger than that of an actor, that the answer to 'who directed it?' could one day make you decide if something is worth seeing or not!

Who would have thought that these master-craftsmen would be revered on a par with scientists or military leaders? But ask them, what is it that they do? And the answers you get will be most unexpected. In principle, they will be of two kinds: some that are figurative and try to capture the poetic essence of the job, and others that stress its organisational nature.

Knebel turned her attention to the director as an author of the project, a creator, an inspiration and a poet composing a poem for the stage. But poets cannot be raised on a diet of prose.

It is so tempting to try to describe her productions of Chekhov or of Dostoyevsky's *Uncle's Dream* … But instead let's talk about the Central Children's Theatre[24] without which the story of her life is unimaginable.

Knebel who ended up there by lucky chance, used to say, 'There had not been a theatre like this in the old days. As a child I was taken to the MAT to see Maeterlinck.[25] And here I am now, see, all grown-up …'

She noticed that in the 'Soviet theatre' archipelago there started to emerge a few islands where other interests prevailed. The 'Academic' theatres were antediluvian, fossilised. But in children's theatres, with a new generation of artists, a spirit of freethinking could be felt.

Not too large, agile, these theatres could respond swiftly to the fickle swings of theatrical weather. Just like small boats that instantly feel the impact of a single wave (while it takes a storm for a big fishing boat to be affected or a huge billow of a wave coming over a liner's railings to cause it any concern). At children's theatres, the young directors did the rowing.

There, on the outskirts of the theatre empire, those who were forced out from the centre found their foothold. Children's theatres were out of sight.

24 The Central Children's Theatre, founded in 1921 by Natalya Sats, was given its name in 1937. In the 1950s and 1960s the directors working there included Maria Knebel, Anatoly Efros, Georgy Tovstonogov, Oleg Yefremov. Now it is called the Young People's Theatre (ed. note).

25 A reference to Stanislavski's famous 1908 production of *The Blue Bird* by Maeterlinck (ed. note).

Soviet bigwigs did not bother to visit them, nor did they expect from them any offerings for the Party's anniversaries. In the meantime, within these theatres, forces were maturing that would come to disrupt the seemingly eternal calm reigning over the country's theatrical waters.

Maria could not have known the consequences of her work at the Children's Theatre. But intuition can take artists far beyond the confines of the tasks they set themselves. Her hunch ultimately proved to be more significant than a detailed plan could have been.

Anatoli Vassiliev, the director who absorbed the spirit rather than the letter of Knebel's work, is justified in thinking that the 'thaw' in Soviet theatre began with his teacher, with her arrival at the Central Children's Theatre.

At the time, the theatre landscape presented a revolting spectacle: imperial style, grand scale, static, pose-striking, ostentatious sets, rousing music and bombastic speech. And the rampant naturalism to boot! Such was the outcome of force-feeding Stanislavski by executive order. This vulgarised interpretation of the 'System' turned it into a nauseating dogma. The image of the experimental risk-taker was distorted and deformed beyond all recognition. But the young no longer trusted everything that was being drummed into them.

And it was the young that worked at the Children's Theatre. For the first time since leaving the MAT, Knebel, who had begun to doubt her usefulness, felt that she was needed again.

Most of all, Maria was preoccupied with introducing the actors to the methodology. That's what creating a theatre company is, isn't it? Discovering the common artistic language with a company of actors and finding the joy of unity.

It was not in a touring production, nor in a collaboration with someone else, but at a theatre all her own that Knebel took a risk and put the method of active analysis to the test.

The results exceeded all expectations. Her actors were fired up by etudes, enthusiastically exploring the subtleties of the new approach. It was also clear that the proposed method was revitalising the theatre. Not only did it liberate the actors' improvisational natures, revealing their unique individuality and wiping the dust off hackneyed old plays, but it also transformed the life of the company beyond all recognition.

The new climate in the theatre was such that any sort of posturing, bragging, or backstage gossip, would shrivel up. Stanislavski knew all too well that what happens in the upstairs offices, or in the cloakroom where the audience leave their coats, could infest every corner of the theatre, and above all the stage. But the opposite can also be true: whatever was happening in Maria's classes began to transform the theatre's life as a whole. When Anton Chekhov first met the Moscow Art Theatre company, he was astonished: 'I say, what cultured and sophisticated people you have here!' Thanks to Knebel's efforts, this came to pass again.

A sense of ease and joy set in. As if the energy of childhood, and the readiness to expect miracles so characteristic of young audiences, poured into the actors onstage. It seems now that *In Search of Joy* was not just the title of the celebrated Central Children's Theatre production but also the leitmotif of everything that went on there.

'The true secret of establishing faith in the miraculous lies in finding such psychological changes as can bring the audience right up to the point of believing in the very possibility, moreover, in the essential need for the miracle they are witnessing.' Although Knebel is referring to the audience, it could equally be applied to theatre-makers.

She inspired those for whom theatre was not only an escape from dogma and unbridled ideology but also a means of standing up to them. Both Oleg Yefremov[26] (the founder member of the Sovremennik Theatre, and later the Artistic Director of the Moscow Art Theatre), and Anatoly Efros,[27] a director of rare talent, found their voice with Knebel's encouragement. Having recognised their singular individualities, she safeguarded and protected them. She enjoyed grasping the sense of someone else's nascent concept, then helping it to grow and sparkle.

Alongside her own productions where traditions of the highest order were the attraction, there emerged productions by Anatoly Efros, full of inner agility and elasticity, iridescent like mercury. Life onstage – forgive my tautology – came to life. The ugly face of that period's comfortable inertia, in which Communist postulations were closely interwoven with conservative bourgeois attitudes, was revealed. The ice broke.

Everything started to bubble up, twirling and spinning. The ripples of it began to spread around the country. This turbulence gave a new lease of life to well-known concepts, and gave rise to new ideas. There was a revival of interest in Stanislavski's discoveries, and in those connected to him as if by an umbilical cord – Michael Chekhov, Meyerhold and Vakhtangov.

The theatre run by Knebel had become truly 'central'. Not central according to the Ministry of Culture's hierarchy but rather to the place it now occupied in the cultural context of the country. After watching a few of the shows and struck by the level of freedom with which the actors lived onstage, Alexei Popov uttered, 'Only dogs can out-act this lot.'

Young playwrights were drawn to Knebel's theatre. They were warmly greeted, nourished and nurtured, and later many of them became household names. Most remarkably, brilliant productions often grew out of weak plays. This was a testament to the theatre's mastering the art of subtext and the second plane, and learning to analyse the play's underlying action rather than its lines.

26 Oleg Yefremov (1927–2000), an actor and director, the founder of the Sovremennik (Our Contemporary) Theatre, was appointed as Artistic Director of the Moscow Art Theatre in 1970. He and his Sovremennik company were the embodiment of the theatrical renewal of the 1950s and 1960s (ed. note).

27 Anatoly Efros (1925–1987), a director and teacher, without doubt one of the greatest Soviet directors of the post-war generation, an indisputable theatre innovator (ed. note).

They mastered the technique that once helped the Moscow Art Theatre preserve their actors' stagecraft when they were compelled to perform socialist realist plays.

Maria's feat was the saving grace for the Russian theatre: she established a spiritual and professional connection between her teachers and the new generation.

Only the poet's words[28] could provide an epigraph to the story of how, after ten years, Knebel was forced to leave the Central Children's Theatre. But it is not worth going into any details of the deviousness of those whose names are only remembered because of the intolerable conditions they created to oust this remarkable pedagogue. The abusive tactics of the faceless against the talented are as old as the world itself.

On the surface, much was incidental. How apt is Pushkin's confession: 'What a mischance to have been born in Russia with brains and talent.'

I joined Maria at the time when, due to the initiative of people aware of the great wealth in Knebel's possession, she was asked to run a laboratory for the Heads of Youth Theatres under the auspices of the Theatre Society.

Without a theatre company, she was bereft. Her inclination to bring people together would not let her rest. All of a sudden there was an opportunity to continue what she had begun: an opportunity to pass on her methodology to directors, and in doing so to influence the theatrical life of the country.

The spirit of Khrushchev's Thaw was gone. The climate turned cold again. The petty tyranny of the apparatchiks knew no bounds. Free vibrant thought was driven underground. The refrain of Bulat Okudzhava's song sounded like a call to action: 'Let's stand together, hand in hand, my friends, so we don't vanish one by one, alone.'

The only thing that could bring together the people most resistant to being part of any group, i.e., theatre directors, was the method of active analysis rather than highfaluting manifestos. That was the 'lure', and with its help – an ensemble of directors[29] began to take shape.

One day someone will write about the unique phenomenon of Moscow kitchens in the last stages of Soviet power. They preserved the warmth of human communication. There we shared our thoughts about new productions, or decided to go on living when life became unbearable. Maria transformed her final series of masterclasses into a Soviet Union-wide kitchen of that kind.

The composition of this group was surprising. Alongside the young there were well-known directors with honorary titles and awards. One of them was sprinkled with medals like a Christmas tree with tinsel. But he too was keen to find out: who is this Knebel? What is she up to? She offered places to every single one of them – there's tolerance for you!

---

28 A reference to Alexander Pushkin – see below (trans. note).

29 The term 'ensemble' implies that actors in a company get soldered together into a certain artistic entity. The ensemble of Stanislavski's Moscow Art Theatre was a model of such a collective (ed. note).

Maria could be biting, without raising her voice, she would take you down a peg or two, with a single ironic comment, or extinguish arrogance with a smile, and yet she had a lot of patience … It is hard to say if it was in her nature or the result of her upbringing. In any case, she knew how to listen, even when there was nothing to listen to.

One day as we tried to follow a wild rant of one of the student-speakers, she picked up my notebook, scribbled something and gave it back to me. Taken aback, I read, 'I think he's a hard-boiled fool!' In the break I asked her, 'Why are we wasting time on him? You listened to him for a whole hour, and then asked questions!' She gave me a perplexed look, 'But what if he had come up with something worthwhile out of the blue!'

Knebel, no doubt, loved smart and gifted people but she was interested in everyone. She knew how to draw out absolutely everything from the person she spoke to, even things they would have preferred to keep to themselves. That's how I remember her – always listening.

When she heard that I was from Latvia (I ran a theatre in Riga), her face lit up: 'Father used to take us there as children to the seaside every summer.' I wanted to find out more about it. But she somehow turned it around, and before I knew it I was talking about myself and revealing the details of my life I rarely shared with anyone.

I made a conscious choice to join her laboratory, fully aware of its whys and wherefores. Initially we study because that is what we are supposed to do; then, for the sake of our nearest and dearest; and later, to obtain the right to be independent. But when it is time to work things out for ourselves, we do it consciously. Then our learning is filled with a sweet sense of being initiated into a cultural tradition.

We wanted to get the secrets of psychological theatre out of Knebel, to master the method. Soon it became apparent that this method was closely connected with the quest of artists during the time when the new artistic forms of the urban age had begun to emerge. The search for 'the life of the human spirit' – the definition whose grand solemnity can be off-putting – in fact expresses that quest precisely.

The desire to capture the singularity and uniqueness of each moment in the theatre as well as in the paintings of the Impressionists: both of these were stages in the development of the same artistic idea. It was as if Knebel linked all that enthralled us in the visual aspects of a theatre spectacle to the ways and means of the actor's existence onstage. She laid bare the nature of the actor's creative work.

With sensitivity and care she attuned our inner sight. Etudes, deconstruction of texts, analysis of paintings – all of these increased our immunity to parochialism, superficiality and crassness, and developed our ability (almost into a reflex) to tell the genuine from the fake, irrespective of the vagaries of fashion or the vicissitudes of life.

Yes, I did make a conscious choice to study with Knebel, but there was a twist to it too. Psychological theatre seemed to me to be pretty dull. Distorted interpretations of Stanislavski had prevailed. So I infiltrated, spy-like, the ranks of the enemy to ferret out their secrets. But, unexpectedly, I was captured. Even though some of what was irrefutable at the time no longer seems so today, it does not matter. What matters is to have something you can reject. Otherwise, how can you grow as a director?

Maria handed on to us the most precious thing – a working method. She did so with hope, demanding no oaths of allegiance. Try it ... see for yourself ... She knew that for a student it was vital to feel like a pioneer, a participant in an experiment. At our first group meeting, as she shared with us the tasks of our Laboratory, Knebel announced: 'We shall have to specify, clarify and analyse the methodology of active analysis.' The very first word, 'specify', instantly transformed our mindset from that of primary school pupils learning their ABCs to that of true explorers on an enticing path of discovery.

She created a set-up in which any opinion, any unfinished thought, any crazy idea – anything at all – had the right to be discussed. And every one of us directors (even those covered in medals) became a little bit more talented than we had been before.

There is nothing more dangerous for a teacher than his or her interpreters (Stanislavski–Knebel is an exception). Each one of us was convinced that they were the only one who could really understand Maria. Many still have that feeling now. How did she ever put up with our drivel about how the etude method should be employed in our own theatres? Apart from the desire to master the method, it is essential that the student's talent is aligned with the fundamental artistic principles of the method. And yet – we did find unity based on our shared professional interests.

Knebel turned our eyes into our very soul. The Laboratory members came to revere their profession, rather than brag about it. That was a result of our initiation into the science of theatre. And another thing: we inhaled the intoxicating aroma of a culture we had never had even a whiff of before. The effects of it spread to our theatres, defining the life within them.

Maria wanted to shield the directors from becoming dismayed by the reality of life at the time and help them develop defences against its nightmares. She encouraged us to talk about whatever was going on in the world. Once she invited a prominent playwright to tell us about his trip to the USA. In a moment of generosity he shared stories with us not only about their official meetings but also about American universities, and visits to strip clubs. When it was time for questions, Knebel was the first to ask, 'Forgive me, but what in God's name is the Department of State?' Yet she would always have practical advice for us on how to dodge censorship or manage pig-ignorant bosses. I suspect she must have analysed them with the tools of events and actions, too ...

The Laboratory would go and visit the cities and towns where its members worked. That was a life-changing event for them and for their theatres, too. If we keep in mind that during those visits we met up with actors, as well as having classes with guest specialists in literature, with playwrights and theatre critics, then the pedagogical intention of these visits becomes apparent.

The Knebel Workshop became our Tsarskoje Selo's Lycée.[30]

In 1983 Maria wrote to me: 'I often think that the Laboratory played quite a complex role in all our lives. While dedicated to the study of the methodology, it intertwined our personal relationships in a much deeper and subtler way than we could have ever imagined!'

Primarily, it happened because Knebel wanted us to understand the fundamentals: theatre is made up of curiosity about life and of contact between people.

She saw her purpose as eliciting an individual working style from each of her students. She rejoiced as she watched their work developing its own distinctive character. She never clipped their wings, acknowledging that each one had the right to fly.

And once they were strong enough, they did fly: they flew away to create new theatres or put themselves to the test on other stages around the country. By the rapid ascent of those who grew up under Knebel, it was easy to appreciate the sort of nest they came from.

'What's that you've written here?!' The hotel administrator stared at the registration form, full of indignation. 'What's that?', she continued officiously, pointing at the date of birth: 1898. 'But it is true', said Knebel.

The last time I saw Maria in the hospital. She was in bed reading Stanislavski. She offered me some coffee. 'Are you allowed it?' I asked – 'I can do whatever I want now.'

I don't feel like finishing yet. It seems, I have missed the most important thing. And I have. The most important thing is to be found in Maria Knebel's books. She said to me once, 'The pedagogue's first commandment is: thou shalt not expect thanks from thy students.' But Vassiliev has collected her writings and offers them now to the English-speaking reader, and I have dared to write an introduction.

Adolf Shapiro was born in 1939 in Kharkov, where he studied theatre. He was the Artistic Director of the Young People's Theatre in Riga from 1962 to 1992. His productions gave a new lease of life to the Latvian theatre. He directed Chekhov, Tolstoy, Ibsen, Kleist and Brecht in Riga and in other Baltic countries; he took part in Maria Knebel's Directing Laboratory in the 1970s. Political changes that followed Latvia's independence forced him to resign from his theatre. Since then he has been working in Russia, mostly at the Moscow Art Theatre but also in St Petersburg and abroad.

---

30 The Imperial Lycée, where Pushkin studied at the beginning of the 19th century (ed. note).

Book One

On Active Analysis of the Play and the Role

Author's foreword

Such is the interest in Stanislavski's creative legacy in every corner of our country that it is difficult to imagine any drama group that does not to some degree apply his system to their own practice.

In this book, I would like to discuss the new method of working on a play and a role – the so-called method of active analysis, which Konstantin Sergeievich[1] arrived at in his final years, having reviewed the theoretical and practical experience of a lifetime.

Since this part of the work cannot be examined in isolation from the Stanislavski system as a whole, I consider it essential to touch upon some of its most important elements.

The art of the theatre is a complex one. It comprises many parts. But the most important of them that impacts on the audience, affecting it directly, is the *word*.

Verbal action is the cornerstone of theatre, the foundation of the actor's creative work onstage.

The ability to deliver the playwright's text onstage is entirely linked to actors' ability to think and clothe their thoughts in the words provided by the author. Battling against mechanical line-delivery and striving to achieve genuine thinking onstage is the task that should be given the highest priority in the work of every theatre company. Because of this I have to address such issues as 'the second plane', 'inner monologue', 'mental images' that are closely related to the subject of this book.

The book brings together basic propositions on active analysis of the play and the role that I have written about in my earlier articles.

I will attempt to summarise some of my conclusions.

---

1 Stanislavski, Konstantin Sergeievich (17 January 1863–7 August 1938) (trans. note).

DOI: 10.4324/9780203125205-4

General principles of active analysis

For the Stanislavski system, and particularly for its later discoveries related to the new rehearsal method – active analysis of the play and the role – to be accepted in theatre practice, we need to examine what led Stanislavski to change the established format of rehearsals.

It is well known that the Moscow Art Theatre introduced the so-called 'table' period as the basis of the initial work on a play, that is, analysing the play at the table before getting it up on its feet in rehearsal.

During this period the company, under the guidance of the director, would undertake a scrupulous analysis of the play: the inner motives, the subtext, the relationships, the characters' personalities, the throughaction,[1] and the supertask,[2] etc. This work allowed the actor to get an in-depth understanding of the play, determining its ideas and artistic tasks. Above all, the 'table' work compelled the actor to delve deep into the character's inner world, the very foundation of the process of creating the show.

As he perfected his creative method, developing and deepening the system, Stanislavski became aware of a number of disadvantages to 'table' work.

One was the increasing passivity of the actors, who instead of actively searching for a way to get closer to their roles from the very start, relied on the director to show them the way.

And indeed, during a lengthy period 'at the table' it is the director who tends to take on an active role: explaining, describing, firing the actors' imagination, while they become accustomed to the director resolving the play- and character-related problems for them all.

Performers are often quite happy for the director to act out all the roles at the start of the 'table' rehearsals. Working this way, actors inevitably grow passive and follow the director's instructions, no questions asked. This, naturally, disrupts a creative process where the actor is a conscious creator.

There is a particular thread running throughout Stanislavski's life: the dream of a fully conscious actor, an actor-creator, capable of interpreting the play

---

1 See below the chapter 'Throughaction' (ed. note).
2 See below the chapter 'The supertask' (ed. note).

DOI: 10.4324/9780203125205-5

independently and of taking effective actions in the play's given circumstances. When he first started, Stanislavski was delighted to find his actors malleable. But later he realised that this very 'malleability' reduced their initiative, that the actor's inertia was a deadly evil in art.

Stanislavski declared war on the actor's passivity, in whatever form it took: in the individual's work on a role, or in the work of the company as a whole, in rehearsals, or in the actual performance. But whilst Stanislavski placed high demands on the actors, the tasks he put to the director were even more challenging.

It is quite natural that at the start of rehearsals the director is better prepared than the actors. The director must not only have thought about the content of the play, but must also have pictured the casting possibilities for each role, and considered all the technical resources at their disposal.

The director must visualise the entire production, organise the process of rehearsals, and have a clear idea of the direction in which to steer the company as they create the show. But being prepared does not mean that directors should impose their creative will on performers. They must inspire each individual actor as well as the company as a whole. By setting up certain conditions, they must enable each actor to feel a personal responsibility for their role, to be as active as possible.

Throughout his artistic life, Stanislavski warned directors against imposing their will on the actor, even in the first read-through, since he believed that even at that stage there could be a risk of imposing certain inflections, adaptations[3] and colours on the actors.

The more cultivated the director, the greater their life experience, the deeper their knowledge, the easier it is for them to help the actor. But the actor can only receive concrete help when the director has previously studied all the inner workings of the play's action, the nature of the characters' relationships, their interactions, their inner worlds and their dispositions revealed as they strive to fulfil the supertask.

Unquestionably, the director must be ready for the first rehearsal, that is, they must have a clear idea of what they want to bring to light in the play. But it is also perfectly natural for the director's ideas to be enriched by the actors' contributions during the course of rehearsals. Naturally, as they work, the actors must familiarise themselves with the period in which the action of the play is set, its iconography, literary and critical studies of the play, and so on.

Stanislavski said that directors must avoid introducing this kind of material to the actors in the first days of rehearsals, and do it only after the actors have familiarised themselves, to some extent, with the characters they are to embody. Then the actors will be able to relate the information they receive to the characters being explored in rehearsals.

---

3 See Book Two, the chapter on 'Adaptations' (ed. note).

Sometimes, however, directors talk about the concept, the period and the style of the piece at the very start of rehearsals. What they say may be true, they believe they are helping the actors, but in fact their words fall on barren soil and become dead weight.

Stanislavski warned directors against revealing their ideas too soon, in too much detail. He believed that in the early stages the actor's imagination should not be overloaded, since this will, to some degree, prevent the actor from actively seeking their own way into the role.

Nemirovich-Danchenko, a close colleague of Stanislavski's, has come up with well-defined teaching on the creative role of the director. He called the director 'a three-faced creature' that combines the following qualities:

1)   the director as interpreter, actor, pedagogue, helping the actor create a role;
2)   the director as mirror, reflecting the actor's personal qualities;
3)   the director as organiser of the entire production.

The audience is familiar only with the third 'face', since it is in plain sight, revealed in every aspect of the production.

But the first two of the director's functions are hidden from the audience. They only see actors, who have fully absorbed the work so generously invested in them by the director.

For the director to be an interpreter of the play and the role, their concept and intention must have depth and integrity.

For the director to be an actor and a pedagogue, they must, in the first instance, personally get a feel for every nuance of the inner and outer work-ings of the role. They must be able to put themself in the performer's shoes, without losing sight of the actor's individuality, cherishing and developing their creative attributes.

For Nemirovich-Danchenko[i] the tasks of the directing pedagogy were to detect each person's individuality; develop it; improve their taste; battle against their bad habits and petty vanities; be able to request, insist and demand; watch, with care and pleasure, for the tiniest little shoots of anything living and genu-ine that would bring the actor nearer to the truth of their onstage sense of self.[4]

If directors develop these qualities in themselves, they can become highly polished mirrors that reflect the subtlest shift in an actor's psyche, the smallest, barely perceptible internal mistake.

---

4   The 'sense of self' (*samochuvstviye* in Russian): the phrase refers to one of the fundamental concepts of the Stanislavski system. It is usually translated as a 'state' or a 'state of mind'. To avoid the passive connotations of the word 'state' and to express the fact that *samochuvstviye* is always in a kind of 'flux', it is translated literally as the 'sense of self'. To an extent, the fundamentals of the Stanislavski system are in particular concerned with producing conditions that would allow for *samochuvstviye* (the 'sense of self') to be conducive to creativity as such, as well as analysing and working with the elements that constitute it (trans. note).

When Stanislavski introduced his new rehearsal method, he emphasised the need for the director as pedagogue to be tactful and not to share their knowledge of the play until such time when it was actually useful to the actor and their work. He poses the question of finding a tactical device, a kind of 'teaching ploy', which would ensure that the director's view of the role and the play did not 'weigh the actor down', but discreetly corrected them, integrating their independent search into an artistic whole.

The initial prerequisite for changing the rehearsal practice was the actors' passive attitudes which Stanislavski had decided to fight.

Another equally important reason was the realisation that the old method of rehearsals maintained – against nature – an artificial gap between the physical and mental aspects of the actor's existence in the given circumstances of the play.

Onstage it is important to be truthful in showing particular actions of each character, and this can only happen when the person's physical and mental sense of self merge.

Human physical life is a concrete realisation of the psychophysical sense of self. Actors, therefore, cannot confine themselves to abstract psychological reasoning, since no physical action can ever be cut off from a mental action. Stanislavski says that there is an indissoluble link between stage action and its cause, that 'the life of the human body' and 'the life of the human spirit' are one. For him this was the basis in his work on psycho-technique.

In my notes, there is an example Konstantin Sergeievich used to clarify his ideas regarding this unity, the indissolubility of the psychophysical process.

['Sometimes a man says nothing', he told us, 'but from the way he sits, stands or walks about we can understand his state of mind, his mood and attitude to what's going on around him. So, often, as we pass by people on a park bench, we can tell, without hearing a single word, whether they are doing business, having a row or speaking of love.

['And yet we cannot tell what goes on in someone's life from their physical behaviour alone', Stanislavski continued. 'We can tell that someone coming towards us in the street is in a rush on a matter of some importance, or that someone else is looking for somebody. But then the person comes up to us and asks, "Have you seen a little boy in a grey cap? He ran away when I went into a shop."

['When he hears your answer, "No, I haven't!", he walks away from you, calling out from time to time: "Vladimir!"

['Now that you have seen not only the man's physical behaviour, not only the way he walked and looked around, but have also heard what he said to you, how he called out to the boy, you can grasp quite clearly what's happening to him, what's on his mind.

['Imagine that this man, who is looking for his son, came up to you and asked you the same question but in a sort of sing-song fashion, melodramatically, stressing the wrong syllables. You would conclude that he is either mentally ill, or simply making a fool out of you.

['But can anything genuine and true occur onstage if the physical behaviour is inaccurate or fake? Imagine that this same man, looking for his son in the street, came up to you, stopped you in your tracks, took out a packet of cigarettes from his pocket, leaned against the wall of a house, lit a cigarette and leisurely enquired about his son. Once again you'd think there is something wrong, that he isn't looking for his son at all but needs you, for some reason.

['It is clear then that our inner state of mind, our thoughts, desires, relationships must be expressed both in words and in a specific physical behaviour.

['We have to be able to decide at any given moment how people are going to behave physically, whether, for some particular reason, they are going to walk, sit or stand, and also *how* they are going to walk, *how* they are going to sit or stand.

['Let's imagine that we have to act the man who is looking for his son.

['If we try and speak his lines at the table, we will find it hard to do so properly. Our body, sitting down, at rest, will prevent us from finding a true sense of self of the man who has lost his son. And without that our words will sound hollow. We won't be able to speak the lines as the person would speak them in real life.

['But then I say to you', continued Stanislavski: 'You are looking for your son who ran off when you popped into a shop. Get up from the table, imagine that this is the street and these are passers-by. You urgently need to find out if they have seen your son. Now do it, and take not only verbal but also physical action.']

The gap between the sense of self of an actor sitting calmly at the table, pencil in hand, and the actual experience of the psychophysical life of the role, which actors should strive for from the outset of their work, obliged Stanislavski to analyse the existing rehearsal practice in depth.

Stanislavski's starting point was that deconstructing a play 'at the table' was, essentially, analysis of the psychological aspects of the character's life. 'At the table' the actor always viewed their character, from the outside, as it were. So when it was time for the actor to get up and do something, *that physical doing always proved difficult.* There was an artificial gap between the psychological and the physical aspects of the character's life in the given circumstances of the play.

By affirming that the unbroken line of physical actions – that is, *the line of the life of the human body* – has an important place in creating the character and provokes internal action, i.e., experiencing,[5] Stanislavski urges actors to under-

---

5 'Experiencing', *perezhivaniye* in Russian, borrowed from everyday speech, consists of the root 'to live' and the preposition that signifies a transition, a transformation, going beyond the boundaries of the 'self'. Going from 'one's self' to 'the other'. The word hovers in between a few different semantic fields, such as 'to live through', 'to experience', or to have a 'strong feeling', 'strong emotion', 'strong impression', etc. As part of the Stanislavski system, *perezhivaniye* refers to the process of undergoing an experience as it occurs. Theatre as 'the art of experiencing' is the new definition of theatre introduced by Stanislavski and the Russian school; feelings, or life, experienced here and now as

stand that *the link between physical and mental life is indivisible, and that consequently, we must not split apart the creative process of analysing the character's inner and outer behaviour.*

The actors must know from the outset of working with the director that they are going to analyse the play through action. Once they have deconstructed the play logically, which Stanislavski called 'mental reconnaissance', the director asks the actors to go to a rehearsal space and perform their actions in the concrete setting. All the objects the performers might need in the course of action, all the personal props, *every* single thing that can help the actor believe in the truth of what is happening must be set up in advance.

Does that mean that once they move on to the etude[6] phase, in which they look for the logic and sequence of their psychophysical behaviour, the actors never go back to the table? Not at all. They go back after each etude to make sense of what they have found, verify how precise they have been in carrying out the playwright's intentions, share with each other the lived experience they have just acquired, get the director to answer the questions that have come up so that they can grasp the author's text in even greater detail, and having discarded what they did wrong, go back and seek again to merge with their role in action.

The third and, perhaps, most important reason that prompted Stanislavski to talk of active analysis was the primary importance he attributed to words onstage.

Verbal action was for him the principal action in performance, and he saw words as the basic means of embodying the author's ideas. He strived to ensure that onstage, as in life, words were inseparably linked to the character's thoughts, tasks and actions.

The entire history of theatre is linked to the problem of how to speak onstage.[7]

Ever since the plays of the Russian realist school began to take their rightful place on the Russian stage, the best actors have given primacy to 'words sung from the heart',[ii] the expressive word that Gogol wrote about as '... sounds of the heart and soul, conveyed in words, so much more diverse than the sounds of music'.[iii]

Shchepkin,[8] who considered the delivery of the author's text onstage to be subject to the character being created, believed that the prime requirement

---

contrasted to the theatre of representation or imitation. In the 'theatre of experiencing' you must live, rather than appear to live. In English, the term is mostly translated as 'experiencing', but sometimes it is translated as 'to sense' or 'to feel', or their derivatives 'sensation/ sensations', 'feeling/ feelings', 'emotion/ emotions'. However, none of them ever imply the result the actor strives for but always the *source of action* itself – that which literally sets things in *motion* (trans. note).

6 See below the chapter 'Etude rehearsals' (ed. note).

7 See Book Two, the chapter 'Technique and logic of speech' (ed. note).
   The notion of 'stage speech' covers a wide semantic field of voice and speech (trans. note).

8 Mikhail Shchepkin (1788–1863), a great Russian actor, known for his roles in plays by Gogol. He kept notebooks on theatre (ed. notes).

for transforming into the character was a truthful delivery of the lines. He made it a mandatory condition for the actors in the company to have a clear understanding of the thoughts the text contained and study their course and development.

Another major figure at the Maly Theatre, the actor Alexander Yuzhin, believed that stage speech must be individually tailored for each character. It is not possible to demand that all the text should be delivered with the same simplicity and natural spontaneity. It all depends on who is speaking. 'Hamlet's lifelike and natural speech is neither lifelike, nor natural for Chatski[9]', he used to say.[iv]

Of great interest are Gogol's assertions on the way words are delivered onstage. He said that achieving a natural and sincere delivery of lines onstage depended on the rehearsal process. He wrote, 'they [the actors] must learn the lines together, and the role must enter their minds of its own accord during rehearsals, so that each of them, immersed in the immediate circumstances, involuntarily picks up the right tone of their role. ... But if the actors learn their lines at home, they can deliver nothing but a studied pompous response that will be fixed in them for ever: nothing will ever break through it ... with the play as a whole turning for them into something indistinct, remote'.[v]

Having observed and analysed the experience of the great masters as well as his own lifelong experience, Stanislavski considered the word to be, in Nemirovich-Danchenko's memorable phrase, both the crowning glory and the starting point of the creative act. He came to the conclusion that the greatest danger for an actor in search of natural behaviour onstage was a linear approach to the author's text.

And that was the third and decisive reason for changing the rehearsal practice.

Stanislavski often said that the more talented the playwright, the more vivid is the effect of their play on you when you first read it. The way the characters behave, their relationships, their feelings and thoughts seem so clear, so close to your heart, that you automatically assume that all you have to do is learn the lines and you will, without even noticing it, master the character.

But as soon as the actor learns the lines, everything that was so alive in their imagination withers and dies.

How can we avoid this danger?

Stanislavski came to the conclusion that the actors can only bring words to life if they do the preparatory work that leads them to a place where the author's text becomes essential in expressing the character's thoughts.

Mechanical line-learning inevitably leads, as Stanislavski put it, to the words getting 'lodged in the muscles of the tongue', that is, turning into dead clichés.

In the initial stages of their work, according to Stanislavski, actors should crave the author's words in order to discover the thoughts they contain, not merely as lines to learn by rote.

9 Chatski is a leading character in a verse comedy *Woe from Wit* by Alexander Griboyedov (1795–1829), Russian diplomat, playwright, poet and composer (trans. note).

Mastering all of the character's inner motives, dictated to the actor by this or that word, is an extremely complex process.

In *An Actor's Work on Himself* Stanislavski wrote:

> To believe in someone else's fictional invention and genuinely live it – you call that a trifle? Don't you know that creating something based on someone else's idea is infinitely more difficult than making up a story of your own? ... we rework dramatists' creations. We discover what is hidden beneath their words. We invest someone else's text with our own subtext. We establish our own relationship to people and the circumstances of their lives. We filter all the material given to us by the author and the director through our own personalities. We reshape it, give it life, fill it with our own imagination. We become bound to it, we live in it psychologically and physically. We produce the 'truth of the passions' in ourselves. The end result is genuinely productive action, closely connected with the ideas hidden within the play. We create living, typical images through the passions and feelings of the characters we portray.[vi]

Stanislavski sought new ways to generate the actor's creative sense of self, in which genuinely creative ideas arise and their embodiment takes place in the most organic way possible.

This primarily concerns that initial period of work, which ultimately plays a decisive role in all subsequent work.

Stanislavski maintained that, if the work started with learning lines by rote, the actor would at best just report them, more or less competently, to the audience. This is only natural since, in life, we never speak unless *'our verbal action is genuine, productive and to the purpose'*. In life, we express our thoughts by using a great variety of words. We can be repeating one and the same idea over and over again, and every time, depending on who we are speaking to, we will find new and appropriate words to express it. In life, we know that our words can bring joy, hurt, pacify, insult, and when addressing other people, we lend our words a definite meaning. In life, our words express our thoughts, our feelings and that is why they affect others, producing a reaction in those around us. Something very different happens onstage. Without having fully made the character's thoughts and feelings our own, with no belief in the play's given circumstances, we are obliged to deliver lines that belong to the character we portray, lines which are quite alien to us.

What do we need do to make the author's text 'our own', an organic part of us, the one and only text that we need? What do we have to do to make the word an instrument of action?

Stanislavski suggested we closely study the course of a character's thoughts so as to be able to express them in our own words. When we know exactly what we are talking about, we can, even before we have learned our lines, express the author's thoughts in our own words.

Stanislavski wrote: 'There are thoughts and feelings you can express in your own words. They are what matters, not the words. The line of the role follows the subtext not the text itself. But the actors are too lazy to dig deep into the subtext, so they prefer to skim the surface, the outward form of the word which can be spoken mechanically without using up energy to penetrate the essence.'[vii] Stanislavski said the secret of his approach was to forbid the actors learning their lines for a certain period of time, which saved them from mindlessly learning the lines by rote, and made them dig into the essence of the subtext and follow its internal line. When learnt by rote, words lose their actual meaning and turn into 'mechanical gymnastics', with 'the tongue gabbling off sounds that have been learnt'. But when actors have to make do without someone else's words for a time, they have nothing to hide behind and can't help but follow the line of the action. By using their own words, actors understand that what is said is inseparable from their tasks and actions.

Regarding the stage of the etude rehearsals in which actors speak using 'their own words', Stanislavski writes:

> This protects you from forming a mechanical habit of uttering empty words you have not experienced. *I have held on to the author's splendid words for you to use them better,*[10] not for the sake of gabbling, but for the sake of action and fulfilling the basic task.[viii]

Once we are able to navigate our character's train of thought with ease and fluency, we are no longer slaves to the text, and will go back to it when we feel the need to use it for expressing those thoughts that we have already understood during the etude. We will fall in love with the text since the author's words will express better and more precisely the thoughts we have come to know through the process of active analysis.

Notes

i   Vladimir Nemirovich-Danchenko, *Iz proshlogo*. Moscow, Academia, 1936.
ii   Mikhail Shchepkin *Zapiski. Pisma*. Moscow, Iskusstvo, 1952, p.237.
iii *Gogol i Teatr*. Moscow, Iskusstvo, 1952, p.387.
iv A.I. Yuzhin, *Vospominaniya. Zapisi. Statji. Pis'ma*. Moscow, Iskusstvo, 1951, p.318.
v   *Gogol i Teatr*. Moscow, Iskusstvo, 1952, p.388.
vi K.S. Stanislavski, *Rabota aktera nad soboj, Sobranie Sochinenij*, vol.2, part 1. Moscow, Iskusstvo, 1954, pp.63–64 (*An Actor's Work*, trans. by Jean Benedetti, Routledge, 2008, p.54. Adapted by Irina Brown).
vii K.S. Stanislavski, *Sobranie Sochinenij*, vol.4, Moscow, Iskusstvo, 1957, p.217 (trans. by Jean Benedetti).
viii Ibid., pp.217–218 (trans. by Jean Benedetti).

10 Knebel's italics (trans. note).

Given circumstances

Alexander Pushkin wrote: 'Truth of the passions, feelings that seem true in the supposed circumstances, that is what our intellect requires of a dramatist.'[i]

Stanislavski made this renowned quote the basis for his system, changing the word 'supposed' to 'imposed'. For an actor in a play the circumstances are not supposed but imposed: given.[1]

So, what are these 'given circumstances'?

> They are the plot, the facts, the events, the period, the time and place of action, the living conditions, how we as actors and directors understand the play, the contributions we ourselves make, the mise-en-scène, the staging, the set and costume designs, the props, the lighting, the sound effects, etc., etc., everything that is 'given' for the actors to take into account in their creative work.[ii]

Stanislavski covers here an unusually wide range of all the factors that actors should give credence to.

What seems to me of primary importance in this chapter on the 'given circumstances' is everything that relates to the study of a play.

Let's take Griboyedov's *Woe from Wit* as an example. What are the 'given circumstances' of Griboyedov's comedy? What is its historical context?

The play was written between 1822 and 1824, the time when all progressive Russians realised that the people had been duped and their hopes betrayed.[2] Once more they found themselves at the mercy of soulless bureaucrats and military blockheads. The finest representatives of the intelligentsia among the nobility formed secret societies and prepared for the uprising on 14 December 1825.

---

1 Stanislavski makes a play on words which it is difficult to translate. 'Supposed' means 'hypothetical'. But for the actor these circumstances are 'proposed' (prescribed) by the playwright. In her original translation Elizabeth Hapgood, who worked closely with Stanislavski, used the term 'given', and this has now been generally adopted (trans. note).
2 A reference to the Tsar's failure to carry out the promise of liberal reforms in the wake of Napoleon's defeat by the Russian people in the Great Patriotic War of 1812 (trans. note).

DOI: 10.4324/9780203125205-6

The acting ensemble need to know that in 1812 Griboyedov volunteered for the Russian army and was also a member of a secret society: probably the reason why in 1826 he was arrested and accused of having taken part in the Decembrist Uprising. He was released only because of a lack of evidence. We know, however, that he had been warned of his impending arrest and managed to burn any compromising papers. Furthermore, at their trial the Decembrists covered up for him just as they did for Pushkin.

To understand the period the characters live in is to discover one of the key given circumstances.

By studying the period, we begin to study the characters' environment.

The Famusov family, their relatives, friends and guests lived in a Moscow we can hardly imagine today. This was a Moscow that was being rebuilt after the fire of 1812.[3] The newly built houses were spacious but quite modest in scale (palaces were an exception) with an enfilade[4] of numerous rooms on the ground floor, and a more cramped upper floor with a rather low ceiling. The house façade was inevitably embellished with columns and a stuccoed pediment, and at the back there was a yard with some out-houses and, often, a large garden. People moved slowly around the Moscow of that time, either on horseback, or in large carriages and small carts. So, if the actress playing old Khlestova pictures the long exhausting journey she had to take to get to Famusov's drawing-room, her opening lines will convey Khlestova's actual experience:

> At sixty-five 'tis no easy matter to drag myself
> To see you, niece. Sheer torment!
> An hour or more just from Pokrovka! I am drained;
> It is not night. It's doomsday!

Of course, we cannot cover here the full extent and variety of the given circumstances in the comedy *Woe from Wit*.

We need to picture not only the period, the character's everyday way of life, and their relationships with one another, but, crucially, we must understand that besides this present, the characters also have a past and a future.

Stanislavski wrote:

> The *present* cannot exist without the *past*; nor can it exist without the *future*. Some will say that we can neither know nor predict our future. However, we not only can but we should desire one, and have designs for it …
>
> If in life there can be *no present* without *a past or a future*, then on the stage which reflects life, it cannot be otherwise.[iii]

---

3 The 1812 Fire of Moscow started on 14 September 1812 after Russian troops and most of its remaining residents abandoned the city just ahead of Napoleon's vanguard troops entering it after the Battle of Borodino. The fire all but destroyed the city. (Wikipedia, 'Fire of Moscow (1812)', viewed 15 December 2020, https://en.wikipedia.org/wiki/Fire_of_Moscow_(1812))

4 'Enfilade' is a suite of rooms with doorways in line with each other (trans. note).

How can we penetrate Chatski's *past*? Our imagination will be helped by studying the text of the play.

Chatski has been away for three years. When he left Moscow, he was a youth in love. He lived abroad. We don't know exactly where, but we can imagine both Italy and France. It was the beginning of the 19th century. There was intellectual ferment everywhere. Famusov may not have been very far from the truth when he exclaimed in response to one of Chatski's outbursts, 'Ah, dear God, he is a Carbonaro!'[5]

Chatski spent some time in St Petersburg. We learn this from Molchalin:

Tatiana Yurievna once spoke,
On her return from Petersburg,
Of your connections in the Government
And then the break-up ...

Let the actor's imagination suggest to them what it was that prompted the break-up with the government ministers, and who else Chatski might have been in contact with while in St Petersburg. Perhaps, they were the very same people that Griboyedov himself was associated with.[6]

Chatski is finally back in Moscow, where he had left behind his first love. He has missed her, he has been impatient to get back to her –

... for five and forty hours, with no sleep at all,
I hastened across seven hundred miles – the wind, the storm ...

He delights in Moscow and even more in seeing Sofya again – his love for her having grown deeper and stronger while they were apart.

So, if the actor gets a feel for Chatski's past, conjures it up, he will then run onto the stage not out of a vacuum, but out of life itself, which will continue to nourish his imagination.

Only then will his first words carry his passion and sincerity:

It's barely light – but you are up! and I am at your feet.

That is where Chatski's *present* begins, and we are to witness it for four acts. But for his present to be vibrant, full-blooded and compelling, the actor must clearly see where Chatski will disappear to after his final words:

Away from Moscow! Never to return.
No looking back. I'll run away and search the world
For the smallest corner where my outraged heart can find shelter ...
My carriage! get my carriage!

---

5 The Carbonari, or 'charcoal burners', were a secret revolutionary society. The organisation involved itself in secret rituals rather like Freemasonry. It attracted thousands of ex-Napoleonic officers and officials (trans. note).
6 A reference to the secret societies and the Decembrists (trans. note).

What is Chatski's *future* like? Here the actor must ask himself a number of questions that will undoubtedly help him with the *present* of the role. For example: maybe Chatski would come to his senses, resign himself to the status quo, and as the years go by turn into a well-meaning respectable member of the establishment, another Famusov? Or maybe he will join the civil service and turn into a functionary, like Molchalin, only a little more intelligent and noble-minded? No, impossible! Perhaps then in his passionate protest against the system, he will immerse himself in the activities of a secret society? Maybe he is going to share the fate of the 120 who were sent to Siberia after the events of 14 December 1825?[7] Or maybe his fate will be that of Griboyedov, who was sent a thousand kilometres from his homeland into an honourable exile as an ambassador to Persia, and perished as a result of political intrigues at the hands of the Persian insurgents?

Indeed, that might be a feasible *future* for Chatski. And the anticipation of this kind of *future* does colour the twenty-four hours that Chatski spends in Moscow, the twenty-four hours of his *present*, in as much as it carries traces of his *past*.

Let us take another example.

The past, present and future of Sofya, a young lady from Moscow: she is a spoilt young lady, the only daughter of a rich and high-ranking father, who grew up without a mother. Famusov, her father, managed 'to hire Madame Rosier to be her second mother'. Madame Rosier, without applying either her mind or her heart to the girl's upbringing, let herself be 'lured away by someone else for five hundred roubles more a year', having nevertheless taught Sofya 'to dance! and sing! and flirt! and sigh!'. Sofya, lonely and longing for love, developed a close bond with Chatski, but, offended by his departure, made Molchalin her hero – and now Sofya's *present* unfolds in front of Chatski's eyes.

It is easy to picture her *future*. She will either wilt away at her Auntie's house in 'the 'village, in the back of beyond, in Saratov', or will be happy to marry, if only to Skalozub, or will possibly forgive Molchalin one day ... All this stems from Sofya's *past* and *present* so vividly described by Griboyedov.

Having immersed our imagination in the past and the future of the characters, having studied their relationships, their milieu and period, we now understand the huge importance of the given circumstances in the specific detailed reconstruction of the author's intentions.

Notes

i   *Pushkin i Teatr.* Moscow, Iskusstvo, 1953, p.393 (*An Actor's Work*, trans. by Jean Benedetti, Routledge, 2008, p.52).

ii K.S Stanislavski, *Sobranie Sochinenij*, vol.2. Moscow, Iskusstvo, 1954, p.62 (*An Actor's Work*, trans. by Jean Benedetti, Routledge, 2008, pp.52–53. Adapted by Irina Brown).

iii K.S. Stanislavski, *Sobranie Sochinenij*, vol.4. Moscow, Iskusstvo, 1957, p.235 (trans. by Jean Benedetti).

7 14 December 1825 is the date of the Decembrist Uprising (trans. note).

Events

As we stated earlier, Stanislavski categorically rejected learning the lines mechanically and insisted on an in-depth analysis of the circumstances that produce a given text.

Stanislavski shows us the way of truly getting to the core of a play. He believes that the easiest way to do this is by analysing the facts, or the events, that is, the plot.

That is why he suggested starting the systematic analysis of a play by defining the events, or, as he put it, the operative facts, their sequence and interaction.

While identifying events and actions, the actor involuntarily grasps wider and wider strata of the given circumstances of the life of the play. Stanislavski insisted that actors should learn to break the play down according to its major events. He advised them to test each situation in the play against an instance drawn from their own life. His suggestion was that every time an actor sought to define the main event at a certain point in their own lives, they should take note of smaller events that occurred at the very same time but did not affect their life for more than a day, or just a few hours, until a new event distracted them, overshadowing the one before.

So Stanislavski advised that during the initial analysis of the play the actor should not get bogged down in details, in tiny bits or chunks, but should keep looking for what was the most important, and through that, comprehend the particulars:

[Think what happened in the Famusov household on Chatski's unexpected arrival?]

[What are the consequences of the news that the Government Inspector is on his way?]

These kinds of questions make us realise the logic and sequence of actions and events. But they are by no means enough to understand *what* happens in the play. This is understanding in the abstract. The most important and complex process comes next: putting oneself into the character's place.

Both the director and the actor must be able to think in images, and possess a dynamic creative imagination.

DOI: 10.4324/9780203125205-7

In getting a grasp of the play, of the author's intentions, his thoughts and motives, an actor must get to the heart of the play's events and given circumstances. He must live amid imaginary objects, in the thick of a fictional, imaginary life.

Without the assistance of his creative imagination the actor will never gain access to this fictional life. What kind of imagination is this? Stanislavski used to say that everything our imagination comes up with must be well grounded. Questions such as who, when, where, why, what for and how stimulate the actor's imagination, producing a vivid picture of a fictional or imagined life.

He said that there are times when this artificial life is created intuitively, with no conscious, intellectual input. However, with an active imagination we can always stir up our feelings and create the imaginary life we need. Still, the subject matter of our make-believe must be specific and clear. There is no such thing as daydreaming 'in general'.

For the imagination to arouse in the 'human being/actor' a life that is true to nature, he must, says Stanislavski, 'surrender to the role not only psychologically but physically'.[i]

The actor must make the character's actions their own, only then can they achieve truth and sincerity. They have to put themselves into the character's place in the circumstances given by the author.

For that to happen, they must start by performing basic psychophysical actions linked to specific events.

The actor must, above all, have '*a real sense of the life of a role, not only psychologically but physically*'.

> Just as yeast causes fermentation, so the sense of the life of a role produces an inner heat, a rising to the boil necessary for the process of creative exploration. We can only speak of approaching the play and the role once the actor has reached this creative state.[ii]

A method of work in which the actor explores only the psychological life of the character gives rise to considerable errors, since the split between the psychological life and the physical life does not allow the actor to get a sense of the life of the character's body, leaving them impoverished.

A person's inner state of mind, their wishes, thoughts, feelings must be expressed both in words and in specific physical activity.

From the very start the actor must analyse the play in action.

Here is Stanislavski's definition of his method:

> ... the new secret, the new aspect of my technique for creating the life of the human body of a role consists in the fact that the simplest physical actions, while being actually embodied on the stage, oblige the actor to create, in accord with his own motives, imaginative ideas, given circumstances, and magic 'ifs'.

If one simple physical action requires such a huge effort on the part of the imagination, the whole line of the life of the human body needs a whole, unbroken series of ideas and given circumstances throughout the play.

It is only possible to grasp and to extract them through detailed analysis carried out by all our creative forces. My technique stimulates that analysis naturally, spontaneously.[iii]

In the early stages of his work Stanislavski often asked the actors, 'What do you want in this episode?', then later he formulated his question differently: 'What *would you do* if this or that happened?'

If the first question makes actors reflective and quite passive, the second makes them active. They start to ask themselves, 'What would I do today, here, now, in these given circumstances?' They become aware of the reasons that compel them to take action; they start to performs actions mentally, and in doing this, if only in their mind, they discover the way to their feelings and their subconscious.

By discovering their character's actions, the actor discovers the storyline, and through it, the essence of their role. Grasping how the conflict develops forces the actor to actively work out the action and the counter-action and brings them nearer the concrete supertask[1] of the role. Using events as the starting point draws the actor into the world of the play by the shortest possible route.

It might seem that this only concerns plays with a vividly expressed external action, with an external plot. Not so. Even when everything in a play is subject to hidden inner development, the living link between its events lays bare the characters' behaviour.

So, if we do not study the play through its events, or from the point of view of the continuity of events that nourish it, we disregard the basic law of drama – the law of action, since in a play the events are of primary importance. In one of his rehearsals Konstantin Sergeievich said to us:

> [Go back to some period in your life, recall the most important event at the time, then you will immediately understand how it affected your behaviour, your actions, your thoughts and feelings, your relationships with other people.]

The events, or, as Stanislavski called them, *the operative facts*, constitute the foundation on which the playwright constructs the play's action.

The actor must study the chain of all the operative facts in-depth.

But this alone is not enough. The action cannot exist without a motive behind it. We cannot imagine asking a question, 'What am I doing?' without a complementary question coming up, 'Why am I doing it?', in other words, for every action there is a motive.

---

1 See below the chapter 'The supertask' (ed. note).

While studying the play's events, the logic and sequence of the character's actions and behaviour, the actor gradually starts to assess them, developing an awareness of the character's underlying motives.

In any play some characters want one thing, some another. Some have one goal, some another. This leads to conflict and to struggle.

To define the reasons for these conflicts, to understand the goals and motives of characters on either side is the primary task in the initial period of rehearsals. To understand the basic events, without getting distracted by smaller details that can lead you astray, to understand what makes the action and the counter-action, is to define the dramatic conflict on the basis of active analysis.

Stanislavski wrote:

> What does it actually mean to assess the facts and events of a play? It means finding their hidden inner meaning, their spiritual essence, and the degree of their significance and influence. It means digging underneath the external facts and events, and discovering deep under them some other well-concealed events that often are the cause of those external facts. It means following the course of the psychological events, getting a sense of the extent and nature of their impact, following the lines of aspiration of every single character, observing the lines clash, criss-cross, intertwine, separate. In a word, grasping the inner pattern that determines people's relationships. Assessing the facts means to find the key to the many secrets of 'the life of the human spirit' of a role, hidden underneath the facts of the play.[iv]

Notes

i   K.S. Stanislavski, *Rabota aktera nad rolyu. Sobranie Sochinenij*, vol.2. Moscow, Iskusstvo, 1954, p.94 (*An Actor's Work*, trans. by Jean Benedetti, Routledge, 2008, p.84).

ii   K.S. Stanislavski, *Rabota aktera nad rolyu. Sobranie Sochinenij*, vol.4. Moscow, Iskusstvo, 1957, p.316 (*An Actor's Work on a Role*, trans. by Jean Benedetti, p.47. Adapted by Irina Brown).

iii   Ibid., pp.340–341. (*An Actor's Work on a Role*, trans. by Jean Benedetti, pp.68–69. Adapted by Irina Brown). See also: K.S. Stanislavski, 'O fizicheskikh dejstviyakh' (On physical actions), *Teatr*, 1948, No.8, p.16.

iv   K.S. Stanislavski, *Statyi. Rechi. Besedy. Pis'ma.* Moscow, Iskusstvo, 1953, p.587.

Assessing the facts[1]

Stanislavski demanded that actors learn to get to the very essence of the facts selected by the playwright.

But establishing the facts is not enough. The actor must be able to put themself in the character's shoes, and then consider the facts and events as themself, from their own point of view. In order to assess the facts through their own feelings rooted in their personal, direct relationship with the facts, the actor must internally question themself: 'Which of my own personal human intentions, wishes, aspirations, characteristics, good qualities or character defects could make me, "the human being/actor", relate to the people and events in the play in the same way as the character I portray?'

Let us try and follow the process of 'assessing the facts' in an example.

Let us take an episode from the role of Sofya from Griboyedov's *Woe from Wit*.

An assessment of the event that starts the play will be decisive for Sofya's inner characterisation.

The event is: her secret tryst with Molchalin.

How could Sofya have fallen in love with Molchalin? How could she prefer him to Chatski, her childhood playmate?

From the very first moment of being onstage the actress must know what it is that she intends to reveal in Sofya and Sofya's thinking about the facts and events, otherwise she will not be able to 'be', 'exist', 'behave' in the given circumstances. Once she has understood Sofya as a person and has looked at everything that is happening in the play through her eyes, the actress discovers traits in herself that bring her nearer to the character. In seeking a psychological approach, her imagination targets – as it were – the author's given circumstances.

We know of a number of different interpretations of the role of Sofya as performed by our leading actresses.

---

1 The Russian term has been variously translated as 'appraising the facts' or 'evaluating the facts'. Jean Benedetti also proposes 'weighing up the facts' to capture the subjective nature of the process for the actor. After some consideration, I have decided on 'assessing the facts' (trans. note).

DOI: 10.4324/9780203125205-8

In the Moscow Art Theatre production Angelina Stepanova,[2] with her characteristic social astuteness, created in the role of Sofya a typical figure of 'Famusov's' Moscow. With wit and malice, she exposed those who 'cannot plainly speak the simplest word'.

Imperious and cold, her Sofya mostly craved admiration; she needed 'a boy-husband, a servant-husband, a wife's page-boy'.

With cunning and determination she implements her plan to wed Molchalin. She is not bothered by his poverty. She believes in his ability to make himself indispensable to Famusov, Khlestova and others in her circle.

Chatski irritates her with his unwelcome love, he is in her way, so with her every word she does her best to insult and humiliate him. She does not want to remember the past that binds her to him, and she is clever enough to understand that Chatski is someone hostile to her social world. She fights against him in every way she can. She deliberately spreads the rumour that he is mad:

Ah, Chatski! You love to make the others look like fools
See if you'd like to wear a fool's cap yourself?

She revels in the effect her words produce, watching as the rumour snowballs into an avalanche that buries Chatski.

We are also familiar with another interpretation of Sofya's character: Vera Michurina-Samoilova[3] played the role very differently.

Her Sofya's nature was fervent, passionate. She had loved Chatski once, loved him as ardently and sincerely as he loved her. But Chatski had gone away. And he stayed away for a very long time. Abandoned by him, alone, she is trying to stifle her feelings. Having suffered separation from the man she loved, with no news from him, she does all she can to forget him. She invents her love for Molchalin, it pleases her to think that there is someone at her side for whom she is the most precious thing in the world. This brings her the possibility of solace and peace of mind.

But her feelings for Chatski are not dead. They are alive, they disturb and torment her, urging her to find another romantic interest and, finally, to rid her heart of the man who had left her of his own free will.

In her scene in Act 1 Michurina-Samoilova abruptly interrupted her servant Lisa, when Chatski's name came up, and her interjection –

Ah! If someone loves somebody
Why go far away in search of answers?

2 Angelina Stepanova (1905–2000), a Moscow Art Theatre actress, who was trained at Vakhtangov's Third Studio. She first appeared as Sofya at MAT in the 1924/1925 season (ed. note).
3 Vera Michurina-Samoilova (1866–1948), an actress at the Aleksandrinski Theatre in St Petersburg (ed. note).

– burst out with all the pain of a woman scorned. It seemed like all the years of separation had done nothing to alleviate it. And when Sofya spoke of Molchalin –

> The man I love is of another sort
> Molchalin always thinks of others, not himself …

– it seemed she was speaking not to Lisa but to Chatski, justifying to him, in her mind, her love for another man who was both better and more deserving of her than him.

The meeting with Chatski shook her to the core, she could scarcely find the strength to hold a civil conversation with him.

The line, 'Why did God bring this Chatski back again!', was tragic on her lips. And in Act 3 when Chatski pressed Sofya to acknowledge, 'Who is it, after all, that she holds dear?', Michurina-Samoilova stubbornly battled with both Chatski and herself, hiding her true feelings with biting sarcastic remarks. Having blurted out, 'He's lost his wits', she saw, bewildered, how the words she had spoken in nothing more than a fit of pique were quickly picked up by others and gained a powerful momentum.

'… Sofya's attraction to Molchalin is, essentially, merely the prism through which the genuine deep love the girl feels for Chatski is refracted', writes Michurina-Samoilova, '[…] My Sofya loved only Chatski'.[i]

'In *Woe from Wit*', wrote Wilhelm Küchelbecker,[4] 'the plot hinges precisely on Chatski's opposition to other characters … There is Chatski. Then there are other characters. They are brought together, and we are shown the inevitable outcome of the meeting between the two opposite poles …'[ii]

The playwright's dramatic intention was embodied both in Stepanova's and in Michurina-Samoilova's interpretations. Stepanova's approach is more direct. Michurina-Samoilova, by making Sofya more human, in the end may have made her Sofya more frightening since she was capable of greater feelings! Naturally, in the process of searching for the personal traits that would bring them nearer to the character, the two actresses developed different psychophysical qualities and used different parallels to evoke the feelings they needed that corresponded to their ideas.

It must be stressed that 'assessing the facts' is a creative process that enables the actor to grasp the essence of a play, requiring from them the ability to feed their personal experiences into the understanding of the play's every detail.

'Assessing the facts' requires the actor to have both a broad overview of the piece and an ability to examine individual moments in it from the point of view of the whole:

> … although real drama manifests itself as a known event, the latter only provides a cause for bringing to an end all the contradictions that have

---

4 W.K. Küchelbecker (1797–1846), a writer and poet, a friend of Pushkin and Griboyedov; took an active part in the Decembrist Uprising in 1825 and died in exile in Siberia (ed. note).

been feeding the drama long before the actual event takes place. These contradictions, concealed in life itself, have been gradually and indirectly paving the way for the event itself. From the point of view of the event, the drama is the final word, or, at least, the decisive turning point of all human existence.[iii]

Notes

i   V.A. Michurina-Samoilova, *Shest'desyat let v iskusstve*. Moscow/Leningrad, Iskusstvo, 1946, p.104.
ii Quoted by M.V. Nechkina in *A.S. Griboyedov i dekabristy*. Moscow, GIXL, 1947, p.219.
iii Saltykov-Shchedrin, *O literature i iskusstve*. Moscow, Iskusstvo, 1953, p.109.

The Supertask

We cannot ignore here one of the most important principles of Stanislavski's aesthetic.

The terms 'supertask' and 'throughaction' are widely used by us all.

While we cannot claim to examine fully the whole of the Stanislavski system here, we have to stress yet again that to understand clearly the method of active analysis of the play and the role we must study every single one of its elements. Therefore, it seems advisable to *remind* ourselves what Stanislavski meant when he talked of the supertask and the throughaction.

First, let us quote Stanislavski himself:

> The Supertask and the Throughaction are the living essence, the arteries, the nerves, the heart-beat of the play. ... The Supertask (wish), the Throughaction (intention) and its fulfilment (action) establish the creative process of experiencing.[i]

How can we decipher this?

'Let us agree that in the future', writes Stanislavski, 'we will call this fundamental, principal, all-encompassing goal, which draws together each and every Task, and stimulates the creative efforts of the inner drives and the Elements that comprise the sense of self of the actor-role: *the Supertask of the writer's work*.'[ii]

The supertask must be 'conscious', generated in the mind by the actor's creative thought. It must be emotional, stimulating the whole of his human nature. And finally, it must be volitional, arising from their 'spiritual and physical being'. The supertask must awaken the actor's creative imagination, arouse their faith, stir up their mental and emotional life.

A properly defined supertask, one and the same, and compulsory, for all the performers, will elicit a personal response, a unique emotional resonance in each of them.

> Without the subjective experiences of a creative artist, it [the Supertask] is arid, dead. It is essential to find a response in the actor's heart and mind if the Supertask and the role are to become living, vibrant, resplendent with all the colours of genuine, human life.[iii]

DOI: 10.4324/9780203125205-9

When we are looking for the supertask it is essential to define it exactly, to name it precisely, to express it in words that will spur us into action because an incorrectly defined supertask often sends actors in the wrong direction.

Stanislavski gives an example from his own acting practice. He tells a story of how he once played Argan in Molière's *Le Malade imaginaire*.[1] Initially, he defined the supertask as: 'I want to be ill.' Despite all his efforts Stanislavski got further and further away from the essence of the play. Molière's joyous comedy turned into a tragedy. All because Stanislavski set off with an incorrectly defined supertask. Finally, he realised his mistake and searched for an alternative, eventually coming up with: 'I want people to think that I am ill.' Then everything fell into place. He instantly struck up the correct relationship with the quack doctors in the play, and Molière's sarcastic, comedic talent resounded loud and clear.

Notes

i   K.S. Stanislavski, *Sobranie Sochinenij*, vol.4. Moscow, Iskusstvo, 1957, pp.151, 154 (*An Actor's Work on a Role*, trans. by Jean Benedetti, p.160. Adapted by Irina Brown).
ii   K.S. Stanislavski, *Sobranie Sochinenij*, vol.2. Moscow, Iskusstvo, 1954, pp.332–333 (*An Actor's Work*, trans. by Jean Benedetti, p.307. Adapted by Irina Brown).
iii Ibid., p.335 (*An Actor's Work*, trans. by Jean Benedetti, p.309. Adapted by Irina Brown).

1 *Le Malade imaginaire* (*The Imaginary Invalid*) by Molière, written in 1673. Stanislavski appeared in it as Argan at the Moscow Art Theatre in 1913.

Throughaction

throughline

Let us take another example from Griboyedov's *Woe from Wit*. If Chatski's supertask is defined as 'I want to strive for liberty', then the whole of the character's inner life and all of his actions must be directed at achieving it. This gives rise to his merciless condemnation of everything and everyone who stands in the way of his striving for liberty, his striving to unmask and battle the likes of Famusov, Molchalin, Skalozub.

This unified action, directed towards the supertask, is what Stanislavski called the 'throughaction'.

Stanislavski says that '… the Throughaction brings everything together, strings all the elements together, like a thread through unconnected beads, and points them towards the common Supertask'.[i]

Unless the actor pins all their actions to the pivotal core of the throughaction, the performance of that role can never be considered a serious artistic success.

More often than not, when the actor replaces the throughaction with minor, less essential actions, artistic failure awaits them.

Imagine the actor playing Chatski saying to himself, 'I aspire to many things: to find rest in my native land after my travels, to mock a host of buffoons, to marry Sofya, to free an old friend from his wife's influence, etc.'.

What would happen then? The role would be fractured into separate tiny actions, and however well they were performed, nothing would remain of the author's supertask.

In combating this phenomenon, rather frequent in the theatre, Stanislavski wrote:

> That is why the individual bits of your role, beautiful as they were, made no impression and were not satisfying as a whole. You are breaking a statue of Apollo into bits and showing each of them separately. Fragments will hardly capture an audience.[ii]

In a work of fiction, for every throughaction there is its counter-throughaction that reinforces the throughaction.[1]

---

1 See Appendix A (ed. note).

DOI: 10.4324/9780203125205-10

Famusov, Skalozub, Molchalin, Famusov's other guests and the mythical Princess Marya Alexeievna represent the counteraction to Chatski's throughaction and thereby strengthen it.

Stanislavski says: 'If there were no counter-Throughaction in the play and everything just worked out, there would be nothing for the cast and the characters to do, and the play itself would be actionless and therefore ineffective on the stage.'[iii]

Notes

i   K.S. Stanislavski, *Sobranie Sochinenij*, vol.2. Moscow, Iskusstvo, 1954, p.338 (*An Actor's Work*, trans. by Jean Benedetti, p.312).

ii Ibid., p.340 (*An Actor's Work*, trans. by Jean Benedetti, pp.313–314).

iii Ibid., p.345 (*An Actor's Work*, trans. by Jean Benedetti, p.318. Adapted by Irina Brown).

Etude rehearsals

Before starting active analysis through etudes with improvised dialogue, there is preliminary work to be done that Stanislavski called 'mental reconnaissance'.

Even during 'mental reconnaissance' the skeleton of the play begins to be fleshed out for the actor. Usually, after this analysis the actor sees clearly what his character does in the play, what he aspires to, who he fights against or sides with, and the nature of his relationships with other characters.

It is only after an in-depth 'mental reconnaissance' that an ensemble, of now like-minded actors, can get down to active analysis.

We must keep in mind that before doing any etudes we have to delve into the major events of the play as well as the minor, secondary ones.

This is essential so that actors, when moving on to etude rehearsals, neglect none of the inner and outer tasks the author has given their characters; essential so that in making an etude on a given fragment, actors are fully aware of the goals they pursue in the etude, and of the functions particular themes within the etude have in the play itself.

A detailed deconstruction of the script in terms of events, actions and themes enables the performer not to diverge from the play in etudes but to make each episode their own, in and through action, by putting themself in the given circumstances of the role.

But how can we make sure that all the actors understand their characters' goals and the path they have to follow? Stanislavski suggests a very useful exercise in this regard: each actor must recount their character's storyline from the beginning of the play to the end.

This exercise will instantly reveal how far the actor understands not only the text the author gave their character but also the character's actions, goals and relationships with other characters. In recounting the story, the actor becomes aware of the material of the play as a whole, of its fundamental throughaction.

It is far from easy to recount the storyline of a role. The actor cannot do it until they have a clear idea of the play as a whole, when not only they but the other actors have figured out the logic and sequence of their actions.[1]

---

1 See Appendix B (ed. note).

DOI: 10.4324/9780203125205-11

Having come to understand the logic of their actions and the sequence of the events, having defined what happens in the play, we have to move on to the most crucial and rather complex process of putting ourselves in the character's place, transferring ourselves into the situations and circumstances the author suggests.

We must make the character's actions our own since we can only live truthfully and sincerely through our own actions. So we have to perform someone else's actions as ourselves. We do not yet know our lines by heart but we do already know the major events, what the characters do, and the way they really think. Do an etude and improvise your own dialogue! Then, as Stanislavski put it, you will begin to feel yourself in the role, and later on you will feel the role in you.

An etude rehearsal forces the actor to become aware of all the details of their physical being in any given episode, which, of course, is closely linked with all their psychological experiences.

So how does this method of rehearsals differ from the old order? Here's how: when analysing the play at the table, the actor had little concern for the physical side of his character's being since he did not actually have to do it. With the new method, the actor has to master everything as soon as he starts working on the role, without separating the psychological (the internal) from the physical (the external).

If previously we analysed the play and the role intellectually, exchanging our views on it from the outside, as it were, with the new rehearsal method, by doing etudes based directly on the themes of the play and the situations within it, we study the play in action and in reality. As if the actor is instantly placed in the circumstances of their character's life, into the world of the play itself.

It is important for the actor to grasp each rehearsed episode not only with their mind but with their whole being. Stanislavski writes:

> Look into this process and you will find it was *an inner and outer analysis* of ourselves as human beings in the circumstances of the life of the role. This process is nothing like the cold, cerebral study of a role which actors usually undertake in the very early stages of creative work.
>
> The process of which I speak is accomplished simultaneously by all the intellectual, emotional, mental and physical forces of our nature ...[i]

For this we must, of course, have the right conditions. So, as we move on to etude rehearsals, the actor must be placed in conditions approximating those of the future production: with the rehearsal space set-up as it will be in the show, with the suitable stand-in accessories, furnishings and props.

We must rehearse in costumes that fit the period of the play. Wearing a modern jacket instead of a period costume will inevitably affect the actor's sense of self.

That means the director must make a decision concerning the time and place of the action since he has to place the actor, from the very start, in conditions to which the actor must become accustomed.

Finally, the rehearsal space is set up, all the props are in place, the actors have put on the right costumes. The actor goes on for his first etude rehearsal.

It is very important in an etude rehearsal, just as it is throughout the rehearsal process, that there is an atmosphere of heightened creative interest and support for the performer. It is no secret that during the initial period of etude work actors often have difficulty overcoming their self-consciousness, their physical tension and inhibitions, that the improvised lines are not easy to come up with and the result is often clumsy. If their fellow-actors, instead of producing the right creative atmosphere in such difficult moments, sit there loudly commenting on the etude, they not only make the method meaningless but, perhaps, paralyse the actor's efforts to approach their role creatively for a long time to come.

The words the actor uses are of absolutely no importance. *What is important is that the words should be prompted by the playwright's ideas within the particular fragment of the play the etude is based upon.*

One caveat: even when the play and the role have been thoroughly assimilated during 'mental reconnaissance', producing an etude is still far from simple. In the initial stages, it is hard for the actors to grasp the material as a whole: the actor is still struggling to remember lots of things. So the company must go back to the play as soon as the etude is over and analyse the scene they have just done. It is essential for the actors to be able to check everything they have done in the etude against the play itself.

Such checking against the playtext is necessary because if, during 'mental reconnaissance', the actor does not take up their character's position physically, in the etude they have already put themself in the character's place, and have *taken action* on their behalf.

Setting the etude against the text, instantly enables actors to see what was right and what was wrong in what they did, if they made any new discoveries, and where they only touched the surface. This immediately raises lots of questions which the director must answer in order to steer actors in the right direction.

Stanislavski wrote:

> … just to be able to walk onto the stage as a human-being, not an actor, you need to know: who you are, what has happened to you, what your life is like, what your days are like, where you have come from and many other given circumstances that influence what you do. In other words, just to make a proper entrance, you have to know the world and how you see it …[ii]

I feel the need to emphasise once more that all the etudes must be done with the actor using only improvised dialogue.

That means that etude rehearsals place actors in conditions when for a certain period of time they replace the author's words with their own, while strictly preserving the author's ideas. It cannot be otherwise: we base our etude on a particular episode of the play, knowing well the themes of the whole play and of our own role, knowing all the situations, all the relationships, in short, everything we learnt during the 'mental reconnaissance'. Improvised lines that are not dictated by the themes affecting the characters in the episode our etude is based on will lead the actors away from the play rather than towards it.

The actors' psychophysical sense of self will in the end, in a properly structured etude, call for the verbal action dictated by the contents of the play as a whole.

The etude method has one other crucial distinction.

We have already stated that as soon as an etude with improvised dialogue is over, the actors should read the scene or episode again and check what they did against the original text.

During this re-reading and analysis, the actor's attention should be drawn not only to the logical connection between the improvised lines and the author's wording but also to the choice and order of words, and the grammatical structures the playwright uses to express a particular character's thoughts in a particular scene. Focusing the actor's attention on this is important since an individual's speech is unique, it is an integral part of one's personality.

The actors' attention must be drawn to the fact that the writer never interrupts the dialogue with pauses unless there is a good reason for it; that sometimes their characters are verbose, and sometimes quite terse. There is always a psychological cause behind it.

Shakespeare provided Othello with speech that is rich, charged with imagery and spiritual depth characteristic of the world-view of the time. Studying the nature of Othello's speech helps us understand the essence of his character. Anfisa in Ostrovsky's *Wolves and Sheep* is given trivial words, all those endless interjections of 'No way!' and 'Oh, well!' indicative of the inner landscape of someone who has no language, thoughts or vocabulary.

If a play is in verse, if it is written with that inner excitement that compelled the author to think in verse rather than prose, then actors approaching etudes must tune into the poetic frame of mind that will bring them closer to the verse later on. What if initially the improvised lines are clumsy? That should not stop them.

The purpose of etudes is to bring the actor as close as possible to the author's text. When after etude rehearsals actors go back to the original text, they greedily soak up the words in which the writer expressed their ideas. Comparing the writer's vocabulary with the words they have just spoken, actors become aware of their own stylistic errors.

In etude rehearsals, words come to the actor spontaneously as a result of having the correct inner sense of the dramatist's intentions. The actor's progress in mastering the material can be gauged by comparing their improvised lines with the author's original text.

Let's be absolutely clear about the whole question of learning lines. For Stanislavski and his students, the true champions of active analysis, one, of course, must be word-perfect. That goes without saying. A must for every actor! The problem is how to make the writer's text our own, not learning it parrot-fashion, but organically, so that the writer's words become the only possible expression of the inner content of the character as created by the actor.

Some opponents of the etude method object that the use of improvised text in etude rehearsals allows the actors to ignore both the style of the play and the form the author has given it.

I consider that active analysis, and consequently, the etude rehearsals, in no way draw actors away from the style of the play but, on the contrary, actively propel them towards it.

The style of the play is primarily expressed through people, their nature, their world-view, their relationships with others, their vocabulary. This, of course, by no means exhausts all the particular qualities that define a style, but in the theatre we must, above all, look for those specific stylistic features which we find within human being themselves.

In an etude, as they follow the writer's intentions, the actor, through the method of active analysis, enters the world of the character's feelings, while simultaneously exploring the form in which they are expressed. They cannot help but take in a number of stylistic clues, typical of the given work.

Once the preliminary 'mental reconnaissance' has been carried out with due depth and seriousness, everything drives the actor towards the writer's style, since the purpose of the etude is a deeper understanding of the essence of the play.

Studying the writer's vocabulary, we gradually make the nature of the person the writer has created our own.

In coming to understand both form and content through etudes, the actor develops a feeling for the style naturally, and gets closer to the author's individual way of writing from the very start.[2]

The etude is over. Everything seems to be crystal-clear to the actors. We can now move on to the author's exact text.

By checking what was done in the etude against the original text, the actors not only see for themselves if they have correctly understood and reproduced the play's dramatic intention in the etude but they also imperceptibly and organically start to absorb parts of the text. Sometimes, when the etude is repeated, the actors begin to use some of the writer's own words.

Post-etude return to the table work and the text enables actors to test themselves, and to understand both their mistakes and their progress in relation to the role.

If the actor has done the etude correctly, if their actions and words have correctly conveyed all the author's ideas, they will respond to the original text with enormous creative joy.

At this point a true creative encounter occurs between the actor and the writer, and the pleasure it produces will bear fruit later on the stage.

2 See Appendix C (ed. note).

Undoubtedly, mistakes can occur in the course of etude rehearsals, and quite often they do. They are mainly caused by an insufficient understanding of the logical sequence of ideas underlying the writer's intention, of the play's subtext.

Here is an example from my own practice.

I was rehearsing Pushkin's *Gypsies*[3] with my GITIS students. We had analysed in detail the poem as a whole. We started doing etudes and got to the point of Zemfira's secret rendezvous with the young Gypsy, the rendezvous that proves fatal for them both since Aleko kills both his young rival and Zemfira in a fit of jealousy.

The etude went well, charged with energy and feeling, and the assessing of the facts and events was lively, spontaneous, natural. The students that were not involved in the etude congratulated their fellows warmly. They particularly liked it, when the student playing the young Gypsy courageously confronted Aleko and offered his breast to the dagger, resolved to sacrifice himself and save his beloved, Zemfira. Aleko stabbed him, and then, as Zemfira rushed to defend her lover, he killed her, too.

It all seemed right.

The student playing the young Gypsy was excited by the success of the etude and told us that what he liked most about his role was how the young Gypsy's love was opposed to Aleko's selfishness. The moment he was given the part, he imagined how he would die defending Zemfira.

However successful the etude might have been, it has long been my custom to go back to the table immediately afterward and check it against the original text. We stuck to our usual practice. Here is what we read:

1st Voice
It's time.
2nd Voice
Do stay!
1st Voice
It's time, my love.
2nd Voice
No, no! stay till break of day.
1st Voice
'Tis late.
2nd Voice
How timorous your love. A moment more!
1st Voice
You'll ruin me.
2nd Voice
A moment more!
1st Voice
What if my husband

---

3 *Gypsies* (1827) – a narrative poem by Alexander Pushkin.

Wakes up alone? ...
Aleko
I am awake.
Where to? Haste not away together;
Here's good enough for you, next to your grave.
Zemfira
My friend, flee, flee...
Aleko
Wait!
Where go you, my pretty youth?
Lie you here!
(Aleko stabs him)

The text ignored by the students is italicised here by me.

1) If they had paid attention to Aleko's words 'Where to? Haste not away together', they would have understood that both Zemfira's and the young Gypsy's first reaction was to run away. They *both* flee.

2) After Zemfira's words 'My friend, flee, flee ...', Aleko says, 'Wait! Where go you, my pretty youth?'

That means that the young Gypsy *tries to run away* alone.

It is not the Gypsy who wants to save Zemfira but the other way around. In the etude, the student playing the young Gypsy got carried away by, quite possibly, very compelling ideas, but they did not come from Pushkin's intention.

Comparing the etude to Pushkin's text revealed the mistake. After that the students learnt the lines with ease, organically, and when they repeated the etude, all the actions followed the play's intention.

Occasionally, we encounter another issue that slows work down. When an actor repeats the etude two or three times, they start to fix their own improvised words. Once the etude turns into a mere repetition, rather than the search for a new and deeper understanding of the character, these attempts, leading us down a false path, must be stopped. The etude is a stage in the process of discovery and analysis of the role and the play. Once an actor has worked out what is going on, there is no need to keep them artificially at the stage they have completed.

A detailed analysis of the play in terms of events, actions and themes prepares the actor, as we have said before, for the etude rehearsals.

The volume of the material used in an etude always varies according to the complexity of the play or the episode.

What is important is that the chosen extract should deal with a particular event or turning point in the play's action fully.

I would like to use as an example Stanislavski's analysis of a crowd scene from the first act of *Othello*.

Let me remind you of the story: Iago and Roderigo speak of their hatred for the Moor. Iago is insulted because Othello has not appointed him his lieutenant. He talks Roderigo into causing a kerfuffle outside the windows of Brabantio's house. Brabantio is Desdemona's father. Iago knows that Desdemona is not at home and that she and Othello have become secretly engaged without Brabantio's knowledge.

Roderigo creates an uproar. Brabantio appears at the window. Roderigo informs him that Desdemona has eloped with Othello. Having ensured that Desdemona is not in the house, Brabantio summons his servants, the officers, and some citizens to set off and track Othello down.

What is the main event in this scene then? Desdemona's abduction, or elopement. Stanislavski's analysis of this crowd scene gives a full picture of an extract primed to the point when the actor can start doing an etude.

> Understand, still half-asleep, what has happened. Get to the bottom of things no one really knows about. Question each other, argue, reject the explanations you do not like, accept others, express your own point of view.
>
> Having heard the shouting in the street, look for the windows to see and work out what is happening. Cannot find any room to stand. Do what you must to get it. See who is making a noise, listen to what these troublemakers are shouting in the middle of the night. Find out who they are. Roderigo is recognised as one of them. Listen and try to understand what all the shouting is about. At first do not believe that Desdemona could do such a crazy thing. Keep persuading others it is either a plot or the ravings of a drunkard. Curse the troublemakers for keeping you awake. Threaten them, try to drive them away. Slowly come to believe that they are telling the truth. Share your first impressions with your neighbours, express condemnation or regret at what has happened. The hatred, the curses and threats against the Moor! Work out what is to be done next. Go over all the possible ways out of the situation. Defend your own opinions, criticise or approve the opinions of others. Try to find out the opinions of the powers that be. Support Brabantio in his exchange with the instigators of the scandal. Incite him to take revenge. Hear the injunction to hunt Othello down. Rush off to carry it out as fast as possible.[iii]

Now we need to take a look at a number of the key elements of the Stanislavski system, without which it is not possible to discuss the use of active analysis. As stated earlier, there is no way of examining this method in isolation from the system as a whole.

Notes

i   K.S. Stanislavski, *Rabota aktera nad rolyu. Sobranie Sochinenij*, vol.4. Moscow, Iskusstvo, 1957, pp.340–341 (*An Actor's Work on a Role*, trans. by Jean Benedetti, pp.68–69. Adapted by Irina Brown).

ii   K.S. Stanislavski, *Statyi. Rechi. Besedy. Pis'ma*. Moscow, Iskusstvo, 1953, p.624 (trans. by Jean Benedetti).

iii Ibid., pp.547–548 (trans. by Jean Benedetti. Adapted by Irina Brown).

The second plane

Vladimir Nemirovich-Danchenko's contribution to the development of the theoretical idea and practical application of the 'second plane' is of great significance.

In life we often keep our feelings and thoughts to ourselves.

Nemirovich-Danchenko taught actors how to make use of these unspoken thoughts, this inner line, onstage. Not through external actions but by using a psycho-technique that he named a character's 'second plane'.

For Nemirovich-Danchenko the 'second plane' is the character's inner, psychological 'cargo', that, as a human being, they carry with them into the play. It is made up of the sum total of all the character's life experiences, all the circumstances of their personal history, and includes all the nuances of their sensations, perceptions, feelings and thoughts.

A well-developed 'second plane' makes the actor's reactions to the events of the play more precise, vivid and substantial, it clarifies the motives of everything they do, giving every word spoken the weight of meaning.

Nemirovich-Danchenko insisted that the actors get inside the psychological processes of the 'character/human being', in the same way that realist literature had done.

With exceptional depth and rare understanding of his characters' lives, Tolstoy takes us into their inner worlds, stripping them bare, compelling us to experience with them their worries and joys, their hopes and suffering. Think of Anna Karenina on her way to the station!

For everyone she meets she is just a society lady in her carriage, going about her business, calm and collected. In reality, Anna is taking stock of her whole life, questioning its worth, saying farewell in her mind to her nearest and dearest, and choosing death as the only way out, the only means to free herself and others.

Let us turn to Chekhov, that remarkable writer, who always opens up the inner world of his characters with astonishing depth and subtlety.

In his story 'Misery', Iona is an old coachman from St Petersburg who has buried his son just a few days earlier. People notice only the most obvious

DOI: 10.4324/9780203125205-12

things in that ordinary coachman: his hat covered in snow, the oversized mit-
tens on his hands mechanically holding up the reins. It does not occur to
anyone that:

> an enormous, infinite anguish fills Iona's heart. If his heart were to burst
> open, and his anguish were to pour out, it would drown the whole uni-
> verse, and yet it is not noticeable. It has squeezed itself into such a tiny shell
> that it cannot be seen by day with a light …

But the artist did see what most people were oblivious to. And he leads us
into Iona's inner world with such expressive power that we feel his grief almost
physically.

Imagine that Iona is a character in one of Chekhov's plays. The actor playing
him will have to picture all the circumstances of Iona's life that have created this
boundless, all-devouring pain. This would be Iona's 'second plane'. But externally, his life will continue unseen by others, unobtrusively: with his worn-out
sledge, a mare slowly moving her hoofs, and a passenger who could not care
less that Iona has just buried his son.

The writer unveils the inner life of their characters, concealed from strangers. Actors recreate these characters in their heart and soul. The audience,
perceiving the depth of the characters' thoughts and feelings, believes what is
happening onstage to be true.

Stanislavski and Nemirovich-Danchenko demanded that the actor went
deeply into the inner world of the character they were to create. They said
that the audience, while watching an actor's behaviour that revealed no
'second plane', might sometimes have a good laugh, and sometimes even
weep if the play's circumstances touched them. But, once the play is over,
they promptly switch to other things, and the memories of the performance
evaporate.

But if there is a truly deep 'second plane' beneath the external behaviour,
then the audience says to itself, 'Aha, I know who you are!'. It is the figuring
out of what is motivating the actor beneath their external behaviour that is
most precious in the art of acting, it is precisely what 'I would take away from
the theatre into my life'.[i]

The meaning of what is going on in a scene is not always the same as the
literal meaning of what the characters say. Sometimes the words conceal the
true cause that moves the action of the scene forward.

The actor must strive to have an active inner life when in character, rather
than be immersed in an impotent contemplation of it. The 'second plane' is *not
a fixed state but an active process*. Scene by scene, act by act, the character undergoes inevitable changes that affect not only the external aspects of their life but
also, with every moment onstage, shift the character's internal perception of
the situation: they give something up, overcome some past issues, or build up
new reserves.

If we want every role in a play to be imbued with truth, we must demand of every actor, whether playing a larger or a smaller part, to build up their 'psychological cargo'.

It is this that produces the intense dynamic, which is characteristic of the art of experiencing.

The issue of the 'second plane' is closely linked with another major issue of the Stanislavski system. Namely, communication.

An actor cannot achieve a genuinely organic sense of self if they do not see what goes on around themself, if they do not hear their partners' lines, if, instead of replying to a particular, concrete person, they send their lines out into thin air.

Yet often we have only a rudimentary idea of communication onstage. It is generally assumed that when we say the lines, we have to look directly at our partner. This, on occasion, creates some semblance of truth.

In life the process of communication is exceptionally complex and varied. Sometimes, for example, a group of people gets together, they chat, they argue. But if one of them is expecting an important piece of news, or the imminent arrival of someone dear to them, or is getting ready to do something of grave importance, they will laugh, and argue just like the others but their entire being will be gripped by expectation, they will be focused on things that have nothing to do with the conversation. And that will be the actor's true 'object of attention'.

In Act 3 of *Three Sisters*, the scene of the fire, Masha who has said very little so far, suddenly speaks to her sisters:

> ... I can't get it out of my head ... It's simply disgusting! ... like a fixed spike in my head. I can no longer keep quiet. It's Andrei ... he's mortgaged the house, and his wife has pocketed all the money but the house isn't just his, it belongs to all four of us!

Masha's words are a surprise for everyone else but not for her. So, for the speech to sound convincing, what she says about Andrei must really be 'a fixed spike' in the actor's head throughout the preceding episodes.

When Nemerovich-Danchenko was rehearsing *Three Sisters*, he said:

> In every character there is something unspoken, a hidden drama, a hidden dream, hidden feelings, a whole big life that has not found expression in words. Now and then, suddenly, it bursts out – in this or that phrase, or scene. Then we experience the deep artistic pleasure that is theatre.[ii]

But there are instances when the actor tries to reveal the 'second plane' too directly. When I was working on the role of Charlotta in *The Cherry Orchard*, Nemirovich-Danchenko warned me against revealing that woman's loneliness, her sense of being unsettled and lost too directly. Then he said that Charlotta is afraid to admit to herself that she has no home, that no one cares about her, she is afraid to face the bitter questions reality puts to her. She pushes dark thoughts away, trying to find little sparks of joy in her situation. Charlotta must give herself over to her conjuring tricks and whimsical fancies with genuine pleasure: she is in her element when clowning, it is her way of taking part in life.

But somewhere, in her innermost being, a nagging thought hides itself: '… always alone, alone, I have no one and … who I am, why I am, no one knows'. If that thought is alive in her, hoarded inside, it will finally become unbearable, and will burst out from her heart, if only for a moment. Chekhov anticipates such situations in Act 2 when Charlotta, hurt by Yepikhodov's disregard for her, bitterly mocks everybody but most of all herself, and later in Act 4, in the hustle and bustle of the departure, when she, yet again, will have to look for a refuge in the twilight of her days, move to another family and home. Charlotta should provoke laughter more often than tears, but in the end there will be an impression of a fate that is both bitter and unfair.

The actor must know what the main object of his attention is in every single scene.

For Baron Tuzenbach in Act 1 of *Three Sisters* the main object is Irina. Whatever he is doing — whether arguing, philosophising, drinking or playing the piano — his thoughts and wishes are directed solely towards being alone with Irina. Particularly on this day when they are celebrating her name-day, Irina is especially dear to him. He wants to be alone with her so that he can tell her how he feels.

But then in Act 4, in the farewell scene: Irina is still the person most dear to him, yet his 'object' is no longer the same. The thought of the impending duel, that 'perhaps, in an hour I shall be dead', colours his relationship to Irina and to the beautiful trees in the orchard, near which they could have led such a beautiful life. The thought of the impending duel, like it or not, fills his heart and mind.

But sometimes what matters most to the character is in the 'here and now': in *this* encounter, *this* conversation, in the way the events of *this* day unfold. Then the rest of it, everything that makes up a person's life will automatically fade into the background.

The 'second plane' when carefully devised, the character's inner world dreamt up and 'visualised' by the actor, endows the role with profound content, helps find the right object of attention in the process of communicating, protects the actor from clichés.

The process of accumulating 'inner cargo' must start as soon as you begin your work on a role. It is a process in which observation and a deep understanding of the writer's dramatic intention play an important part. One of the main tools for acquiring 'inner cargo' is the 'inner monologue'.

Notes

i   V.I. Nemirovich-Danchenko, *Statyi. Rechi. Besedy. Pis'ma.* Moscow, Iskusstvo, 1952, p.332.
ii   Ibid., p.322.

Inner monologue

We know that thoughts expressed out loud are only a fraction of the thoughts that arise in human consciousness. Many thoughts are unspoken, and the more concise the sentence provoked by big ideas, the richer and more powerful it will be.[1]

So can we limit ourselves onstage just to the writer's words?

In life, someone listening to someone else will silently agree or disagree with what is being said. All kinds of thoughts will inevitably cross their mind.

Is it conceivable to succeed in creating 'the life of the human spirit' onstage, and for our character to behave naturally in the given circumstances, if we do not use the inner monologue? Of course not.

But for these unspoken thoughts to occur to us, we need to go deep into the character's inner world. *The actor must be able to think onstage in the same way as the character they are creating.*

It is essential that we invent our own inner monologues. No need to worry that we have to devise them ourselves. We have to go deeper and deeper into the character's train of thought so that their thoughts become familiar, innate, and, with time, come automatically to mind during performance.

It is wrong to think that mastering the inner monologue is swift or easy.

The psychological 'cargo' that the actor carries onstage with them requires them, as we have said, to enter the character's inner world. The actor must learn to relate to the character they are creating not as a 'literary' figure but as a living being, and must endow them with appropriate human psychophysical processes.

Only when the actor onstage does not just speak their lines but – just like any person in life – also has unspoken thoughts and words come to mind, only then can they achieve a truly natural existence in the given circumstances of the play.

Nemirovich-Danchenko stated that the text determines *what* you say, and the inner monologue *how* you say it.

1 See Appendix D (ed. note).

DOI: 10.4324/9780203125205-13

Let us take Act 3 of Ostrovsky's *Without a Dowry* as an example.[2]

The actor playing Larissa waits in silence for the moment when she speaks the following words: 'You forbid me? Then, gentlemen, I will sing!'

Can she be merely passive in this scene? Of course not.

She silently makes a comparison between Paratov and her fiancé Karandyshev, with all his buffoonery and cowardly vanity.

Larissa says nothing, but inwardly she does not stay silent. She thinks what a nonentity her fiancé is, how petty he is at heart, she asks why, what sin did she commit to deserve this banquet at which she has endured such burning shame, she thinks about Paratov too, compares him to her fiancé, weighs both in the balance and secretly admits to herself that even today everything could turn out differently ...

Human actions are often sudden, but unless the soil of the heart is fertile and ready, they will not come to fruition, be it Desdemona's murder or Larissa's insane dash across the Volga with Paratov. For her to be able to utter the fatal words, 'Let's go!', she must have gone through a thousand thoughts in her mind, imagined the likelihood of doing this or something like it a thousand times, said the words, or something like them, a thousand times silently to herself. Otherwise these words will be remote, dead, lacking the warmth of real human feeling.

The inner monologue has a significant place in the works of all our writers, both classical and contemporary.

In Tolstoy's novels, for example, inner monologues occur with unusual frequency. All the characters have them: Anna, Levin, Kitty, Pierre Bezukhov, Nikolai Rostov, Nekhludov and Ivan Ilyich as he is dying.[3] These unspoken monologues are a significant part of their inner life.

Let us take for example a chapter from *War and Peace* in which Sonya rejects Dolokhov's proposal of marriage. Dolokhov writes a note to Nikolai Rostov, whom Sonya loves, and invites him to a farewell evening at the Hotel d'Angleterre.

When Rostov arrives, he finds Dolokhov at a card table, as the banker. Rostov is drawn into the game, and gradually he loses vast sums of money.

Tolstoy expresses Nikolai Rostov's inner monologue with exceptional power.

> 'Why is he doing this to me? ... He knows all too well what the loss means to me. Surely he does not want to ruin me? He was my friend. And I loved him ... But he is not to blame; what can he do if he is in luck? Nor am

---

2 Alexander Ostrovsky (1823–1886), an outstanding Russian playwright, the author of 47 original plays. *Without a Dowry* premiered in 1878 at the Maly Theatre, Moscow. Larissa, a young girl from an impoverished family, tries to escape her pitiful state by finding a rich husband. But the only one to propose to her is Karandyshev, a minor civil servant. The scene Knebel comments on is that of a wild engagement party, attended by a few of Larissa's previous admirers, including Paratov, a rich landowner who asks Larissa to sing. Karandyshev instantly forbids this as the husband-to-be (ed. note).

3 This is a list of characters from the following of Tolstoy's novels and novellas: *Anna Karenina*, *War and Peace* and *The Death of Ivan Ilyich* (ed. note).

I to blame', he said to himself. 'I've done nothing wrong. Have I killed anyone, insulted anyone, wished anyone ill? Have I deserved such misfortune? When did it begin?'

Please note that Rostov goes through all these thoughts internally. Not one of them is spoken out loud.

Once the actor gets the role, he must conjure up dozens of inner monologues for the passages in which he has nothing to say. Then they will be filled with invisible content.

A great Russian actor, Shchepkin, said:

> Remember, onstage there is no total silence, apart from exceptional instances when the play requires it. When someone speaks to you, you listen but you are not silent. No. You respond to every word you hear with a look, a facial expression, with your whole being: it's your dumb show that can be more eloquent than words themselves, and God forbid that you should then, for no reason, turn your eyes away, or glance at something else – then all will be lost! That one look will instantaneously destroy a living being in you, cross you out from the list of characters, and you should then be thrown out of the window like a piece of useless muck …[i]

Note

i   Mikhail Shchepkin, *Zapiski. Pis'ma*. Moscow, Iskusstvo, 1952, p.356.

Mental images[1]

The more actively the actor exercises their capacity to see vivid images of reality behind the writer's words, the more they can call to mind pictures of the things being talked about, the greater the effect on the audience. When the actor sees what they are talking about, what they need to convince their partner of, they manage to capture everyone's attention with their mental images, convictions, beliefs and feelings. The range of images and associations that arise in the audience's mind fully depends on what the actor's words are charged with, what they see behind the words and the way they deliver them.

In life we always see what we are talking about, every little word we hear brings up a concrete mental image but onstage we often betray this fundamental aspect of our psychology.

When in life we recount something that has happened to us, we always try to make the person who is listening to us see the pictures imprinted in our consciousness. We are always anxious that the picture we convey should be like the original, that is, like the images produced in our mind by a particular event in our life.

Let us not forget that the imagination is the fundamental factor in the creative process. Using the material provided by the writer as the springboard, our imagination helps us produce such vivid mental images that they closely resemble our real-life impressions.

The process of creating mental images works in two phases. The first, building up an image store. The second, communication, or, the actor's use of images to capture their partner.

'Nature is so ordered', Stanislavski wrote,

> that when we *communicate with others in words, we first see what we are talking about with our inner eye, and then we tell people what we have seen. If we listen to someone, we understand what is being said first through the ear, then we see it with the eye. In our vocabulary listening means seeing what is being talked about, and speaking means making mental images.*

1 See the chapter on the same subject in Book Two, *The Word in the Actor's Creative Work* (ed. note).

DOI: 10.4324/9780203125205-14

For an actor words are not just sounds but stimuli for images. That is why when we are in verbal communication, we speak not so much to the ear as to the eye.[i]

In one of his conversations with his students, Stanislavski said:

[My task, the task of a man talking to someone, persuading someone, is to make the person I am communicating with see what I need him to see through my eyes. It is essential in every rehearsal, every performance to make my partner see events as I see them. If this inner goal is embedded in you, you will use words effectively, if not, then you are in trouble. You are bound to speak the words of your role for their own sake, and they will end up lodged in the muscles of the tongue.

[How are we to avoid this danger?

[First of all, as I have already told you, do not learn your lines until you have studied the content thoroughly, only then will you feel a compelling need for the lines. Secondly, you should commit to memory something else, you must remember all the mental images in the role, all the material that makes up the inner experience you need for communication.][ii]

Since he attached enormous importance to mental images, Stanislavski advocated developing the actor's imagination in every possible way, advising that the actor should store up mental images for each particular section of the role, and in this way assemble a unique 'film' of the role.

This 'film' will always stay fresh since visual images are enriched on a daily basis, giving the actor the necessary impulse that makes the actions and the text come to life organically.

But how are we to build up a store of these essential mental images? This is an independent process of work for each actor, and it must take place mostly outside of rehearsals.

When meeting other people, visiting museums and exhibitions, listening to music, reading poetry, the actor gathers material for their role. They create in their imagination that 'inner luggage' which is inherently right for their character's particular lifelike traits.

The actor's work on mental images lays the inner foundation, as it were, for building the role. This work, to an extent, is similar to that of a writer. When we study different writers' notebooks, filled with their numerous notes and jottings, we get an insight into the considerable amount of preparatory work they need to do.

Like the writer we must collect the necessary basic material for each role but share only a fraction of what we know about it with the audience.

An actor communicates with their partner – this communication means knowing how to hold the partner's attention by their own mental images.

[What does it mean, to listen? It means giving your full attention to your partner, being interested in them. What does it mean, to persuade, to explain? It means transmitting mental images to your partner so that they see what you are talking about through your eyes. You cannot speak in general, you cannot persuade in general.

[Often performers shut themselves off and lose the living contact with their partner. This happens if during their preparatory work they have not drawn in their mind a sufficiently vivid and precise picture of what they are talking about, and instead of engaging their partner with their mental image of it, they are still drawing it.

[If the imagination has been properly trained to produce well defined mental images, it is enough just to call them up for the familiar creative sense of self to be triggered. Frequent recall consolidates visual images and the imagination will continue to add fresh details to them. The efforts to create an illustrated subtext inevitably stirs up the actor's imagination and enriches the author's text.]

Let us take as an example Chatski's monologue from Act 1 of *Woe from Wit*.
Excited by his return to Moscow after a very long absence, moved by his meeting with Sofya, Chatski wants to find out about his old acquaintances, but although he questions Sofya about them, he does not wait for her answer. His mind is crowded, overwhelmed with a surge of memories, and with his characteristic wit and sarcasm he paints ruthless verbal portraits of the Muscovites as he remembers them. He wants to find out if anything has changed in his absence or if everything 'now' is still 'as once it was'.

He wants to chat with his childhood friend about people of whom he was heartily sick, people from whom he fled all those years ago but with whom he is now bound to cross paths again. He wants to talk of it because −

… when, having travelled the world, you get back home
the fumes of fatherland are sweet and pleasant![2]

There is no end to his questions.[3]
This speech of Chatski is the most difficult passage for any actor playing the role.

The actor must picture all the people that Chatski refers to. Often an actor is content with the mental images that any reader of Griboyedov's text might see naturally: at times vague, at times vivid but which sadly tend to evaporate in an instant. The actor must see these people in such a way that his memory of them becomes *his personal memory*, so that when speaking, he shares only a tiny part of all that he knows of them.

Konstantin Sergeievich maintained that if we look at Chatski as a living person and not as a character in a play, we are able to understand that in his

---

2 From a poem by Gavrila Derzhavin (1746–1816), one of the pre-eminent Russian writers of the 18th century. Derzhavin himself quotes a Latin saying 'Et fumus patriae est dulcis' (ed. note).
3 See Appendix D (ed. note).

imagination Chatski sees all the people the way they looked when he left them three years previously.

An actor who sees nothing beyond the lines, merely play-acts an interest in these people, while in reality being indifferent to them, with no 'old acquaintances' in his imagination.

We talk a great deal about the fact that musicians have exercises which enable them to work on their art daily. But theatre actors supposedly have no idea what they should do at home, outside of rehearsals.

Working on the mental images associated with a role is precisely the way of training the imagination that delivers incomparable results. Drawing detailed mental sketches of the outward appearance and the relationships of the men and women of Famusov's time, repeating these sketches over and over again in ever greater detail in a variety of episodes from their lives, and most importantly, specifying *your own attitude to them*, will stir up the imagination to such a degree that soon it will no longer be satisfied with these people-portraits alone but starts drawing a thousand scenes from life in Famusov's Moscow, a life that Chatski rejects with all his passionate, young heart.

Nemirovich-Danchenko said of this stage when the imagination is actively engaged:

> You should talk about it as though you had been there yourself … as though you had really seen it all. And, perhaps, one day, you will see it in your dreams, because *your imagination has been so vigorously stirred to action by working on this passage.*[iii]

Now imagine the case when an actor only *vaguely* sees the people he wants to talk to Sofya about. He has made no effort to practise the required mental images, and at the same time, he understands that, without picturing every single figure in this spectacular gallery of portraits from the Moscow society of the time, he will not be able to be convincing or compelling in delivering his speech.

Having set himself the task of seeing what he is talking about, he will give his all to the task and shut himself off from his partner. He will be absorbed by a technical problem that has nothing to do with the actions of the character called Chatski.

To earn the right to 'implant mental images in the partner's mind', to 'infect' them with the pictures of your imagination, you must collect and sort out all the basic material for your communication. You have to know the facts you are talking about, the given circumstances to be taken into account, and create the appropriate mental images in your inner eye.

When an actor begins to work in this way, and in the process actually 'accumulates mental images', they will come up against the fact that initially the image is indistinct. Yet they have only to ask a few specific questions: How old is she? What does her face look like? What is she wearing? etc., and their imagination, using the whole of their life's experience, produces a range of diverse details so that the mental image starts to become more concrete.

By doing this kind of simple work, we imperceptibly become immersed in the process, the fruits of our imagination become a part of us, and we are keen to go back to them in our minds and look for even more details.

The object that our imagination is working on becomes a personal memory, the precious cargo, the basic material without which we are not able to create.[4]

The wider our observations and knowledge of life, the easier and more fruitful is the work of our imagination.

In the art of theatre this is a decisive point, since as a result of doing this work the actor appears before an audience as a living human being, from a particular historical period, and the tiniest false note in their inner or outer behaviour rings untrue and puts a perceptive audience on its guard.

Notes

i   K.S. Stanislavski, *Rabota aktera nad soboj. Sobranie Sochinenij*, vol.3, part 2. Moscow, Iskusstvo, p.88 (*An Actor's Work*, trans. by Jean Benedetti. Adapted by Irina Brown).

ii   Notes made by Maria Knebel at the Opera Studio session in 1936.

iii   Vladimir Nemirovich-Danchenko, *Statyi. Rechi. Besedy. Pis'ma.* Moscow, Iskusstvo, 1952, pp.236–237 (Maria Knebel's italics).

4 See Appendix E (ed. note).

Characteristics/Characterisation[1]

When we speak of creating a character, we cannot ignore the question of their individual characteristics.

Characteristics that are random rather than gradually cultivated, are stuck to the character like a label. Characteristics reveal essential problems of the character's psychological life, they are not external, accidental tokens of personality.

Stanislavski spoke of the indissoluble link between the person's inner world and all its outer, everyday aspects.

When, for example, Khmelev was working on a character, he tried to picture even the smallest details of their life. He had to know everything about the person he was to embody onstage: the way he walked, spoke, his gestures and mannerisms, his smile, the way he rumpled his shirt collar, the size of his finger joints. Khmelev could not rehearse until he knew everything about the person he was to play, down to the smell of his skin and the timbre of his voice. He devoted a great amount of his time, strength and inner energy to creating a vivid portrait of his character. As a result of this colossal work Khmelev astonished people with the originality of his creations, be they Ivan the Terrible in Alexei Tolstoy's play, or Kostylev (in Gorky's *Lower Depths*), or Baron Tuzenbach (in Chekhov's *Three Sisters*). No one who saw him perform could escape the feeling that they had encountered somebody just like these characters in real life.

Often all an actor finds is some external colours for the character without realising that this diminishes the whole idea of who the character is.

This is a harmful sort of characterisation since it fails to reveal the character in all its complexity and depth, it lessens them.

Characterisation is a much subtler notion than is commonly assumed in the theatre. It does not just imply being short-sighted, lame or hunched over. Much more important than these external signs and characteristics is the way

---

1 In Russian the term 'characteristics/characterisation' (*kharákternost*) is a theatre term that has no general usage outside of theatre. It defines the sum total of someone's distinguishing characteristics. The term refers not just to physical characteristics. It rather marks out that which makes each character a unique individual. In the Russian tradition this is understood to be an outcome of a particular internal process. (trans. note).

DOI: 10.4324/9780203125205-15

the person speaks or listens, and the nature of their communication with other people. Some people never look at you, it is hard to catch their eye, others, as they listen, look around with suspicion, and some listen with their eyes wide open, full of trust. It is each person's distinctive way of communicating with others that reveals their character and expresses their inner substance.

To find for each concrete character their unique, inherent characteristics, the actor must first learn to make detailed observations of all the different sorts of people they meet in life, storing up all the observations they have made in their creative piggy-bank. The actor has to develop their powers of observation.

Let us take *Dead Souls* as an example. Gogol provides the actor playing Sobakevich with extraordinarily vivid material for the role:

> Chichikov glanced sidelong at Sobakevich, who now seemed to look like a medium-sized bear. [...] His complexion was red-hot, burnt, like that of a copper coin. As we know there are many faces in the world that nature fashions without puzzling over it too much, or bothering to use any precision instruments, that is: files or gimlets, or such like; it simply hacks them out with an axe, one chop for the nose, another chop for the lips, a large drill to dig out the eyes, and, without sanding it down, nature lets it out into the world and cries, 'It lives!' Sobakevich's visage was just like that, powerfully and miraculously hewn: he carried it with more of a downward than an upward slant, never turned his neck, and being in such a fix, he hardly ever looked up at the person he talked to, with his eyes either on the corner of the stove or the door. Chichikov glanced at him out of the corner of his eye again as they crossed the dining room: a bear! An absolute bear!

Here's another example from *Dead Souls*. Let us see how Gogol describes Plyushkin.

> Outside one of the huts Chichikov soon picked out some figure. [...] For a long time he could not tell the figure's sex: a woman or a man. The garment it was wearing was impossible to identify, rather like a woman's housecoat with the hat like that of a female house-serf and only the voice seemed to him to be a bit too hoarse for a woman. 'Oh well, a peasant woman!' he thought to himself, and immediately added, 'Oh, no!'. 'Surely, a woman!' he said finally, having had an even closer look. [...]
>
> The side door opened and in walked the very same woman, the house-keeper he had met in the courtyard. Only now he saw that it must be a man rather than a woman. [...]
>
> Chichikov had seen all kinds of people, even some, the likes of which neither the reader nor myself will ever get to see; but he had never seen anyone like this. His skinny face, like the skinny faces of all old men, had nothing special about it. It was only his chin that jutted out so far he had to cover it up every time to keep his spittle off it. His tiny eyes have not yet

burnt out; they darted about underneath his highly overgrown eyebrows like mice when their sharp little noses peep out from the dark holes, with their ears pricked up, moustache twitching, and peer out for a cat or a mischievous boy as they sniff the air with suspicion.[i]

Leonidov's[2] performance as Plyushkin automatically comes to mind. He was at once tragic and comical, naive and callous. Having absorbed Gogol's characterisation of Plyushkin, he did not omit even the smallest detail and had made everything so much his own that not a single gesture or inflection seemed contrived.

Of course, no such detailed characterisation can be found in any of the plays. Sometimes a character says something that gives us a glimpse of what another character is like. Sometimes the playwright gives their sparing description in the list of characters at the beginning of the play.

This is when the actor's imagination, their powers of observation, and capacity to create a characterisation stemming from the role's inner content become essential.

It is not enough just to detect in others particular traits typical of your character. You must know how to make them your own, to cultivate and nurture them in yourself.

When he was rehearsing Karenin[3], Khmelev was mocked by many of his fellow-actors because he kept cracking his finger-joints in an attempt to capture Karenin's characteristic mannerism as described by Tolstoy. He ignored the mockery and continued to practise the gesture until it had become part of him, his very own. This gesture enabled him to find the key to Karenin's character, to feel that he had turned into Karenin.

Stanislavski always distinguished between *illustrative* characteristics and *experienced* characteristics. He did everything he could to ensure that physical characterisation arose from the psychological content of the role. Since every human being is unique, the actor must seek a distinctive physical way to embody each character.

At the beginning of this book we said that etudes enabled the actor to experience the physical nature of a scene or episode from the very first moment of rehearsal.

Etudes enable us to analyse how this or that person behaves or thinks in a set of given circumstances. Vitally at this time, actors need to be helped to discern characterisation not only in external, physical signs – their gait, gestures – but, above all, in the way they *communicate* with each other, how they perceive things, specifically, how any given person thinks and reacts to their surroundings.

2 Leonid Leonidov (1873–1941), an actor at Moscow Art Theatre. He played many leading roles, among them Dmitry Karamazov, Lopakhin, Peer Gynt, and Othello (ed. note).
3 An adaptation of *Anna Karenina* based on Leo Tolstoy's novel produced at MAT in 1937 (ed. note).

The new rehearsal method, naturally, also raises the question of mise-en-scène, of staging.

We know that, normally, this is mainly a matter for the director. The only questions that concern the actors before they come on are where they are to enter from, who goes where, where do they cross to, etc. The principle of the new method is very different – it forces actors to take an active part in the process of staging.

During etude rehearsals, once the mock set has been assembled and furnished as required, and the rehearsal costumes and props are all in place, the actor, having, thanks to the set-up, the correct sense of self, cannot help but move through the space in line with the tasks stipulated by the play's action.

All the moves that have emerged from the etudes must be critically analysed in the post-etude discussions. What is right and essential must be retained, what is wrong and contrived must be discarded. Of course, none of the moves produced by the etude can be automatically transferred into the final production. It is part of the director's creative work to select them. But in the process of etude rehearsals the essential qualities of the staging are revealed and may be retained in the final production itself.

The subject of staging during the course of active analysis of the play is fascinating and profoundly important. It is not possible for me to develop the idea further in the present book.[4] However, I feel obliged to say that during the staging of the production itself the fruits of etude rehearsals become strikingly palpable. Actors who have learnt to move freely in the performance space, learnt to analyse their own physical behaviour, freely contribute, on their own initiative, to the process of creating mise-en-scène.

Finally, the period of etude rehearsals is over. Now begins a period when, as Stanislavski put it, 'you cannot tell where you end and the character begins'.

The actors' transition to being word-perfect in rehearsals is accomplished gradually and organically. On occasion, alongside the scenes in which the author's exact text is used, there will be scenes still worked on through etudes. It is important that actors are not consciously aware of the transition process.

If, during the period of active analysis, the actors have made the content of the play their own, they will become aware of how much the author's actual text enriches them, allowing them to savour the well-honed form of the original dialogue.

All the work the actors have done in the course of 'mental reconnaissance', a complex process of discovery made through etude analysis, the return to the text for post-etude dissection and discussion, getting deeper into the role, the storing up of mental images and an illustrated subtext of the play – all of these allow the actor, almost unconsciously, to absorb the original text.

Directors must be absolutely vigilant and rigorous about the accuracy of the actor's lines. They must fight mercilessly against 'ad-libbing' or the lines being

---

4 See the chapter 'Analysis through action' in *The Word in the Actor's Creative Work* (ed. note).

'close enough'. They must insist that the actors do not learn the lines by rote, but have a deep knowledge of them and respect the distinctive quality of the writer's voice expressed in the sentence structure, the interjections and the punctuation.

There must be an individual approach to each actor as they make the lines their own. Some have a good memory and absorb their lines just by checking them after an etude. Others take quite a bit longer to master the text.

If, through the process of active analysis, the actors have gained an in-depth understanding of the play and the writer's intentions, then they must and should learn the lines. It will no longer be a mechanical memorisation but an organic assimilation.

Many ask, when do we make the transition to rigorously exact text-work? Some of those who vulgarise the new method of work consider the accuracy of the writer's lines an irrelevance. If you happen to memorise it, well and good, if not, let us express the thoughts in our own words.

The actors must work on the text throughout the process of character-development. Hard to say when exactly they should start learning the lines. It seems to me, no time-limit should be fixed. If the work proceeds normally, not mechanically, then the improvised dialogue will inevitably give way to the writer's dialogue. The director must sense when the ensemble is ready to move on.

The method of active analysis of the play and the role leads the actor to the naturally sounding word, which is the basic task and goal of the art of the stage. We must never forget that the raw material quarried by the actor must be cast into a magnificently sounding word.

Note

i   N.V. Gogol, 2008, *Dead Souls*, viewed 18 December 2020, www.gutenberg.org/files/1081/1081-h/1081-h.htm

Creative atmosphere

It is vital for students of active analysis to be convinced of its usefulness so that they establish the necessary creative atmosphere in rehearsals. Initially, etude rehearsals can make some participants either too self-conscious or unduly flippant, and provoke cynicism in those watching instead of creative engagement and camaraderie. A badly timed comment from the sidelines, a chuckle, or whisper can jerk the actors in the etude out of the necessary creative sense of self and lead to long-term damage. They can lose faith in what they are doing, and having lost it, inevitably turn to posing and overacting.

A deep engagement with the exercise, the etude, by every single participant will lead to the precise quality of the creative atmosphere without which there can be no access to art.

The whole complex process by which an actor creates a character is not confined only to rehearsals with the cast and the director. This process simply cannot fit into the framework of rehearsals exclusively. When preparing a role, an actor must be obsessed by it the entire time they are working on the play.

Stanislavski often said that this was very much like being 'pregnant with the role'. The actor carries the character within them, just like the mother-to-be. Throughout the process they constantly think about it. At home, on the metro, in the street, in their free time, they are looking for answers to the questions the playwright has put to them.

We all know how often we can be haunted by the tune of a favourite song, how sometimes we cannot get it out of our head, singing it over and over again. It must be the same with a role. It must constantly stay with the actor, they must be obsessed by it. And the enormous creative joy the actor feels when vague traits in the character they love and have to portray surface in their mind, when, quite unexpectedly, they are struck with mental images of new character traits, when the full structure of the thoughts and actions of the role they are creating is revealed to them.

So, when an actor comes to rehearsal and brings with them the result of the enormous inner work they have done, it is essential that the director and the rest of the cast treat the birth of this new human being with caution and sensitivity. And that can only happen when there is a genuinely creative atmosphere in the rehearsal room.

DOI: 10.4324/9780203125205-16

Are there many young actors who can boast of being as obsessed by their role, of doing as monumental a preparation for it as the celebrated masters of the Russian stage used to do, when creating the roles that brought them recognition and glory?

I think with awe and veneration of those masters who having *created* unforgettable characters, still continued to reflect on them. I cannot help mentioning one example that is particularly dear to me.

Some years ago I happened to be in Yalta when Olga Knipper-Chekhova[1] was convalescing there. I called on her. She was in bed, gaunt and pale, not having recovered yet from a serious illness. Hardly had I entered the room when she said, 'You know, I am not allowed to read, so I lie here and think about Masha'.

At first I did not understand who this Masha was. She turned out to be one of Knipper's most dazzling roles, Masha in Chekhov's *Three Sisters*. She spoke of her as of someone infinitely dear to her, talking of her inner world with amazing depth and subtlety. She relived whole scenes in her mind, occasionally speaking an individual line. I left, astonished by the creative memory of this great artist and the fact of her having maintained such a direct living connection with the role she had created.

Need I say more? If the role already created leaves such an indelible imprint in our memory, how much more must we love and cherish the role we are *still 'carrying'*!

That love for a role, that creative obsession that exists at the birth of a character is for me inseparable from the creative atmosphere that must surround the actor when they are creating and then embodying the role. So far I have only spoken about the atmosphere in rehearsal but it is no less important to talk about the atmosphere backstage during performance.

I know too well the special anticipation and nervous excitement that accompanies a performance, but, unfortunately, I am also aware of the many negative occurrences that sometimes accompany the performance and can be detrimental to it. We must work to establish a truly creative atmosphere and sweep away everything that interferes with the process of creating and embodying a performance.

A creative atmosphere is one of the most powerful factors in our art, and we must remember that creating a good working atmosphere is particularly difficult. The director cannot do it alone, but the company as a whole can. Unfortunately, anyone can destroy it. All it takes is for one cynic to laugh at the fellow-actors who are working seriously, and the virus of mistrust infects and corrodes the company's healthy body.

---

1 Olga Knipper-Chekhova (1868–1959), an actress. Having trained with Nemirovich-Danchenko, she was part of the original acting company at the Moscow Art Theatre. In 1901 she married Anton Chekhov. Among her many roles, she was the first to play Masha in *Three Sisters* and Ranevskaya in *The Cherry Orchard*. (ed. note).

We all know of the enormous effort it took Stanislavski and Nemirovich-Danchenko – the rigorous demands they had to make on themselves, the actors and all the production departments – to produce the amazing creative atmosphere at the Art Theatre which has been studied by companies the world over.

I would like to tell you about the atmosphere backstage during performances of *The Cherry Orchard* in which I played the role of Charlotta for many years.

Despite the play opening with a big scene between Lopakhin and Dunyasha and, a little later, Epikhodov, those of us involved in the 'homecoming' – Ranevskaya, Gaev, Anya, Pishchik, Varya, Charlotta (when I first started they were played by Knipper, Kachalov and Koreneva)[2] – were sitting backstage, before curtain-up, on a bench waiting for their entrance. After Leonidov as Lopakhin delivered his line, 'I think they're here …', a prop-master – always the same one – crossed from the opposite side of the stage with a leather collar stitched with jingle-bells, shaking them in rhythm, increasing the sound as he grew nearer. As soon as the sound of the bells was heard, all involved in the 'homecoming' went upstage, from where we were to enter chatting away, bringing with us the excitement of the arrival.

Taking this scene which the audience could only *hear* as a model, made me realise once and for all how subtle Stanislavski was in convincing the audience of the truth of what was happening. As to the 'veterans' who had been playing *The Cherry Orchard* for many years this backstage scene seemed to have entered into their flesh and blood. And every time they played it as if the curtain were up. Already in the wings Knipper-Chekhova was in that amazing state of elated animation, in which it seemed perfectly natural to say with a mixture of laughter and tears, 'Nursery, our nursery …'.

With exceptional ease – achieved, of course, only through incredibly hard work – everyone involved in the scene, as soon as the bells began to jingle, was plugged into that special sense of self of people who have come back to their homeland, who have not slept all night, who are struck by the dampness of the air in the spring dawn, by the joy and excitement of homecoming, the acute bitterness of loss, and the feeling that life has been absurd.

I was also amazed by the atmosphere on 'the bench' even before the 'backstage arrival' scene. Knipper, Kachalov, Tarkhanov and Koreneva came, sat down, greeted each other and even exchanged a few words that had nothing to do with the performance, yet at the same time they were no longer Knipper, Kachalov, Tarkhanov and Koreneva, but Ranevskaya, Gaev, Firs and Varya.

The great strength of the Art Theatre was the actors' ability to live in the 'core' of their character. It is a great pity that young actors are not willing to believe that this core, which is a subtle restructuring of the whole nervous system, does not come easily, and that they simply cannot just chatter idly in the wings, and then instantly take control of the complex character they are to portray.

---

2 The first generation of actors at the Moscow Art Theatre (ed. note).

Yet another moment of waiting for my entrance comes to mind. Act 2 opens with a scene between Dunyasha, Yasha, Epikhodov and Charlotta. At a certain moment Charlotta exits, but she has to come back a little later. Having exited, I again sat down on the 'bench'. A few moments after Charlotta, Epikhodov, played by Moskvin, also leaves. Every time he uttered in a tragic voice a warning, 'Now I know what I have to do with my revolver', we heard how the line was greeted with a gale of laughter. Then Moskvin exited into the wings over the little bridge, passed by us and went towards his dressing room, looking injured, disheartened. This slightly exaggerated earnestness was one of the facets of Moskvin's enormous talent for comedy. A prop-master went up to him, and Moskvin gave him his guitar but his expression never changed. And every time I asked myself, 'When does he "wipe off" this extraordinary expression from his face?'. At what point did Epikhodov's tragically witless eyes, showing someone trying to resolve an impossible problem, become Moskvin's eyes again, the ones we knew so well? And what compelled Moskvin, even in the wings, still to be Epikhodov? Later on I understood that art was just that: when the actor, taken over by the thoughts and feelings of his character, cannot cast them off easily.

This kind of art does not come to you quickly. It requires a highly strenuous effort.

'Labours of theatre!', wrote Nemirovich-Danchenko:

> That is what we, theatre people, love most in the world. Persistent, unstinting, multifaceted work that fills the backstage world from top to bottom, from the flies above the stage to the traps below it. The actor's work on a role – what does that mean? It means working on oneself, on one's gifts, nerves, memories, habits …[i]

These words, I think, have great significance.

Note

i   Vladimir Nemirovich-Danchenko, *Iz proshlogo*. Moscow, Academia, 1936, pp.105–106.

Conclusion

Book One is basically concerned with the new method of work Stanislavski discovered in the last years of his life. My own practice has convinced me of its considerable advantages, of the enormous creative drive it provides, making the actor's work on the role and the play easier.

Many of those opposed to this method do everything they can to prove that the method of active analysis of the play and the role is no more than an experiment, insufficiently backed up, either theoretically or practically, by Stanislavski himself. I do not think we should be frightened by the word 'experiment' when it is used in close proximity to the name of Konstantin Sergeievich Stanislavski.

The time when Stanislavski's ideas were passed on by word of mouth is over. Now we have the eight-volume edition of his works. Anyone interested in the theoretical position of the great director-researcher is able to study Stanislavski's original statements on any particular aspect of the system.

I would like to quote something Stanislavski said about working on *Othello*, in which he defended his new method of work with absolute clarity. He began by reminding his students of the time when they worked using their own improvised dialogue. He explained to them why at the beginning he would take their scripts away and make them speak their characters' thoughts in their own words. He reminded them that during rehearsals he had often needed to prompt them with the order the writer's thoughts came in. This forced the actors to clarify over and over again their grasp of the logical sequence of the ideas as they are laid out in Shakespeare's play. The sequence had become so familiar and essential to the actors that they no longer needed to be prompted. As he watched the actors gain a deeper grasp of the line of tasks, actions and thoughts, Stanislavski gradually began to feed them Shakespeare's words, which became essential for them to express fully the actions that they had found. It was only when the score of the role was clear that Stanislavski finally allowed them to learn their lines by heart.

'Only after this preparatory work', writes Stanislavski,

> did we have the ceremony of handing the play's printed copy and your parts back to you. You scarcely needed to learn your lines, since long before that

DOI: 10.4324/9780203125205-17

I took care to feed you the lines, prompting you with Shakespeare's words whenever you really needed them, when you started looking for them, and chose them to carry out this or that verbal task. You seized on them avidly because the writer's words expressed this thought or fulfilled that action better than your own. You learned Shakespeare's words because you had come to love them and could no longer do without them.

What was the result? Someone else's words became your own. They were grafted onto you in a natural way, without being forced, and so they never lost their most vital quality: that of being active when spoken. No longer do you merely rattle through your part, but use the words as a means to fulfil the fundamental tasks of the play. That is exactly what the writer's text is for.

'Now think,' continued Konstantin Sergeievich,

consider it well, and tell me, do you believe that if you had started your work on the role by cramming the lines by rote, as is usual in most theatres across the world, you would have achieved what you did without my way of working?

Let me tell you straight away – no, you would never have achieved the desired results. You would have forcibly crammed the sounds of words and lines into the mechanical memory of the tongue, into the muscle memory of your vocal mechanism. And then the thoughts of your character would have dissolved and vanished, and the text would have been separated from your tasks and actions.[i]

My goal has been to help students investigate one of the most significant sections of the Stanislavski system, to explain those final discoveries that have given us a new vantage point for its application.

I have tried to demonstrate, using concrete examples, the methodology of the new way of rehearsing through active analysis of the play and the role. At the same time, I wanted to show readers the strong link this method has with the principal tenets of the system, which Stanislavski maintained and developed throughout his active and productive life.

Action, to which Stanislavski attached such great importance, the supertask and the throughaction, words (verbal action, which Stanislavski considered to be the major action), mental images, the subtext, and communication, are all links in the chain of a single creative process, the path to which is organically revealed in the course of active analysis. Let us not forget that the creative work of the actor and the director transforms analysis into synthesis in a way that is both imperceptible and complex. It is not always possible to tell where one process ends and the other begins, but that does not mean they are the same. The selection of the material needed for producing the character and the performance is in itself a clear indicator of the transition from analysis to synthesis.

When this process occurs through using the approach described in this book, it is even more organic, and provokes the highest level of creative activity in those making the work.

The responsibility and the initiative for creatively organising rehearsals using active analysis, rests, naturally, with the director. And, for that reason, the director must master the methodology of the rehearsal process.

The ability to tell the grain of truth from the germ of a lie in the actor's work, to correct it in good time, to bring together the discoveries made by individual actors towards the common task: these are, among many others, the director's functions.

But even the best directors are powerless unless the actors want to work creatively. This means not only being disciplined, attentive and serious but also that every actor must be actively engaged in their work both in rehearsals, and at home.

The question of working independently in the course of etude rehearsals is extremely important.

However talented the director, there is one area in which they are powerless to help. The director cannot 'see' for the actor, cannot 'think' or 'feel' in their place. They can uncover the supertask and the given circumstances for the actor, be a true mirror reflecting back the slightest touch of falseness in the actor's performance, but they cannot live as the character, cannot be, see, listen and hear like them – only the actor can do that.

But as soon as the actor stops living by spontaneously assessing everything that goes on around him, as soon as living mental images, living contact and a genuine physical sense of self are replaced by a demonstration, magnificent though it may be, of the director's suggestion, a wave of boredom rolls off the stage. Without the actor's living, genuine, passionate thoughts and feelings, everything on the stage becomes dead.

Approaching the text of the role through etudes, in which the actor must set their imagination to work on the circumstances, the mental images and the thoughts that they will later express using the writer's words, activates this independent work.

Inevitably, the actor has to face the task of their independent preparatory work. They must build up a store of mental images, if they are to have the right to speak of them in their own words in the etude. Gradually they will be drawn into the more complex tasks of acquiring an intimate understanding of the character's inner and outer world, and come to realise that independent work on a role is not just a matter of learning their lines (as some actors assume).

When you consider why the Stanislavski system has continued to develop and take on new deeper meaning, the answer is: Stanislavski's life-long idea was that, to produce authentic life on the stage, we must create according to the laws of nature.

Expressing the ideas of the play within each character, creating 'living beings' onstage, benefiting from the experience of the greatest masters of the theatre, doing our work with the sense of responsibility, which alone will lead us to positive results – these are our common tasks.

Note

i   K.S. Stanislavski, *Sobranie Sochinenij*, vol.4. Moscow, Iskusstvo, 1957, pp.271–273.

Book Two

The Word in the Actor's Creative Work

Author's foreword

In March 1936 Konstantin Sergeievich Stanislavski invited me to come and see him.

I knew that at the time he was making every effort to complete his book *An Actor's Work on Himself* [1] as well as dealing with the practicalities of setting up the Opera–Dramatic Studio[1] that he had such great hopes for. He believed that by doing experimental work with young performers he would be able to put new theoretical propositions of his system to the test. I also knew that despite serious health problems, Stanislavski was going through one of the greatest possible upsurges of his creative powers, each day filled with the promise of new insights into the nature of the actor's creative work.

As soon as I approached the familiar mansion on Leontievski Lane[2] I felt the deep excitement that had always gripped me, even after all these years, on one of my frequent visits to see Stanislavski.

Having sat me down in a huge soft armchair, he looked at me for a little while, searchingly and affectionately.

'Have you heard of my Studio?', he asked finally.

'Yes, of course, Konstantin Sergeievich.'

'Would you like to teach Artistic Recitation there?'

'I have never studied it myself or given any concert recitals',[3] I answered.

'Even better', he said, 'then you haven't had time to develop any bad habits. There hasn't been much practical exploration in the field so far. It needs to be considered at length. We need to find a new approach to it. How about: teach and learn?'

1 Stanislavski created his Opera–Dramatic Studio to test the latest 'elements' of his system in practice. The Studio was intended as the final link of artistic interconnections Stanislavski endeavoured to establish between opera and dramatic theatre ever since he began his work at the Bolshoi Theatre Opera Studio in 1918. The Studio produced many outstanding actors and theatre-makers, and later merged with the Moscow Drama Theatre named after K.S. Stanislavski (ed. note).

2 In 1921 Stanislavski moved in to the first floor of a detached house on Leontievski Lane, where he lived till the day he died in 1938. Due to Stanislavski's bad health he conducted most of his directing and teaching over there. It opened as Stanislavski's House Museum in 1948 (ed. note).

3 Maria Knebel refers to the widespread practice of concert recitals, very popular in Russia at the time. Mostly it presented 'poetic declamation' (ed. note).

DOI: 10.4324/9780203125205-19

I was delighted to accept the offer, embarking on a new and fascinating period of my creative work under Stanislavski's guidance. Since the significance of this work goes far beyond my personal experience, I consider it my duty to try and share it with my students and everyone else who treasures the art of the spoken word.

Now, as I am writing these lines, there are a whole host of new materials that shed light on the final period of Stanislavski's experimentations.

Back then at the Studio, as we, guided by Stanislavski, devoted ourselves to the problems of the spoken word, his newest and most mature ideas on the art of theatre, and his latter-day creative discoveries were only just crystallising, taking the form of precise well-honed definitions backed up by a mushrooming number of examples, adjusted and fine-tuned over and over again in the Studio's practice. We were there, witnessing that remarkable process.

This book is based, on the one hand, on Stanislavski's published statements, and on the other, on my personal recollections of his Studio activities at the time. This is the story of what I heard and saw, as well as an attempt to systematise and summarise, at least in the first instance, Stanislavski's basic principles of the word in the art of the stage. It is neither a purely scientific research paper, nor a textbook on verbal action. I see my task as less ambitious than either of these and would consider it accomplished if I simply succeed in raising the question above. As a result, I believe it is feasible for this paper to go from the direct account of the problem as I understand it to my personal reminiscences of what Stanislavski said about the word in his classes at the Studio, how he conducted his classes, describing and explaining to us what he considered to be of radical significance in the development of the actor's psycho-technique.

Stanislavski never separated verbal problems in artistic recitation from the verbal action in drama productions.[4] He clearly saw that there were issues specifically related to each of these cases. But it was important for him to highlight that they shared the *general foundation of the verbal action.* Therefore it would be a mistake to limit the discussion in this book only to the isolated laws of artistic recitation without attempting to uncover fully the notion of the verbal action as the fundamental principle of the Stanislavski system. One way or another, I will have to touch upon the sum of all the questions related to the verbal action in the actor's practice.

Moreover, while for Stanislavski the word was the primary source of the actors' tasks and at the same time the pinnacle, the ultimate destination of the creative process, he never spoke of it in isolation from the system's other principles developed over the many years of his 'life in art'. The process of mastering the author's words in performance – in Stanislavski's thinking – goes

---

4 This refers to the fact that 'artistic recitation' which only uses vocal action must not be artificially set in contrast to a theatre production, where actors deploy an entirety of their expressive means. It was an accepted practice of the Russian and Soviet theatre to separate the two approaches (trans. note).

hand-in-hand with the process of creating a stage character! This obliges me
not to leave out any of the key points of the system or its aesthetic and technical
foundation. I will have to touch upon them in as much as will be necessary to
clarify the role and place of verbal action in the entire intricate structure of the
views of the great founder of stage directing and theatre pedagogy, Konstantin
Stanislavski.

Note

i   Part 1 of *An Actor's Work on Himself in the Creative Process of Experiencing* was published
in Stanislavski's lifetime (the Russian version came out in 1938). Part 2 was initially
published in several issues of *The Art Theatre Year Book*. In 1948 a complete version
of the book came out based on the materials put together by Stanislavski himself
(ed. note).

Word is action

There does not seem to have been a single prominent theatre-maker in the history of Russian [19th-century (trans.)] theatre who failed to consider the great power and impact of the word onstage, to look for ways to steep words in truth, charge them with genuine feeling, and invest them with significant social content.

In the chronicles of the Russian stage there are numerous cherished examples of the masters who build magnificent stage characters using the art of the word as their foundation. Shchepkin, Sadovsky, Mochalov, Yermolova, Davydov, Varlamov, Lensky, Sadovskaya,[1] each of them in their own way, according to the unique nature of their talent, proved to be equally masterful in their delivery of the author's text onstage.

Reading Shchepkin's notes and letters, it is clear how thoughtful and profound was his concern for the problems of stage speech:

> All over Europe they are still satisfied with this type of declamation, that is, with howling, but we cannot stomach this 'singsong' ...
>
> ... I witnessed the declamatory style introduced to Russia by Dmitrevsky,[2] who acquired it during his European travels adopting the fashion typical of the European playhouses at the time. The style manifested itself in a loud, over-exacting stress on every single rhyme, with the couplets deftly rounded off. All of this kept building up and up, so to speak, getting louder and louder, until the final line of the speech was bellowed at the top of his lungs. ... But as soon as we began to grow up here and, with time, grow

1 This is a reference to some of the greatest 19th-century Russian actors. Mikhail Shchepkin (1788–1863) most famously performed in the plays by Nikolai Gogol. His letters are the key source for studying Russian theatre tradition. Prov Sadovsky (1818–1872), an actor of great standing, performed in the plays by Alexander Ostrovsky (ed. note).

2 Ivan Dmitrevsky (1736–1821), a well-known actor of his time. He was twice posted abroad to study the acting techniques of the French and English actors (Lekain, Dumesnil, Clairon, Molé, Garrick, etc.) (ed. note).

DOI: 10.4324/9780203125205-20

wiser, we instantly saw through the absurdity of all this and dropped it. ...
We, too, have many a singing word! But we sing them with our hearts ...[3/i]

Very soon the realistic nature of Russian drama compelled Russian actors to
give up the conventions of the declamatory style ubiquitous on the European
stages of the period.

Since the art of 'singing the word with one's heart' is so much harder and
more complex than the art of false pathos, artificial declamation and bombastic rhetoric, the history of the evolution of the Russian theatre's realist
movement] was a quest for and reflection on the truthful delivery of the word
onstage, and the clearing of the way that led to it.

For Shchepkin the realistic interpretation of the author's text onstage was
possible only if it stemmed from the essence of the person portrayed, from 'the
character's inherent nature'.

> The actor must, without fail, study how best to deliver every single speech.
> It should not be left to chance, or, as they say, to one's own nature, since
> the character's nature and my nature are completely different. If we impose
> our own personality on the role, the individuality of the character por-
> trayed will be lost.
>
> Indeed, every speech must be studied to such a degree that every thought
> is well expressed. Then, even if you fail to breathe life into the thoughts, all
> is not lost. They may say of you, 'Cold', but never, 'Bad'.[ii]

For Shchepkin, transformation into the character was a pre-condition of
delivering the text truthfully. Only then, in Shchepkin's terminology, is the
delivery no longer merely a technical skill but 'artistry'– the highest form of
truth onstage.

Following in Shchepkin's footsteps and developing his legacy, other Russian theatre practitioners continued to penetrate the secrets of speech and
unravel its laws. Ostrovsky dedicated his life to the study of the word, taking
the mastery of verbal portraits in drama to the highest degree of perfection.
Gogol, in his battle against bombastic speech onstage, linked the possibility
of a lifelike and natural delivery of lines directly with the actor's approach to
learning them.

Gogol maintains that prior to learning their role by rote, the actor is able
to receive their partner's lines with an open mind, that on hearing a truthful
actor address them naturally, they are able to respond instinctively, truthfully
and naturally.

---

3 From Shchepkin's letter to Annenkov, 1854. Among other things, this extract on the art of acting
 refers to the French *tragédienne* Mademoiselle Rachel (1821–1858), and her performances on her
 tour of Russia (ed. note).

Anyone, even the most common person, has an innate ability when responding to be in tune with what they have just heard. But once an actor has learnt his lines by rote at home, he spouts nothing but a pretentious and studied response. It is now lodged in him for eternity and nothing can break the mould. Unreceptive to a single word spoken by the better actor, deaf to all the circumstances and characters surrounding his role, just as he is deaf to and cut off from the play as a whole – like a dead man, he wanders amongst the dead.[iii]

But however valid the Russian theatre-makers' comments may have been on the nature of words in the art of theatre, none of them had come up with a *teaching* on the subject of speech. This was to be undertaken by the great founders of the Moscow Art Theatre, Konstantin Stanislavski and Vladimir Nemirovich-Danchenko. Bringing together isolated observations and deliberations on stage speech, they arranged and systematised them, adding to them from their own considerable practical experience. The Stanislavski system does not just reveal to us the *objective laws* of stage speech. The system – the essence of which is that speech is the main *action* onstage – creates a logical chain of *pedagogical devices* and skills that allow the actor to master the author's text consciously, making words active, effective, purposeful and full-blooded.

'It is customary to call what we have been studying "the Stanislavski system"', writes Konstantin Sergeievich. 'That is a mistake. The strength of the method lies precisely in the fact that no one conceived it, no one invented it. The system is an innate part of our nature, both psychological and physical. *The laws of art are based on the laws of nature.*'[iv]

The Stanislavski system, having come into being at the beginning of the 20th century, underwent a complicated creative evolution in the Soviet period. Stanislavski's whole life was a living embodiment of the continuous evolution of his teaching.

The fundamental premise of the Stanislavski system is the concept of the human being/actor's super-supertask. In other words, the artist's world-view is an essential condition for conscious creative work.

The super-supertask makes the artist's vision unusually sharp, helping them to discern the radical and the vital in the life around them and separate it from the petty and the incidental. The super-supertask guides the actor's imagination, activates their fantasy, gives purpose and passion to the process of creating a character. For Stanislavski, the absence of the super-supertask leads to inevitable naturalism in art, to a dismal imitation of everyday life, producing instead of the genuine truth the 'teensy-weensy little truth' that Stanislavski hated so fervently and adamantly.

Persistently and tirelessly he looked for the most profound ways of reproducing 'the life of the human spirit' of the role on the stage.

In striving for art that was insightful and realistic, able, as Nikolai Cherny-shevsky[4] puts it, 'to transport us from the future into the present', Stanislavski was not alone. And together with Nemirovich-Danchenko, his comrade-in-arms, he found the way to achieve that goal. With surprising precision, he defined the specifics and peculiarities of the art of the stage, and the unique conditions needed to allow the creative process to take place. This is what makes his system genuinely scientific.

Even Chernyshevsky points out, as he considers the nature of art, that for an artist it is particularly hard to reproduce simple and natural human behaviour – the human action – truthfully:

> In any group of people, everybody behaves perfectly in accordance with: 1) the nature of the incident they are involved in; 2) the intrinsic nature of their own character; and 3) the circumstances of the situation they are in. In real life, all of these are always taken into account as a matter of course, but in art, it takes a supreme effort to achieve that. 'Always' and 'as a matter of course' in life, but 'it takes a supreme effort' in art. This fact characterizes practically every aspect of nature and art.[v]

Why is it so hard onstage to remain natural in conveying those simple human behaviours that can be carried out with such ease in real life? The reasons for this are concealed in the conditions of the actor's creative work itself, in its public nature. The creative act of a stage artist is on public display and evolves in front of spectators. Under such conditions, if the actor-creator lacks sufficient willpower and has no natural inclination to engage in the creative process 'in public', they will inevitably feel at a loss, out of it, no longer able to feel and think as the character. This inevitably leads to 'dislocation', physical tension and self-consciousness. Then, as Stanislavski puts it, the required creative sense of self gives way to a shoddy 'actorish' sense of self.

'It is much easier for us to "dislocate" our own nature onstage rather than live a genuine human life', Stanislavski liked to say.

His mind searched persistently for devices that could lead to a natural sense of self onstage. In his view, the purpose of his system was to eliminate inevitable 'dislocations' by restoring the laws of our creative nature disrupted by working in public, returning the actor to an organic human sense of self onstage.

---

4 Nikolai Chernyshevsky (1828–1889), the author of a famous novel *What's to be Done?* written while he was imprisoned in the Peter and Paul Fortress, St Petersburg. An economist, materialist philosopher and a supporter of realism in art, he was highly praised during the Soviet period. He is often considered the precursor of socialist realism (ed. note).

Like Chernyshevsky, who believed 'the chief part of a poetic talent to be the so-called creative imagination', Stanislavski maintained that creativity starts with an idea conceived in the imagination of a poet, director, actor, designer, etc.

The first step on the actor's journey to get closer to the character they play is dependent upon their ability to stir up their own creative nature, to give their imagination a push in the direction prompted by the situation and given circumstances of the play. Stanislavski discovered that the best and most effective lever for this was, as he put it, the magic 'if' – an invented imagined truth you can believe in as sincerely, if not more fervently, than the real truth. The magic 'if' instantly transports the actor from the real world into the world of fiction created by the storyteller. It represents reality not as it actually is but as its poetic recreation.

Konstantin Sergeievich used to say that the magic 'if' is not categorical, it is not a command. 'If' neither insists on nor claims anything, and as such, imposes nothing. All it does is to ask, 'what would happen, if …?'. But as soon as the actor tries to answer the question posed by 'if', they cannot help but stir their imagination. Once it is set in motion, there is an inner shift that triggers the creative process.

So, 'if' stimulates the performer's imagination. But the imagination as such is not a free agent; it is bound by the play's given circumstances and must act within their framework. Stanislavski rejected blind, chaotic, aimless imagination that can only take the actor away from the vital material of the play. Here's what he said:

> 'If' always launches the creative act, and the Given Circumstances develop it further. One can't exist without the other, or acquire the stimulating power they need. But their functions are somewhat different. 'If' is a spur to a dormant imagination, and the Given Circumstances provide the substance for it. Together and separately they help bring about the inner shift.[vi]

Consequently, 'if' brings the actors' creative work strictly in line with the author's invention, with the full range of someone else's ideas and the themes encompassed by the play. At the same time, 'if' only raises the questions. The actor answers them independently, according to their own life experience, beliefs, moral and ethical values. In *An Actor's Work on Himself* there are some inspired lines about the poetry of the actor's work:

> To believe in another person's invention and genuinely live and breathe it – you call that a trifle? Don't you know that creating something based on someone else's idea is often more difficult than making up a story of your own? … We rework dramatists' creations. We unlock what is hidden beneath their words. We invest someone else's text with our own subtext. We establish our relationship to people and the circumstances of their lives. We filter all the material the author and the director have given us through

our own personalities. We rework it internally, give it life, fill it with our own imagination. We become bound to it, we live in it psychologically and physically. We produce 'the truth of the passions' in ourselves.[5] The end result of our creative work is genuinely productive action, closely connected with the play's innermost ideas. We create living, typical figures through the passions and feelings of the characters we portray.[vii]

In saying that the end result of our creative work is a genuinely *productive action* closely connected with a play's 'innermost ideas', Stanislavski touches upon the very essence of the art of the stage. Theatre is action. And everything that takes place on the stage is always action, an active expression of the thought, of the innermost idea that is actively and effectively transmitted to the audience. Dramatic art is the synthesis of a variety of artistic disciplines. But Stanislavski believes that the word is and will always be the main and decisive means of affecting the audience.

It is the verbal action that makes the theatre one of the most powerful and impressive forms of human creativity!

'At the *Homo sapiens* stage [in human evolution] there was an extraordinary increase in the mechanisms of neural activity', writes academician Ivan Pavlov.[6]

> Speech constitutes the second signal system, and is specific to humans, since it is the signal of the primary signals. Multiple verbal stimuli, on the one hand, distanced us from reality ... on the other, the word transformed us into human beings.[viii]

And so, the word, being 'the signal of signals', makes it possible for human beings to abstract and generalise the immediate impressions received from the external world at the most profound level of connections and relationships. It is speech that differentiates human beings from animals, since animals are incapable of going beyond the confines of those impressions and images that they receive directly through their sense organs. The whole of the age-long history of different people's experiences is preserved in words. Words, like a sensitive condenser unit, absorb the multifaceted wisdom of mankind. When a word is uttered it evokes in human consciousness a complex chain-reaction of impressions and associations, visual and emotional images, often as fully fleshed-out as the images received through sensory perception of the real world.

---

5 A quote from Pushkin's article 'On National-Popular Drama and on the Play *Martha the Seneschal's Wife*': 'Truth of the passions, feelings that seem true in the supposed circumstances, that is what our intellect requires of a dramatist' (trans. note).

6 Ivan Pavlov (1849–1936), a world-famous Russian scientist, known primarily for his work in 'classical conditioning' and his discovery of 'conditioned reflexes'. In 1904 he won the Nobel Prize for Physiology or Medicine, becoming the first Russian Nobel laureate. In his later life, he showed an interest in theatre. During the Soviet period Pavlov was an acknowledged authority and the point of reference for anything to do with psycho-physiology (ed. note).

'Speech signalling' is the bedrock of the art of the stage.

All theatre work is underpinned by this peculiar ability to see real-life phenomena underneath the text, to conjure up in our mind's eye images of the things referred to, and in turn, affect others with our own mental images. A whole section of the system, defined by Stanislavski as 'mental images', is dedicated entirely to that. If the actor onstage visualises what they are talking about or what they are convincing their partner of, then they manage to capture the audience's attention with their mental images, convictions, beliefs and feelings. The audience's perception of the author's text, the whole range of images and associations that will arise in their minds as they listen to the text, is totally dependent on what the actor has invested their words with, what the actor sees in their mind's eye as they deliver the text, and the way that they speak it.

By setting up a certain goal for themself, the actor directs the verbal actions towards it, taking their partners, individual spectators and the whole audience with them.

That is why the powers of observation, life experience, emotion memory and associative thinking are of such enormous importance for the stage artist.

The closer the actor observes life, the more specific they are in what they notice and retain, the more vivid the mental images, the more active the content they will invest the author's text with.

Stanislavski and Nemirovich-Danchenko, while investigating the problem of the word in the art of the stage, taught us to plough up the full expanse of the content concealed underneath the word in deeply submerged layers of subtext.

A well-developed, rich and diverse artistic subtext, employed in the theatre practice, works on the audience as an intricate and complex stimulus.

Yet the fundamental and principal means of producing this impact is the word!

The whole of the Stanislavski system focuses on the process of verbal communication between people, on making it active and effective, and making the words spoken onstage purposeful, productive, dynamic and intentional. Ensuring that the word is always *action*.

Notes

i   Mikhail Shchepkin, *Zapiski, pis'ma*. Moscow, Iskusstvo, 1952, pp.236–237.

ii   Ibid., p.236.

iii   *Gogol i Teatr*. Moscow, Iskusstvo 1952, p.388.

iv   K.S. Stanislavski, *Rabota aktera nad soboj*. Moscow, Iskusstvo, 1951, p.635 (Maria Knebel's italics) (*An Actor's Work*, trans. by Jean Benedetti, p.611. Adapted by Irina Brown).

v   *N.G. Chernyshevski on Art*. Moscow, Akademia Khudozhestv SSSR, 1950, pp.54–55.

vi   K.S. Stanislavski, *Rabota aktera nad soboj. Sobranie Sochinenij*, vol.3, part 2. Moscow, Iskusstvo, p.66 (*An Actor's Work*, trans. by Jean Benedetti, p.53. Adapted by Irina Brown).

vii   Ibid., p.67 (*An Actor's Work*, trans. by Jean Benedetti, p.54. Adapted by Irina Brown).

viii   Ivan Pavlov, *Polnoye sobraniye sochinenij*, vol.III. Moscow/Leningrad, Akademia Nauk SSSR, 1949, p.568.

Analysis through action

Stanislavski's teaching on the supertask and throughaction is fundamental to the process of the actor's transformation into a character. 'The author's work was engendered by the Supertask and it is towards that the actor should direct his creative efforts',[i] says Stanislavski.

But it is not enough just to define the author's supertask. It is necessary that the actor's own supertask is

> analogous to the writer's idea, however it must also unfailingly evoke a response in the human heart of the actor-creator.
> That is what can evoke not formalistic, not cerebral but genuine, living, direct, human experiencing.
> Or, in other words, we must look for the Supertask not only in the role but also in the actor's heart.[ii]

Stanislavski asserts that the creative process of the actor's transformation into a character is fundamentally dialectical, and elaborates on this statement in his teaching on the two perspectives – the perspective *of the actor* and *of the role*.

I, the actor, know everything that is going to happen to my character in the play, but the character knows nothing of their future. It is only when the actor has mastered the entire complex of the character's psychophysical behaviour, that they have then earned the right to say 'I am' in the role.

At the same time, continuous self-monitoring guides the actor's creative process. This awareness allows us to develop our psycho-technique. And 'that's what our psycho-technique is for, to bring the wanderer, with the help of "lures", back ... onto the highway', writes Stanislavski.[iii]

What sort of a 'highway' is it? It is the way to the author's supertask.

Once he has established the conceptual difference between the perspective of the role and that of the actor, Stanislavski defines the *actor's perspective* as a way to align and apportion the role's constituent parts prudently and harmoniously, while having a full grasp of the whole.

DOI: 10.4324/9780203125205-21

The teaching on the perspectives shows us a way of reaching an understanding of the play and the role. It is organically linked to Stanislavski's ideas on the actor's super-supertask. It teaches us to grasp the character holistically, to be able to subordinate their diverse individual traits to the super-supertask. This teaching protects us from an artistically harmful approach of assessing particular isolated instances in the role or the play without taking into consideration their organic connection to the given circumstances and the play's intention.

The teaching on the actor's perspective also sheds light on some serious questions regarding the arsenal of our techniques but first and foremost it raises the *question of the creative intention!* It would be a grave mistake to ignore this proposition. An artist who amazed everyone who worked with him by the inexhaustible wealth of his imagination, both as actor and director, who believed that the main creative impulse lay in the imagination, Stanislavski *never underestimated the process of conceiving an idea, always protecting that process from the danger of becoming formulaic, trite and hackneyed!* He maintained that the actor who jumps to conclusions about the play, having done little study of it, cuts themself off from a genuine discovery of the author's intention. Their imagination is silent. Without understanding anything about the piece, they already 'know' how to play the role the author has created. Stanislavski warned against such hasty 'conception'.

Each word of the author's text, each event, each of the character's actions must be subjected to analysis so that they nourish the actor's imagination, channelling it along the course that leads to the supertask.

To achieve this, Stanislavski teases the actor's imagination, he holds the director back from giving the actors explanations before they have discovered things through their own experience. He mobilises the actor's creative forces 'so that the Supertask and the role become living, vibrant, resplendent with all the colours of genuine, human life'.[iv]

Stanislavski teaches that a creative idea is before all else a process and not some preconceived given. It is a complex process that goes through a variety of stages, nourished by all of the artist's creative capabilities.

There is no fixed period for creative conception. There have been cases when certain elements of the conception occurred to the actor on the first reading of the play and served them as an effective creative compass in developing their character. The conception can also emerge as a result of committed and persistent work, but emerge it must if onstage the actor is to play a *human being rather than a stage character.*

No human being can be born onstage unless the actor brings together all the traits, given to the character by the author, that dictate the character's behaviour. The actor must get to know the person they embody and, rooted in the author's material, produce a new human being out of the organic nature of their own individuality.

'My goal', writes Stanislavski,

> is to compel you to *create a living person anew* out of your own being.[7]
> You must get the raw material for their spirit from inside yourself rather
> than from an outside source, from your own memories (affective or oth-
> erwise) that you have experienced in reality, from your wants and inner
> 'elements' analogous to the emotions, wants and 'elements' of the character
> you portray.[v]

In his ceaseless search for the creative sense of self that allows a genuinely
creative idea to arise and be embodied in the most organic way possible, Stanislavski suggested to us, during his final phase of work, that we should revise
the established order and practice of rehearsals. Primarily this revision concerns
the initial period of rehearsals, a stage that plays a decisive part in all the work
that follows.

In analysing the initial stage of the actor's work on a role, Stanislavski used a
number of crucial stipulations as his starting point:

1. To become a fully-fledged actor-artist the actor must be *independent* in
    their creative process.
2. Mechanical line-learning slows down and cripples the subsequent working
    process.
3. Without the mind–body unity in the creative process of transformation,
    the creation of the role will be deficient.

'There is the law of creativity', Konstantin Sergeievich said to me. 'Never
force anything! This law cannot be broken – art does not tolerate force.'

As an example he quoted his conversation with the actor Ivan Moskvin[8]
who told him, 'There I am, face-to-face with my role, unable to squeeze
myself into it, but the director keeps pulling me in through a crack.'

Moskvin's words made a big impression on Stanislavski since the image laid
bare the dissatisfaction felt by a true actor in the initial stages of their work on
a role when everything in the play and the role is still completely alien to them.

At that point the strengths of the actor and the director are, as a rule, une-
qual. In preparation for rehearsals the director, naturally, will have done much
more thorough and varied work on the play than the actor. And even the most
patient and tactful of directors still attempts to help the actor merge with the
character as soon as possible, unintentionally robbing the actor of their creative
initiative.

---

7 Italics are mine – M.K.
8 Ivan Moskvin (1874–1946) is one of the most famous Moscow Art Theatre actors. In 1898 he played
   the lead in the theatre's inaugural production of *Tsar Feodor* by Alexei Tolstoy. In 1904 he played
   Yepikhodov in Chekhov's *The Cherry Orchard* (ed. note).

Stanislavski spoke with enthusiasm of an important discovery he had made over the previous few years: he had identified the conditions that must be established to enable the actor's creative process of grasping the role to begin naturally, how to liberate the actor from the 'director's tyranny', making it possible for them to follow their own path towards the role, supported by their own creative nature and experience.

Stanislavski spoke of working in such a way that would be certain to lead to organic, living *stage speech*.

The more brilliant a piece of dramatic writing, the more vivid and infectious it is when we encounter it for the very first time. The character's behaviour, their relationships and their train of thought appear so affecting and clear that we unwittingly assume: once I learn the lines, I'll master the character as written by the playwright.

But as soon as the lines are memorised, everything that was so alive in the actor's imagination dies.

How can this danger be avoided?

In the initial stages of work, according to Stanislavski, the actor does not need the author's text in order to learn it by heart but rather as fundamental source material, the springboard for their artistic imagination. They need the text in order to discover the wealth of the playwright's ideas contained within it.

'In the vast majority of cases,' writes Stanislavski,

> actors *declare the text of the play to the audience* decently or tolerably well. But even that is done crudely, conventionally. There are many reasons for this of which the first is: in life they usually say what they need and want to say for some purpose, some task, some necessity, to perform some genuine, *productive and purposeful verbal action.* ... It is different onstage. There we speak someone else's, the author's, text. Often not what we need or want to say.

What can be done for the actor to make the author's text their own, inherently theirs? What can be done to make each particular word become the actor's instrument of action?

'Besides,' continues Stanislavski,

> in life, we speak of and in response to what we see physically or mentally, to what we genuinely feel and think, to what really exists. Onstage we have to talk about what our characters are living through, what they see, feel and think not what we ourselves see, feel and think.[vi]

To make the author's text one's own by gradually getting inside the character, by reaching the 'I am' state of mind, and, as Stanislavski put it, by 'honestly' studying all the circumstances of the role's life, all of this brings the actor to the major goal of making the author's text their own. This remains the primary goal throughout the rehearsal process and the actor's work on the role.

Stanislavski and Nemirovich-Danchenko used to say that if an actor gives themself a task of living in their character, they must devise for themself the character's train of thought both at the point when they have text to express it, and when they are silent. For Stanislavski and Nemirovich-Danchenko creating such a train of thought meant creating an internal, unspoken text.

They both required actors to devise an internal text for the role without which the genuine 'life of the human spirit' cannot be conveyed onstage.

Stanislavski categorically rejects not only mechanical line-learning done without delving deeply into the circumstances that give rise to the text, but also memorising the text until the actor has rooted themselves in the throughline of the role, gained a firm hold of the subtext and of the need for a productive, purposeful action.

Only then will the author's words become a tool of communication for the actor, the means of embodying the essence of their role.

Having enthusiasm for the play and developing a thorough knowledge of it lay the foundation of the actor's creative work.

> Artistic enthusiasm is the engine of creativity. Rapture that accompanies enthusiasm is a sensitive critic, a keen explorer and the best guide into the psychological depths.

'So, let the actors,' continues Stanislavski,

> after their first encounter with the play and the role, give more time and space to their artistic rapture, let them infect one another with it, enthuse about the play, re-read it from start to finish or in parts, recall the bits they loved, reveal to each other again and again the splendours of the play, let them argue, shout or be moved, let them dream of their own role and those of others, let them dream of the production. Rapture and enthusiasm are the best means of getting closer to the play and the role, and getting to know them.

> The ability to enthral their own feelings, will and mind is one of the characteristics of an actor's talent, one of the major tasks of their inner technique.[vii/viii]

But, while calling for a passionate engagement in the analysis of a play, Stanislavski also points out precise ways of truly getting to the essence of a piece of dramatic writing.

He believed that the easiest plane for the active analysis to access was the plane of facts and events, that is, the plot of the play. So he suggested starting a systematic play analysis by determining events or – as he sometimes called them – 'operative facts', their sequence and interaction between them.

He insisted that actors should learn to break the play down into major events. This allows them to understand the structure of the plot and the action.

Stanislavski also told us that it was far from easy to learn how to identify the major events in a piece of dramatic writing, that we had to cultivate in ourselves a particular perspective that would teach us to separate the essential from the non-essential.

['You'll never succeed in charting the throughaction unless you are able to grasp everything that happens in the play by following very large milestones, large-scale events', said Konstantin Sergeievich.

[When taking the first steps in getting to know the play and the role, it is important to see the logic and sequence of events, and the possibilities in the development of action and counteraction.

[Try to analyse Romeo's line of action based on the largest-scale events.

[The first operative fact – Romeo's infatuation with Rosaline. The second one – Romeo's love for Juliet.

[Make a note, in strict order, of the actions that arise from the above two facts.

[Romeo's infatuation with Rosaline compels him to gatecrash the ball of his family's worst enemies, the Capulets – his only chance of seeing Rosaline. At the ball – his encounter with Juliet. An instant blaze of all-consuming love.

[A new event for Romeo: Juliet is Capulet's daughter.]

This process of 'mental reconnaissance', as Stanislavski called it, helps the actor from the very beginning of working on their role to develop an awareness of the play's operative structure.

In his notebooks from 1927–1928 Stanislavski writes:

The play, like a journey from Moscow to St Petersburg, is broken up by the major station stops – at Klin, Tver ...[9] That's an express train. But there's also a mail-train that stops at smaller stations, like Kuntsevo ...

To explore the territory between Moscow and Klin, or between Klin and Tver, it helps if we stop at smaller stations and examine their environs. In one location there is an abundance of forests, in another of marshland, in the third of meadows, the fourth of hills, and so on. Another option is to travel by a cargo-passenger train that stops at every waypoint, whistle stop, and other stopovers. Getting off there is even better for exploring the environs between Moscow and Klin, or Klin and Tver, and so on.

We can also charter a special train from Moscow to St Petersburg, travelling non-stop. In this case, we gain high momentum – the throughaction, high speed. The special high-speed train is for actors of genius (Salvini). An express train – for actors of talent (us).

As for the mail- or cargo-passenger trains, they are good for study (the analysis, the 'ploughing-up').

9 These are large towns – the main stages on the journey from Moscow to St Petersburg (ed. note).

By identifying events and actions, in rehearsals the actor will unwittingly seize the ever-widening layers of the given circumstances of life in the play.

By uncovering the main event in the character's life that gives rise to a certain behaviour, the actor is able to identify the cause of their conduct. And depending on the character's actions, the actor starts to perceive what kind of a person they are.

Training his students to test all theoretical propositions with an instance taken from real life, Stanislavski advised:

> [Try and look back at a certain period in your life and identify the main event at that time. Let's suppose that at the time the most important thing for you was to get a place at a theatre-school. Now analyse how that event affected your life, your behaviour and your interactions with various people. What was the role it played in shaping your life's throughaction and supertasks, etc.?
>
> [Having determined the main event, you will see that at the time there were also many much smaller events that lasted less than a month, or even a week of your life. They occupied you for only a day or a few hours, until a new event distracted you and overshadowed the one before. Just like this, in the initial stages of play-analysis learn not to get bogged down in the minutiae, the tiny little bits, but seek out the essential, and based on that, figure out the particulars.
>
> [Think carefully of what happened at the Famusov household as the result of Chatski's unexpected arrival,[10]

Konstantin Sergeievich asked, guiding us to determine the actions of various characters in response to that event.

> [What are the consequences of the news of the Government Inspector's arrival?][11]

By asking these questions, Stanislavski instilled in his students the idea that before anything else they needed to scrupulously analyse, 'plough up', the structure of the play's action, its story.

Only having clearly understood the logic and sequence of actions and events, will the actor understand the ultimate goal that their role should aim towards.

---

10 A reference to Alexander Griboyedov's play *Woe from Wit*, 1823. Chatski, the play's protagonist, returns to Moscow in Act 1, having spent a long time abroad. He calls at Famusov's house, where he meets his daughter Sofya, who he is still in love with (see Appendix F) (ed. note).

11 A reference to Nikolai Gogol's *The Government Inspector*, 1836. A small Russian provincial town is in a state of turmoil at the news that a government inspector is on his way from St Petersburg in order to investigate the state of local affairs (ed. note).

But in studying *what* is going on in the play, the actor is still looking at it from the outside. Ahead of them lies the most complex and subtle of the processes: *putting themself into the character's place.*

['You will have arrived at the concise outline of events that the narrative is built on', Konstantin Sergeievich said in his classes at the Studio.

[Let's suppose that the play's storyline is clear to you, and you can see it logically leading to the supertask. What's to be done next?

[The most important thing to do before you start rehearsing is to let go of the tasks that are excessive and are bound to drive you to ham it up and force your own nature. You must make the character's actions your own since you can live sincerely and truthfully only through 'actions of your own'. You must transport yourself into the character's situation in the given circumstances of the story. To achieve this you must first perform the simplest psychophysical actions linked to a particular event. Perform them as yourself. Let it not hold you back that at the beginning you, the actor, know very little about the role. You do not yet know your lines, but you already know the basic events and the actions taken by your character, you know their train of thought, and consequently, you can express it in your own words.

[The very first question that everyone in the production must ask themselves is: 'What would I do, if such and such happened?']

'As a result', Stanislavski maintained, 'you will begin to feel *yourself in the role*. Starting off from there, you will move on and in time arrive at the point where you feel *the role in yourself.*'

We must have courage to change the established method of rehearsals!

Speaking of the generally accepted method of rehearsals, when the director pushes the actor to get up close and personal with an unfamiliar character, and tries to stir their imagination by describing the play's content, its characters, its historical period, and so on, Stanislavski states that the actor perceives the director's ideas coldly and rationally in the initial stages of rehearsals. The actor is not yet ready to receive someone else's ideas and feelings since they do not feel grounded in their character's reality and have no idea of what they need to accept or reject in what is offered to them.

To develop their opinion of the play and the role, the actor first needs to get

a *real sense of the life of the role, and not only mentally but also physically.*

Just as yeast causes fermentation, so the sense of the life of a role generates in the actor an inner heat, a coming to the boil necessary for the process of gaining creative understanding through mental and sensory experience. Only when an actor is in that creative sense of self, can we speak of approaching a play and a role.[ix]

It is fascinating to notice the theme that was running through the whole of Stanislavski's creative work: how to produce the psychophysical sense of self that enables the actor to be genuinely creative in the process of gaining that understanding? In the end, Stanislavski revised a number of his original provisions and set down new principles with the actor's independence as the cornerstone of creative work. Asserting the indissoluble connection between the psychological and the physical, Stanislavski introduces a new *rehearsal practice*. He criticises the old method with the actors sitting around the table for lengthy periods of time, trying to get inside their characters' inner life with the director's help. Stanislavski maintains that this method leads to major errors since the actor, by examining the role at the table, separates the psychological from the physical and, with no opportunity of experiencing the actual life of their character's body, are at a loss.

This inevitably leads to a purely cerebral analysis of the role. The table work in the first stages of rehearsals is required in order to get a clear understanding of the spine of the plot, to determine the sequence of events and the characters' actions. As soon as they have grasped the fundamental structure of the play, actors get a sense (if only a vague one) of the throughline of the play's action, even though it is still quite cerebral.

Stanislavski calls this the period of 'mental reconnaissance'. Once this part of the work is done, he suggests that we move on to the next stage of a more in-depth analysis that takes place away from the table – analysis through action. It is through action that the actor simultaneously investigates their character's physical and psychological life. They experience the actual, concrete sense of unity and indivisibility of psychophysical processes.

In his essay 'On physical actions' – one of the chapters in part three of *An Actor's Work on Himself* [12] – Stanislavski describes the new rehearsal method in detail.

He suggests that a student should recall an episode from Gogol's *The Government Inspector*, and by putting themselves into the given circumstances of the play, perform those psychophysical actions from the life of the role – however minute – that they are able to 'do sincerely, truthfully, as themself'.

The pages that follow relate how the student, attempting to perform a very simple action, finds it impossible to move forward without knowing why they are doing it and what for. They bombard the master-teacher with questions, and the teacher guides them past the hidden obstacles, safeguarding them from clichéd ideas or superficial analysis, and steers the student's attention to the true-to-life existence of their character.

'You have to understand the fact that at the beginning', writes Stanislavski,

> it is vital for actors to seek someone else's help and instructions when they feel the need for it, of their own accord, out of necessity, rather than having it forced on them. In the first instance, the actors keep their independence, in the second – they lose it. Psychological, creative material derived

---

12 This refers to the documents put together for *An Actor's Work on a Role*, written down most likely in 1937 for his classes at the Opera-Dramatic Studio (ed. note).

from someone else, rather than experienced in our own heart, is cold, rational, inorganic. It only gets stale in our psychological and intellectual store-rooms, cluttering up the heart and mind.

By contrast, our own material instantly finds its place and is put to use. That, which is drawn from our own organic nature, our own life experience, which finds response in our hearts, can never be alien to the human being/artist. There is a close bond, a kinship with what is our own. No need to grow and cultivate it. It exists, it springs up spontaneously, begging to be expressed in physical action.

I don't need to repeat that all these 'personal' feelings must, without fail, be analogous to those of the character.[x]

Wishing to make the new method of working even more vivid, Stanislavski gets up on the stage and improvises Khlestakov's arrival at the inn.[13]

He rushes into the room, slams the door behind him, then stands there for a long time peeping into the corridor through a crack. Those watching get a sense that he is hiding, running away from the landlord of the hotel. Having made his entrance, with great sincerity from the students' point of view, Stanislavski instantly starts to analyse his actions.

> I pushed it! ... It should be simpler. Besides, is it right for Khlestakov? After all, as someone from St Petersburg at that time, he considers himself above everyone in the provinces. What prompted me to enter this way? What memories? Can't work it out. Maybe this combination of a braggart and a puerile coward is Khlestakov's inner nature? What brought up the feelings that I have experienced? ...[xi]

Inviting his students to investigate closely the method he was demonstrating, Stanislavski writes:

> Examine this process and you will find that it was an inner and outer analysis of oneself as a human being in the given circumstances of the life of the role. This process is nothing like the cold, cerebral investigation of a role that actors usually undertake in the initial stages of their creative work.
>
> The process of which I speak is carried out simultaneously by all the mental, emotional, psychological and physical forces of our nature ...[xii]

Only through such a method of analysis is the actor's inner sense of self permeated with a real experience of the play's life. Stanislavski describes a whole

---

13 In Act 2 of Gogol's *The Government Inspector* the protagonist, Khlestakov, depressed by his debts and lack of money, checks into a cheap hotel together with his manservant, Osip (ed. note).

series of etude variations[14] on Khlestakov's entrance into the hotel, with each new etude assessing the play's given circumstances with more depth and precision, discovering a greater inner and outer freedom, and the greater truth in the logic and sequence of his thoughts, actions and feelings, as he gets closer and closer to the character.

Summing up the scrupulously selected physical actions in the rehearsed bit of the scene, he gives an exhaustive definition of his new method:

> The novel secret and the novel aspect of my method for creating 'the life of the human body' of the role lies in the fact that the simplest physical action, fully embodied onstage, compels the actor to produce, following his own motives, all sorts of imaginative ideas, given circumstances, and 'ifs'.
>
> If one simple physical action requires such a huge effort on the part of the imagination, then a continuous line of 'the life of the human body' of the role needs a whole unbroken series of ideas and given circumstances, the author's and your own.
>
> We can understand and excavate them only through a detailed analysis carried out by all our creative forces. My approach provokes this kind of analysis naturally, of its own accord.[xiii]

When creating 'the life of the human body' of a role, we continuously stimulate our imagination by checking whether the physical actions we have selected are in line with the behaviour of our character. Keeping in mind Stanislavski's imperative that the actions and feelings of the actor must, without fail, be analogous to those of their character – since 'both the life of the body and the life of spirit of the role are drawn from one and the same source: the play'[xiv] – the actor, by striving in the course of active analysis to select their physical actions with maximum precision, penetrates deeper and deeper into the role.

We must bear in mind that the outline of 'the life of the human body' of the role is only the beginning. The actor's most important challenge lies ahead: immersing themself in this line of 'the life of the human body' so deeply that it reaches the secret recesses where 'the life of the human spirit' of the role is beginning to emerge. Creating that life is one of the main tasks of dramatic art.

'Our first encounter with a particular work of a writer leaves impressions that may stay with us in patches, as isolated moments, often highly vivid, indelible, that set the tone for all of our future creative endeavours.' But only after we have

drawn the line of 'the life of the human body' all the way through the role, and as a result found an inner sense of the line of 'the life of the human

---

14 See above the chapter on 'Etude rehearsals' (ed. note). In theatre parlance, the term 'etude' (from the French *étude*) refers to a particular way of examining the role practically, in action and making a sort of a sketch. The term was used in 18th-century French theatre but became obsolete, and its practical application was lost (trans. note).

spirit', only then can all our isolated feelings fall into place and acquire a new and real meaning ...

Asserting the organic interconnection and interdependence between the physical and the psychological, Stanislavski writes that in his approach to creating the life of the human body there is a most important proposition: 'the life of the body of the role cannot fail but respond to the life of its spirit; of course only on condition that the performer's actions onstage are genuine, purposeful and productive'.[xv]

At first glance this statement by Stanislavski seems contradictory.

Why does he say that 'the life of the spirit' of the role cannot fail but respond to 'the life of the body' at the stage of rehearsals when the actor is only taking their first steps in studying the physical life of the role? After all, the new working method is based on a compulsory demand to begin active analysis with the study of 'the life of the body' of the role.

It is because the starting point of active analysis is the deconstruction of the text, that is, the 'mental reconnaissance'.

'Our reason', writes Stanislavski, 'is like a scout who explores every plane, every direction, every constituent part of the play and the role; it is the vanguard preparing new routes for the forthcoming search for feelings.'[xvi]

Actors, as they take their first steps to investigate the 'life of the body' of the role, arrive at that point carrying a certain amount of the inner creative freight.

Otherwise, they would not be able to compare the results they get in the course of active analysis with their own notions of the character.

The richer the actor's creative personality, the more varied and colourful their life experience and their ability to make sense of the inner workings of the play's action, the more organic is their process of getting to know the life of the role in its psychophysical unity.

By focusing the actor's attention in the initial stages of the work on 'the life of the body' of the role, and by asserting that 'the life of the body cannot fail but respond to the life of the spirit of the role', Stanislavski proves that in creating the 'life of the body' of the role, the actor brings to life their feelings.

'Can you recall', writes Stanislavski,

> if your own feelings stay dormant when you wholeheartedly live through the human life of your own body, through its physical actions. Were you to delve deeper into this process, closely following what takes place at that moment in your heart and soul, you will notice that if you have faith in the physical side of your life onstage, then you experience feelings closely related to that life, logically connected to it.

During one of our meetings, Konstantin Sergeievich said to me:

> [Imagine the following situation: you switch on the radio only to discover that your watch is slow and you may now be late for your train.

[I can see, your imagination is silent. Sitting here, opposite me, in a snug armchair, with no need to rush anywhere, it is hard for you to imagine the situation I have just proposed.

[Then I ask you: what would you do in such circumstances?

[Have a think, then get busy – get your suitcases, pack your things ...

[There you are! As soon as you have taken relevant actions, your imagination started to speak straight away: you looked for the address-book with the number for a taxi, you ran into a few problems: no one picked up the phone at the other end, the key to the wardrobe had gone missing, you could not fit all the books into your suitcase, were still reluctant to take another one, and so on, and so forth.

[How was it that for a few minutes you so deeply believed in your need to catch the train that the thought of being late brought tears to your eyes?

[Once the actor correctly *defines the actions* to be taken in the given circumstances, and then carries them out with sincerity, their feelings can't fail to respond!]

The director's and actor's talents manifest themselves primarily in the *selection of actions* that arise from their insight into the dramaturgical idea and the *essence* of characters as created by the playwright.

Quite often we come across actions that have been defined randomly, sometimes superficially, and even on occasion misrepresenting the author.

Active analysis leads the actor to an in-depth concrete investigation of actions that reveal the inner springs of the forces that set the play in motion.

Striving to produce the most natural conditions to secure elusive, capricious feelings through his new way of working, Stanislavski writes that

> ... the life of the body of the role can become a kind of a rechargeable battery of creative feelings. Inner feelings are akin to electricity: discharge them into the void, and the sparks will fly away and vanish. But when they feed the life of the body of the role as electricity does the battery, then the emotions aroused by the role are secured in a tangible physical action. This physical action soaks up, absorbs the feelings linked to every single moment of the body's life, cementing the actor's volatile, quick to evaporate, feelings and creative emotions.[xvii]

And so, the new method reveals yet another essential problem. Physical actions secure whatever has been accumulated in the course of their embodiment and arouse the intensity of the emotional experience acquired by the actor throughout the rehearsal period.

'Let us suppose', observes Stanislavski,

> that you are about to, for the twentieth or thirtieth time, repeat the carefully fine-tuned 'life of the human body' ... If when doing this you live

correctly in your physical tasks and correctly carry them out, then, as has happened on many previous occasions, you experience not only the life of the body of the role but simultaneously, as a reflex, the inner feelings of the role corresponding to the physical actions. This occurs because the body and the mind are interdependent.[xviii]

Konstantin Sergeievich often spoke to us about how bad we all were at observing ourselves in life, of studying our own physical behaviour, even though the life of the human body made up half of our stage existence. So, from now on we would be obliged 'to study the nature of the physical action, in the course of carrying it out'.

He was passionate in saying that the actor must never have a single moment of inaction, that inaction was out of the question in the art of theatre. We had to seek out action, and the actors had to be trained to go into action straight away.

['In the olden days we used to learn our tasks by rote', joked Stanislavski.

[We divided the role into smaller bits, then defined the idea of each bit and what that idea expressed. That is what we used to do before.[15]

[That was analytical work, with the reason playing a bigger part than feelings. But once I train myself to ask: *what would I do today, here and now in these given circumstances?* – then I can no longer speak about it in a detached analytical way, mentally I begin to take action, and by taking an action I will discover the way to the feeling, to my subconscious.]

['We will no longer be sitting around the table, our heads buried in books', he said to his students.

[Nor will we break the playtext up into bits, pencil in hand. We will search through and in action, looking practically, in life itself, for anything that will help our actions. We will investigate the material but not in a cold, theoretical or rational way. We will come to it from *practice*, from *life*, from our own human experience.]

Notes

i   K.S. Stanislavski, *Rabota aktera nad soboj, Sobranie Sochinenij*, vol.3, part 2. Moscow, Iskusstvo, p.358 (*An Actor's Work*, trans. by Jean Benedetti, p.311).

ii   Ibid., p.354 (*An Actor's Work*, trans. by Jean Benedetti, p.308. Adapted by Irina Brown).

iii   Ibid., p.544 (*An Actor's Work*, trans. by Jean Benedetti, p.457. Adapted by Irina Brown).

15 Stanislavski refers to a particular method of work according to the system presented in his first book *An Actor's Work on Himself in the Creative Process of Experiencing*, for example in the chapter 'Bits and tasks' (*An Actor's Work*, p.135 translated by Jean Benedetti) (ed. note).

iv   Ibid., p.355 (*An Actor's Work*, trans. by Jean Benedetti, p.309).

v   K.S. Stanislavski *Real'noe oshchushchenie zhizni p'esy i roli*. Yezhegodnik MKHT, 1949–1950, Moscow, Iskusstvo, 1952, p.48 (Maria Knebel's italics).

vi   K.S. Stanislavski, *Rabota aktera nad soboj, Sobranie Sochinenij*, vol.3, part 2. Moscow, Iskusstvo, p.490 (*An Actor's Work*, trans. by Jean Benedetti, p.400. Adapted by Irina Brown).

vii   K.S. Stanislavski, *Rabota aktera nad rolyu*, Yezhegodnik MKHT, 1948. Moscow/Leningrad, Iskusstvo, 1950, vol.1, p.317 (all further quotes from this piece of work are taken from this edition).

viii   All the materials for this unfinished book were first published in Russian in K.S. Stanislavski's *Sobranie Sochinenij*, vol.4. Moscow, Iskusstvo, 1957 (ed. note).

ix   K.S. Stanislavski, 'O fizicheskikh dejstviyakh' (On physical actions), *Teatr*, 1948, No.8, p.8 (all further quotes from this article will be taken from this publication).

x   Ibid., p.15.

xi   Ibid., p.11.

xii   Ibid., p.16.

xiii   Ibid., p.16.

xiv   K.S. Stanislavski, *Rabota aktera nad rolyu* (An Actor's Work on a Role)*, Sobranie Sochinenij*, vol.4. Moscow, Iskusstvo, 1957, p.335 (trans. by Irina Brown).

xv   Ibid., p.334.

xvi   Ibid., p.337.

xvii Ibid., p.335.

xviii Ibid., p.348.

Assessing the facts

In the course of active analysis the actor has to address an extremely important proposition made by Stanislavski regarding 'appraising the facts'.
['The essential problem arises', Stanislavski told me,

> [because onstage the actor must behave the same way as the character created by the author.
>
> [But this is impossible to achieve without a thorough investigation of all the circumstances of the character's life, without putting yourself into these circumstances, and then assessing the event the character is living through at that moment from the point of view of these circumstances.]

Stanislavski stated that assessing the facts through your own life experience – and without that no true art is possible – occurs only when an actor compels their imagination – even in the initial stages of the work, during the 'mental reconnaissance' of the play – to treat the play's *dramatis personae* as if they were real people living and operating under specific living conditions.

'What was it like in real life?' This was the main question Stanislavski put to the actors, challenging them, bombarding them with endless questions, leading them deeper into the living circumstances of the play, rescuing them from clichéd theatrical ideas.

There are innumerable obstacles actors have to overcome on this journey!

Preconceived ideas of the role are such a hindrance! When approaching a role in a classical play, the actor, before they have made sense of any of the essentials in the piece, already recalls the way the role was played by actors of renown, and what the critics said of their performances – so, the actor gets trapped by theatrical associations.

Drawing the actor's attention above all to the living circumstances of the play, Stanislavski first demands that instead of thinking about 'the role', the actor places themselves from the very start in the character's shoes and looks at the facts and events provided by the writer from this subjective point of view.

In order to assess the facts with their own feelings, based on a personal, lively interest in them, the actor internally asks themselves the following

DOI: 10.4324/9780203125205-22

question and resolves the following problem: 'Which circumstances of the inner life of my human spirit, which of my own personal, living human intentions, wishes, aspirations, and characteristics, which of my good qualities or character defects could make me, the human being/artist, relate to people and events in the play in the same way as the character I portray?'[i]

This is, essentially, the moment when a complex creative process of developing the character begins.

The actor, wishing to explain the character's behaviour to themselves, embarks on a journey of figuring out the given circumstances of the character's life, and simultaneously tries to put themselves into the character's place. The actor is both the material and the creator. While the actor nurtures and cultivates their idea, their conception of the role, they are fully aware that there is no other material with which to embody the role but their own voice, their own body, thoughts, temperament and feelings. Consequently, they need, as Stanislavski puts it, to find themself in the role, and later on create 'the role in themself'. This is a path of continuous and strenuous work.

Leo Tolstoy used to call this type of work the ploughing up of deep furrows over the literary field where he intended to sow his seeds.

This kind of 'ploughing up' is what Stanislavski called for. By putting themself in the character's place, the actor inevitably begins a complex inner duel between their own idea of life and that of the character.

This impassioned combat gives rise to an understanding of the inner workings of the character's actions and states of mind. It produces an understanding of the inner springs that compel the character to say a particular line.[1]

This process was brilliantly described by the actor Nikolai Khmelev during his work with Vladimir Nemirovich-Danchenko on the part of Tuzenbach in Chekhov's *Three Sisters*:[2]

> When you speak to me of feeling a certain emotion, if I used only myself to get it – it will hardly be Tuzenbach. So I have inwardly shifted things about. I have thrown out all of my own stuff that is of no use to Tuzenbach, and only kept what I need for the character.[ii]

Stanislavski writes:

> What does it mean to assess the facts and events of a play? It means: finding their hidden inner meaning, their spiritual essence, and the degree of their significance and impact. It means: digging underneath the external facts

---

1 See Appendix F (ed. note). An example quoted there (various interpretations of Sofya's role in *Woe from Wit*) is the same as the one used in the chapter 'Assessing the facts' in Book One (ed. note).

2 Nikolai Khmelev played Tuzenbach in Nemirovich-Danchenko's MAT production in 1940 (ed. note).

and events and discovering deep down underneath them some other well concealed events that actually often provoke the external facts. It means: following the course of psychological events and getting a sense of the extent and nature of their impact, following the lines of every single character's aspirations, observing the lines clash, criss-cross, intertwine, and separate. In a word, it means grasping the inner pattern that determines people's relationships. Assessing the facts means to find the key to the many secrets of 'the life of the human spirit' of a role, hidden underneath the facts of the play.[iii]

Making such demands on an actor, Stanislavski speaks of the actor-thinker, capable of examining any isolated occurrence in a play based on the wealth of all the ideas contained in the piece.

Let's compare Stanislavski's view of the matter with that of Gorky's.[3]

A fact – is not yet the whole truth. It is only the raw material from which the genuine truth of art is to be extracted, smelted. You cannot fry a chicken still covered in feathers. That is exactly what worshipping of facts leads to – mixing up incidental and inessential with the fundamental and typical. We must learn to pluck off the inessential plumage of facts, and extract meaning out of them.[iv]

Gorky teaches writers to add up and pick out the typical in the facts of life. Stanislavski demands no less from the actors in order to get to the true essence of selected facts. He teaches actors to find in each line a true meaning that drives them to action and gives them stimulus for speaking a particular thought.

The author's text has to be accepted by the actor with a precision that enables them to express it in their own words. Only then did Stanislavski allow the actor to speak the lines as written by the author.

As an experiment Stanislavski suggested to the actors that they, following the example of great writers, should create their own 'drafts of the text of the role' – to get an even deeper insight into the author's text.

Stanislavski was trying to get actors, when rehearsing a scene, to convey a particular section of the text in their own words. By creating 'drafts', actors expand their notion of the facts reflected in the text, and get used to the idea that words must express the character's train of thought precisely. At the same time, the 'draft' of a role makes actors read the author's text more keenly as they verify its finely honed verbal form.

The wider our knowledge and observations of life, the easier and more fruitful the work of our imagination.

---

3 Maxim Gorky, pseudonym of Aleksei Maksimovich Peshkov (1868–1936), Russian and Soviet novelist and playwright (trans. note).

In the art of the theatre this is a decisive factor since the actor, having done their work, appears in front of the audience as a real-life person from a certain historical period. The smallest absence of authenticity in their inner or outer behaviour instantly puts a perceptive audience member on their guard.

['How often do you consider', Stanislavski said, 'the amount of effort a writer puts into finding a figure of speech to express the complexities of human feelings precisely? Yet you make no effort to get inside the actual thoughts they were trying to express, mechanically rattling off the words.']

Thinking about this quote from Stanislavski, brings to mind Mayakovsky's[4] essay on 'How Poems are Made', where he writes of the enormous painstaking labour that goes into selecting the precise words he needs.

Mayakovsky describes his work on the poem 'To Sergei Yesenin'.

In the opening lines of the essay, the poet writes that in choosing a word, he asks himself, 'Is this the word? Will it be understood correctly? etc'[5]

Actually, if we think of draft manuscripts by Pushkin, Tolstoy or Mayakovsky with their numerous corrections, crossed out words, insertions, if we think of the huge amount of work, determination and self-discipline that distinguishes the creative work of all great writers, and then juxtapose it all with the slipshod thoughtlessness of quite a few actors and directors in terms of stage interpretations of the verbal fabric and actions in a play, it becomes apparent that we have a great task ahead of us – to learn from the masters of the word, learn from Stanislavski.

Notes

i   K.S. Stanislavski, *Rabota aktera nad rolyu* (An Actor's Work on a Role), *Sobranie Sochinenij,* vol.4. Moscow, Iskusstvo, 1957, p.365.

ii   *Yezhegodnik MKHAT* (MAT Yearbook) 1945. Moscow/Leningrad, Iskusstvo, 1948, vol.2, p.442.

iii K.S. Stanislavski, *Rabota aktera nad rolyu* (An Actor's Work on a Role), *Sobranie Sochinenij,* vol.4, Moscow, Iskusstvo, 1957, p.369.

iv   Maxim Gorky, *Sobranie sochinenij*. Moscow, GIKhL,1953, vol.2, p.296.

4 Vladimir Mayakovsky (1893–1930) a Russian Soviet poet, playwright, and artist (trans. note).

5 See below Appendix G (ed. note).

Mental images

Without figurative thinking, there is no art. But getting there is far less simple than it sometimes appears. Quite often the actor lingers so long over the initial process of exploring the play's facts rationally and logically that, without noticing it, they smother their own emerging feelings and emotions.

Meanwhile, whichever individual acting process is used to establish a close bond with the character, it will always demand that the actor uses their imagination actively. Unsurprisingly, Stanislavski is full of praise for the *mighty* ' "if …" without which no creativity is possible'.[1]

One of the devices that arouses imagination is the use of mental images.

When Stanislavski first brought up the subject of 'the film of mental images' and 'the illustrated subtext',[2] it was a genuine discovery in the art of the stage. This discovery completely overturned every single aspect of the science of the actor's creative work. 'Mental images' refers to the law of the actor's figurative thinking onstage. In life, we always visualise whatever we are talking about; every word we hear brings up a specific picture in our mind's eye. But onstage we often abandon this crucial faculty, trying to affect the audience with 'empty' words unsupported by living pictures from the unbroken flow of our existence.

Stanislavski proposed that actors should *practise seeing mental images that relate to various moments in their role, gradually building up a store of these images to produce 'the film of mental images of the role' in a logical and sequential way.*

In life we remember an event that struck us, we reconstruct it mentally, either visually or verbally, or both at the same time. Our impressions of the past are often polyphonic: now there is a cadence that had surprised us once before, ringing in our ears as if heard only a few seconds earlier, now our consciousness renders most vibrant pictures and images, or we recall the meaning of something someone said to us once that had deeply impressed us. Stanislavski bases his teaching about mental images on this particular psychological trait of ours. If an actor consistently goes back to the pictures they need for the role,

1 See *An Actor's Work*, part 1, chapter 3, 'Action, "if", given circumstances' (ed. note).
2 See *An Actor's Work*, part 1, chapter 4 on 'Imagination' (ed. note).

DOI: 10.4324/9780203125205-23

their mental images will grow more and more vivid on a daily basis, building an intricate system of thoughts, feelings and associations.

Let us take an example from life. Say, I am in a rush to get to rehearsals. I am getting off at the next stop. As I go towards the exit, I see that a woman by the door is unwell. After a few moments of hesitation, the fear of being late for rehearsals prevails over my desire to help the sick passenger, and I get off the train. But this is not the end of the story. For the next few days I am haunted by the image of the unknown woman who, her mouth wide open, tries – and fails – to take a deep breath. So the memory of the incident turns into something significantly more complicated than what I felt on leaving the train. Now the image of the sick woman gets all mixed up with thoughts of my indifference and selfishness. I am judging myself for not having helped a person in need, for having mollified my conscience with the excuse that I was in a hurry on important business, that someone else was undoubtedly going to help her instead. For me, this unknown woman has become a source of rather complicated feelings. I am no longer upset by the event as such but rather by my hard-hearted and inhumane behaviour. In worrying about my attitude to the fact, I interweave the fact into a system of moral generalisations. And the more often I go back to it, the more actively and deeply I process my first direct impressions. My feelings are now more acute, more complex and sharper than they were in that first instance.

'Processed' impressions have huge power, and playwrights quite often make use of them. For example, Nastia's recollections in Gorky's *The Lower Depths*, or Sarah's in Chekhov's *Ivanov*. Yet actors often ignore this quality of the psyche, and want to break through to mental images straight away, without any extended and frequently repeated mental 'peering at' an object, while it accumulates further minutiae and details. And at times: if during rehearsals an actor catches a glimpse of something in their mind's eye, that's well and good; if nothing comes to them – nothing to be done. As a rule, nothing comes from such an approach. The character is unable to affect anybody around them with their mental images because their creator – the actor – has failed to accumulate any.

In one of his letters Flaubert recounts how he himself was close to death while he wrote the description of Emma Bovary's suicide.[3] He experienced Emma's suffering so fully that he thought he could taste arsenic on his own tongue.

One day a friend of Balzac's came for a visit and saw that he was not at all well: he was gasping for breath, his face covered in a cold sweat. When asked, if something was wrong with him, Balzac answered, 'You don't know anything, do you? Father Goriot[4] has just died.'

In Tchaikovsky's diary there is a remarkable entry made on the day when the composer finished the last scene of *The Queen of Spades*: 'Cried bitterly when Hermann[5] breathed his last!'

---

3 *Madame Bovary* (1856) is Gustave Flaubert's (1821–1880) debut novel (trans. note).
4 *Le Père Goriot* (1835) is a novel by French novelist Honoré de Balzac (1799–1850) (trans. note).
5 *The Queen of Spades* (1890) an opera by Pyotr Ilyich Tchaikovsky (1840–1893) (trans. note).

The actor must train themself to see all the events of their character's life as clearly and concretely as Flaubert saw Emma's suicide, Balzac the death of Father Goriot and Tchaikovsky Hermann's downfall. For the actor, these mental images must exist just as if they were their personal memories.

Here for example is Juliet's soliloquy from Act 4, scene 3 of Shakespeare's tragedy.[6]

Out of the blue, they announce the day of Juliet's wedding to Paris. Friar Laurence, who secretly married Romeo and Juliet, proposes a ploy that will allow Juliet to escape the loathed wedding and join Romeo who has fled to Mantua. She must drink a sleeping potion; her family will mistake her sleep for death and carry her in an open coffin to the Capulet family burial vault. In the meantime, the Friar will have sent for Romeo to come back and save her.

The action in the soliloquy seems to be very straightforward: Juliet must drink the sleeping potion. But in order to feel how hard it is for Juliet, in love, to follow the Friar's advice, the actor must experience the moral battle that takes place in her character's heart. Shakespeare, with a tragic power, reveals the depth of what Juliet is going through. She has made up her mind to follow the Friar's advice, promising him that she will find strength and courage in her love for Romeo. But when the time comes for Juliet to take the potion she is overcome by terror and is ready to abandon her plan, and call for her mother or the nurse who she has just sent away. Juliet pictures what will happen to her, if she gives in to her fears and fails to drink the potion: eternal separation from Romeo, the loathed marriage to Paris. And she makes her decision. 'Come, vial', exclaims Juliet. Then a mortifying thought stops her:

> What if this mixture do not work at all?
> Shall I be married then tomorrow morning?

The very thought of marrying Paris is so revolting to Juliet and seems so impossible that she is ready to die even if the potion does not work. She gets an idea: she must have a weapon handy. Juliet hides a knife under her pillow, while her imagination draws pictures of how in twenty-four hours, when the effect of the potion wears off, there will be her Romeo, how happy they will be to be together again after all they have suffered. Discarding her doubts, she brings the vial up to her lips, then stops again.

> What if it be a poison which the Friar
> Subtly hath ministered to have me dead,
> Lest in this marriage he should be dishonoured
> Because he married me before to Romeo?

6 See Appendix E (the same example as in Book One) (ed. note).

Another frightening picture comes up in her mind's eye. Friar Laurence, fearful of being exposed, decides to kill her to save himself. But straight away Juliet remembers everything that she knows of him. She recalls how respected he is by everyone, how known for his life of holiness, how eager he was to help her. No, the image of Friar Laurence that comes to her mind is incompatible with such treachery. 'Everything will work out as the Friar said: I won't die, I will just go to sleep.' But the imagination draws a picture of a new danger:

> How if, when I am laid into the tomb,
> I wake before the time that Romeo
> Come to redeem me? There's a fearful point!

Horrified she imagines a harrowing picture of waking up: the cold, the night, the foul smell in the vault where many a generation of her ancestors are laid to rest, Tybalt's bloody corpse, spirits wandering about in the night. Suddenly a terrible thought strikes her, 'What if I lose my wits and go mad?' Her imagination produces horrendous pictures of insanity, but then the same imagination brings up Romeo and her fear is forgotten. Romeo! Romeo is in danger! And without another thought, seeing only Romeo in her mind's eye, she drinks up the potion.

To transform fully into the character of Juliet, to experience what it feels like to be in her place, the actor will have to produce in her imagination a sequence of mental images akin to those that arise in Juliet's mind.

['My task, the task of a person telling something to another person, persuading that other person', began Stanislavski in one of his talks to us,

> [is to make the person I am talking to see through my eyes whatever it is that I may require. It is crucial to do this at each rehearsal, in every single performance – make my partner see events the way I see them. If this inner goal is embedded in you, you will be using words as actions, if not, then you are in trouble. You are bound to speak words for words' sake, and then they will inevitably get lodged in the muscle memory of the tongue.
>
> [How can this danger be avoided?
>
> [First of all, as I have told you before, do not learn your lines until you have thoroughly studied *their contents*. Only then will you feel the need for them. Secondly, you must commit something else to memory: *the mental images* for your role, *they are the source of the inner feelings* required for communication.]

['Having created "the film of mental images"', Stanislavski told us,

> [you can get up onto the stage and unroll that film to a thousand-strong crowd of spectators, as you watch it and speak of it the way you feel about it in the here, today, now. Consequently, *the text, the verbal action must be fixed in pictures, in mental images, and those images conveyed through thought — with words.*

[With frequent repetitions, the text of the role becomes overfamiliar and humdrum. But mental images, on the contrary, get strengthened through multiple repetitions because with every repetition the imagination adds more and more fresh detail to the picture.

[When an actor aspires to develop an "illustrated subtext", their imagination inevitably gets stirred, continuously enriching the author's text with more and more novel creative characteristics since we have a boundless ability to take in new phenomena. The more we focus on the fact, the more we learn about it.][7]

Later, on more than one occasion, I had an opportunity to see for myself the huge importance of this device of the psycho-technique in theatre practice.

Roughly speaking, the process of creating mental images has two phases. The first one is the storing up of mental images.

This enormous job is mostly undertaken outside of rehearsals. The actor gathers up and stores material that helps them to create the living past of their character, their 'inner freight', those inherently unique ideas and beliefs that firmly bind the actor to the unfamiliar author's text, and help them to breathe life into it.

Konstantin Sergeievich spoke of yet *another phase* in the process of working with mental images – of perfecting the actor's ability to entice their partner with their images by 'speaking to the partner's eye rather than their ear'.

This is an integral part of the process of communication.

['What does listening mean?', continued Konstantin Sergeievich.

[It means giving your undivided attention, your consideration to your partner. What does it mean to persuade, to explain? It means to pass your mental images over to your partner: it is necessary not only for you but also for your partner to see what you see. It is not possible to tell a story 'in general', or to persuade someone 'in general'.

[Examine the process of communication – of *interaction*. No authentic action can ever arise without a natural process of communication.]

[You should communicate [Stanislavski pointed out] without forcing it. Otherwise, the moment an actor begins 'communicating', they just stare at their partner. Communication is *the prelude to action*. Tasks and actions arise from it. Learn to impress pictures, mental images rather than the sounds of words on your partner.]

Even nowadays we rarely follow these instructions left for us by Konstantin Sergeievich.

[Imagine that once upon a time, a long time ago, when you were young, you visited a city. You walked through its parks and streets, saw the sights,

---

7 See Appendix F (uses the same example as in Book One – Chatski's soliloquy) (ed. note).

went down to the river, lingered on the bridges. And then you left. You never got another chance to go back there. But whenever someone mentions the name of the city in your presence, an emotional and visual memory instantly flares up in you, tied to that city, with the combination of the sounds in its name. You may not able to see the full picture, its details, but something that particularly struck you at the time, instantly appears in your mind's eye. It may be a small corner of a courtyard with a bench under old lime-trees, or a market square with scraps of straw on the dirty snow, or the man you talked to for two hours straight. Instantly the memory of the way you were then comes up, in short, in the blink of an eye a thousand sensations are stirred up in you because a long time ago these emotional sensations were preceded by a vibrant fully fleshed-out concrete reality, because you really did visit that city and saw it all with your own eyes. Something similar should be happening onstage to an actor whose mental images of the role are well stocked.

[So, the more thorough, in depth and conscientious the actor's approach to conjuring up the character's mental images, the more powerful the impact on their partner and – it goes without saying – on the audience.

[But if the actor cannot see the things they are talking about with their stage partner, there's no chance of them 'infecting' anyone else, try as they might: no living emotional connection will occur between the actor and the audience. Until the actor can carry out, by affecting the audience through living mental images, the very best of the director's discoveries, the production is dead, and can never become an affirmation of life, a spiritual revelation. Without an actor, who here and now, this very second, is 'seeing' and infecting the audience with the vibrancy of their images, the essence of theatre – that which makes us consider it a school of laughter and tears – is missing.]

The actor must be continually collecting mental images for the role, and that should include mental images for those facts in the character's life which may have occurred either prior to the events revealed in the play, or in between two events, even facts that the character may never refer to.

Of course, as directors, we draw the actor's attention to the illustrated subtext of the words they deliver onstage. And if the actor clearly starts to lose this mental thread of images, the director says to them, 'No. You are not seeing anything!'. Often the actor says exactly the same and stops themself, 'I can't see what I am talking about.' However, we don't take the character's past history or what happens to them in between the acts seriously enough. We discuss the significance for the character of all the events not shown in the play, and sometimes in the course of rehearsals we point out a particular fact missing from the character's life-story. But considering that none of these parts of the story are rehearsed, for most actors they become just dark patches within the role.

What can we make out of *Hamlet* unless we clearly visualise and comprehend the reality of how the king's murder turned Hamlet's life upside down, revealing to him, without a shadow of a doubt, that 'the time is out of joint', and plunging him into a state of extreme mental strain? And yet all this takes place before the start of the play.

There is a minor character in Gorky's *Children of the Sun*. The moment he enters, this is how he introduces himself: 'Allow me! First things first ... Let me introduce myself – second lieutenant Yakov Troshin, an ex-deputy station-master at Log ... the same Yakov Troshin whose wife and child were crushed by a train ... I have other kids, but no wife ... Yes-s-s! Who do I have the honour to speak to?'

Just one phrase – but behind it, no end of work for the actor. The whole of the man's past life is contained in these few terse words carefully selected by the writer: the daily life of a poor but honourable family, the terrible disaster that befell them, and the mire of the provincial life that gradually, step by step, sucked the man in, his slow descent to the lower depths. Behind this tirade, a glimmer of pride of the man down on his luck, who having by chance found himself in the polite society of educated people, 'intelligentsia',[8] aspires to appear as one of them. As soon as all this is not only understood but also *pictured* in the tragically condensed colours of the man's life envisaged by Gorky, the actor, having *transposed himself* into it, will enter the scene as Yakov Troshin – one of the many down–and–outs in Gorky's plays who may have had their backbone crushed but not their living soul.

If there is a concrete mental image behind each line spoken by the actor, then a living human feeling, which is never accessible directly and can only be reached in this roundabout and lengthy way, will spontaneously arise in action the moment the actor touches upon these memories.

The nature of the actor's independent work on what their character undergoes in the time between each of their entrances is exactly the same, regardless of whether this is an interval of ten years, a few hours or even a few minutes. A talented actor will not fail to follow their character on the journey through those times of their life which are left out of the play, and their next entrance on the stage will reflect everything that their character has been through in the interim.

Is it possible to perform Act 4 of *The Seagull* truthfully unless you have travelling along the way of sorrows next to Nina from the day when, young and in love, she first meets Trigorin at a Moscow hotel until the two stormy autumn days when she aimlessly wanders in the rain by the 'bewitching lake'?

People's recollections of their past experiences not only throw light on a part of their life but also reveal a lot about themselves, of who they are now, at this moment in time. Were Chekhov to cut Nina's final speech in *The Seagull*, and replace the story she tells with a series of isolated scenes of her 'sorrows, and

8 The intelligentsia is a class of intellectuals or highly educated people as a group, especially when regarded as possessing culture and political influence (trans. note).

rootless wanderings', her character would have lost a lot of its depth and poetry. And we would have learnt much less about Nina, of who she has become.

In all these cases, it is not the plot that sustains our interest. Usually, we know in advance what happens to a character in between their entrances, just as we know everything in advance about Nina from Dorn's story. This is what makes us so keen to meet up once again with the 'seagull' who has been mindlessly shot down.

Why does Ostrovsky feel the need in *More Sinned Against than Sinning*[9] to recap what we have already seen in Act 1, in Kruchinina's detailed retelling of it in Act 2? Do all the performers who play the part properly assess the facts of Kruchinina's life over the preceding seventeen years? Do they understand how much she has suffered? Do they all follow her, an actress and an outcast, as she roams the country from one provincial stage to the next? Are they storing up all her bitter thoughts exacerbated by time and the memories, that flood her with a particular intensity the moment she is back in her hometown? Well, when Yermolova,[10] as Kruchinina, spoke of her past, the audiences were shaken to the core! Her memories were more vivid, more intense than the event that had produced them.

When the actor manages to capture their character's life in its entirety, without skipping over the periods omitted from the action of the play, what emerges is a living human being rather than a stage character. This process gives rise to a genuinely truthful behaviour, which leads to unexpected shades of meaning and adaptations so surprising that the actor could never have invented them by design but only discovered them by sharing with their character all that they have been destined to experience in their life. And yet it is this unpredictable truth, which we have missed a hundred times before, to which an artist draws our attention for the very first time, it is this truth that takes our breath away and makes us, '*co-experience*'[11] the character's joys and sorrows. Only such acting can be a revelation, allowing us to grasp the new and the uncanny in life, which which we have never been able to unravel before!

Stanislavski always reminded us that powers of observation are the basis of the actor's creative imagination. He advised actors to keep a journal and make

9 Alexander Ostrovsky's *More Sinned Against than Sinning,* written in 1881–1883, tells a story of a young girl Lubov Otradina, whose child, born out of wedlock, dies at the end of Act 1 when she is abandoned by her lover. In Act 2, seventeen years later, she is back in town starring at the theatre under her stage-name Elena Kruchinina (trans. note).

10 Maria Yermolova (1853–1928), an actress at the Maly Theatre, Moscow. Played many parts in Ostrovsky's plays and was an idol of the Russian youth at the end of 19th century, including Stanislavski (ed. note).

11 The literal translation of the Stanislavski system concept of *Soperezhivamiye* is 'co-experiencing', which denotes neither the inner feeling, nor action, nor the actor's physical sense of self, nor their experiencing. It denotes the audience's ability to share their feelings, communion and empathy with the actors. So 'co-experiencing' is an instant reminder of an ideal relationship between the stage and the audience that Russian theatre has always aspired to achieve (trans. note).

notes of things that strike them in life. He said that in this respect actors should follow the example of writers.

Konstantin Sergeievich attached great importance to our ability to absorb knowledge and discoveries. He constantly spoke of the concealed wealth in painting, music and poetry, and called on actors and directors to study those art forms adjacent to theatre not only out of necessity, for a production of a particular play but, as he put it, as a 'prudent reserve'.

['Learn to look into life', Stanislavski said.

[Scrutinizing life is a form of high art for the actor. Now you must learn to 'gobble up knowledge'. Chaliapin always comes to mind at this point.[12] Once I was with Repin, Serov[13] and a few other master painters. Chaliapin listened to them greedily. Mamontov nudged me and said, 'Look, Konstantin Sergeievich, how Chaliapin "gobbles up knowledge".' So there you are, learn to 'gobble up knowledge'.]

Stanislavski suggested that before they start working on a literary story (or a monologue), the student should do an exercise that would allow them to understand the kind of organic process that structures a story in real life. He suggested that they should recount an incident that happened in their own life.

The student must reconstruct in their mind – fully, vividly and in as much detail as possible – an incident from their own life, and then recount it to a listener.

Creative imagination will compel the student to conjure up circumstances in which they would feel like telling the story today, here, now to this particular partner about this particular incident from their own life.

Once the student has mastered the exercise, they need to see that when talking about an incident from their own life, all they need to do is to recall it. But when working on a monologue or a story, the student will have to dream up such clear mental pictures and images of what they are going to recount, become so familiar with them that the student could claim them as their personal memories.

---

12 Feodor Chaliapin (1873–1938) is not only one of the greatest basses of Russian opera but also a particular type of an actor, who was an inspiration to the whole of the Russian theatre. That is why he can be considered a part of the theatre tradition (ed. note).

13 Ilya Repin (1844–1930), the most significant Russian realist painter, endowed with a genuine historical and epic insight. Valentin Serov (1865–1911), one of the greatest Russian painters of the early 20th century, also belongs to the realist tradition, but his work is more chamber and intimate; well-known for his portraits, in particular that of the great Russian actress Maria Yermolova (see above), as well as his still-lifes. These artists alongside with Chaliapin and Stanislavski belonged to the circle of Savva Mamontov, an industrialist, merchant and passionate patron of the arts, who brought together the most important painters, musicians and actors of *fin de siècle* Russia (ed. note).

['The main point is', Stanislavski told us in our classes at the Studio,

[to find a way for genuine communication. The tentacles of my soul must sense my partner's soul. We need to discover the organic process to which we will add the layer of words further down the line. So firstly, it is necessary to probe your partner, secondly, make them receive your mental images, and thirdly, test your partner's understanding of them. For this, you must give your partner time to see what is being transmitted to them.

['The actor who simply learns their lines', said Stanislavski,

[will always speak without waiting to see if their partner has received them. But in real life, however far you are from each other when you speak, you always wait for the other person to see and absorb what you have said. How can the words spoken onstage make sense, if the actor just spits them out? Such words are just frittered away! They will never be active.]

If the student knows precisely which facts they want to share, to what purpose they tell their story, and what kind of response to these facts they can expect from their partner, they will never be rushed.

The action is brought about by its motives. Each action is linked to the throughaction and the supertask.

The throughaction is a channel. When the actor has no supertask and starts to follow minor tasks, they fail to get anywhere. Logic and sequence must be the foundation of the creative process.

For the students to better absorb this idea, Konstantin Sergeievich advised me to offer them to put it to the test by using examples from life.

[Let them recall an incident from their own life, and present an account of it strictly following the course of events and the actions provoked by these events.

[When someone shares something they have lived through themselves [said Stanislavski], even if they only want to talk of their feelings, in reality they talk of nothing but their actions.]

Interestingly enough, Anton Chekhov, in contemplating the writer's craft, wrote in one of his letters: 'It is best to avoid describing the character's psychological state; we should instead make an effort to reveal it through the character's actions.'[i]

Note

i   Anton Chekhov, *Sobranie sochinenij*. Moscow, Pravda, 1950, vol.12, p.42.

Studies in artistic recitation

I remember to this day how – just before starting my classes in Artistic Recitation at the Stanislavski's Studio – I was frantically trying to make sense of everything that Konstantin Sergeievich had shared with me. I knew all too well that even if I did understand what Stanislavski urged me to do, it was not enough. His words were ingrained in my mind:

'In art, to know means to be able to do it.'

How should I structure my course? How to avoid taking the wrong turn that leads to the widely accepted clichés for teaching Artistic Recitation?

These thoughts kept me awake at night. But Konstantin Sergeievich, in response to my many questions on the practical aspects of the studies, always said:

[If you have understood what I am after, you will definitely find ways of getting there. And if a question you cannot answer on your own does come up, you can phone me any time. Don't forget, I expect you to do experimental work, so I will be delighted to be of help.]

I was concerned about the nature of the actor's sense of self in the recitation of the short literary story.[1] In a play, the actor encounters each event as it occurs, in that very second, and reacts to it on the spot, spontaneously since the actor portrays a person who has no knowledge of what is going to happen next. Or to put it another way, that is precisely the nature of the art of acting: the actor must, despite knowing the play backwards, respond so spontaneously to what is happening at any given moment that it is as if they are unaware of where it is all going.

The more talented the actor, the more compelling they are in making the audience believe that everything on stage happens to them 'as if for the first time'. The play's action always takes place in the present! But how can we

---

1 The Russian term 'story' means both a certain literary genre (a story or novella, such as Chekhov's stories) and the act of narrating in general. Here Maria Knebel refers us to the practice when an actor, or a student, performs a literary story, written by a writer (ed. note).

DOI: 10.4324/9780203125205-24

hold on to this sense of 'as if for the first time' when working on stories? The story covers different periods in a person's life. In building the plot, the writer introduces us to the characters' past and gives us a chance to follow them over a long period of time. The actor–narrator must have, without fail, a perspective on the recitation they perform, on what they are going to talk about. In a story the actor must know the full course of events in advance, and lay out the facts in a way that leads us to understand what they are after as they share with us all they have been through.

I tested myself by recalling what stories sound like in real life. Suppose I wanted to tell the story of how I got into the Arts Theatre. I may begin the story with my childhood, it may abound with all sorts of details that I will need later to support the basic fact that I want to relate. So as I tell my story I make every detail serve the main fact.

The more I considered the problem of delivering a short literary story onstage, the better I understood Stanislavski's words:

> No matter what speech or short story the student chooses to do, it is essential that they conjure up such a clear picture of what they are going to talk about and become so familiar with it, that *it will turn into their personal memory.*

One of Stanislavski's adamant demands, regarding the work of the Artistic Recitation Department at the Studio, was that our way of working on this particular subject was no different from the approach to teaching the Mastery of Acting.[2] And so the active analysis that he had introduced the actors to in their initial work on a role, was made compulsory in our work on stories.

For the pictures painted by the writer in the story to become part of the student's personal memories, we had to start from a long way away. Before doing any practical work in class, I was supposed – following Stanislavski's instructions – to break down the chosen stories into events, define their narrative action, and select a few of them for doing etudes. Some stories use the device of being narrated in the first-person singular; in others, the writer, without using the first-person singular, tells the story about people they have encountered in life, and tells us of their attitude to those people. There is also the third device: for the writer to tell us first about something they have witnessed in life, then share their personal reaction to it, thus weaving themself into the narrative of the story.

I was given a list of stories to work on, selected by Konstantin Sergeievich. When I got home, I tried to work through them in the new way, that is, by first defining the specific events in the story, the facts on which the writer built the development of the plot. I started by analysing Chekhov's story *Champagne.*

---

2 'Mastery of Acting' – the art of acting, mastering the art of acting. This is still the title of actor training courses in Russia (ed. note).

Here's a brief reminder of what happens in it. A down-and-out man tells us how his monotonous and hopelessly grey life of a station-master at a minor local railway stop was torn apart by his passion for a woman, an unexpected visitor, and how it destroyed him.

In the first bit of the story Chekhov introduces us to the given circumstances of his character's life. A minor railway stopping place in the middle of a steppe with no human habitation for fifteen miles around.

> The only possible diversion was in the windows of the passenger trains, and in the vile vodka … Now and then there would be a glimpse of a woman's head at a carriage window, and he would stand there, like a statue, not breathing and stare at it until the train turned into an almost invisible speck; or he would drink his fill of the revolting vodka, black out and no longer have any sense of the passing of the long hours and days.

Having painted a picture of the circumstances of the station-master's life, Chekhov starts to develop the plot.

The station-master and his wife (who he does not love but who is still in love with him) are having supper to celebrate the New Year.

> In spite of the boredom that was consuming me, we were preparing to see in the New Year with exceptional ceremony, and were awaiting midnight with some impatience. The fact is, we kept in reserve two bottles of champagne, the genuine article, with the label of *Veuve Clicquot* …

At five to midnight the husband, having uncorked the bottle, dropped it on the floor.

> Not more than a glass of the wine was spilt, as I managed to catch the bottle and put my thumb over the foaming neck.
> 'Well, happy New Year, may it bring new joy!', I said, filling two glasses. 'Have a drink!'
> My wife took her glass and fixed her frightened eyes on me. Her face was pale and had a look of horror.
> 'Did you drop the bottle?', she asked.
> 'Yes, I did. So, what of that?'
> 'It's not good', she said, putting down her glass and turning paler still. 'It's a bad omen. It means something bad will happen to us this year.'
> 'What an old gossip you are!', I sighed. 'You are a clever woman, but you are talking gibberish like an old nanny. Drink.'
> 'God grant, it's gibberish, but … something is sure to happen! You'll see!'
> She did not even touch her wine, but moved away, deep in thought. I made a few stale remarks about superstition, drank half a bottle, paced up and down, and then went out of the room.

The short episode, an irritation with his superstitious wife, makes the station-master rethink his whole life. He comes to a conclusion which is full of anguish and bitter irony.

> I have known nothing but failure and trouble all my life. What further misfortune can strike me?'
>
> The misfortunes we have endured already, and those facing us now, are so great that it is difficult to imagine anything worse. What further harm can you do to a fish which has been caught and fried and served up with sauce?

On his return home, after a miserable walk, the station-master learns that while he was out his wife's aunt arrived for a three-day visit.

> A little woman with large black eyes was sitting at the table. My table, the grey walls, my rough-hewn sofa … everything to the tiniest grain of dust seemed to have grown younger and more cheerful in the presence of this creature, new, young, and oozing a curious scent of something beautiful, and dissolute.

Once again they start their supper …

> I can't remember what happened next. Anyone who wants to know how love begins may read novels and long stories, but I will put it briefly, and in the words of that silly old romance:

> When first I saw you,
> It must have been an evil hour …[3]

> Everything hurtled downwards, head first, to the devil. I remember a terrifying, violent whirlwind that swirled me around like a feather. It lasted a long while, and swept from the face of the earth my wife, and her aunt, and all my strength. From the little station in the steppe it flung me, as you see, onto this dark street.
>
> Now tell me: what further misfortune can strike me?

Chekhov reveals to us the inner world of a 'little person'[4], deeply shocked by what had happened to him. Suddenly a woman, who has no connection to

---

3 Words of a famous Gypsy romance 'Black Eyes' (trans. note).

4 It is generally considered that Russian literature, starting with the publication of Pushkin's *Belkin's Stories* and Gogol's *St Petersburg Stories*, is distinguished by its concern with the 'little person' – an insignificant character like a lowly clerk or the head of a post office (ed. note).

any circumstances of his 'existence', arrives at his house, he is destroyed by his love for her, and terrified by life's complexities asks, 'What further misfortune can strike me?'

The more I thought about it, the clearer it became to me that in the story to which Chekhov gave two titles: *Champagne* and *The Rogue's Story*, we should look for the throughactin from the 'rogue's' point of view:

I want to grasp the tragic absurdity that occurred in my life, find an explanation for the inexplicable fact I cannot even begin to comprehend: the ill omen that proved to be true.

That is why I need to speak about it out loud, tell someone about it, and find in that person's eyes the solution to this riddle.

That is why I need to build up mental images that will provide raw material for my communication. In my imagination, I must live through the station-master's life which by force of circumstances took such a turn that it turned me into a rogue.

The basic event that pushed Chekhov's station-master into the abyss was the passion that unexpectedly flared up sweeping away the past like a furious hurricane.

First of all, it is necessary to picture this man's life before the fateful event.

Place of Action. A minor stopping place on a railway line. No human habitation for fifteen miles around. The steppe!

Society. Wife. A deaf telephonist. Watchmen.

Relationship with his wife. He does not love his wife. Irritated by her love. She forgives him everything, even his cruelty, when he gets drunk and torments her with endless rebukes since there is no one else he can vent his anger and anguish at.

What was his life like? Before he was deemed useful enough to 'be shoved into the station master's position at the railway stopping place'? His parents died when he was still a child. Born into an aristocratic family, he was given neither education, nor upbringing. He was kicked out of school. Got married very young. Dreamt of love, but found none.

Recreation. Catching glimpses of female faces in windows of the passing passenger trains. And vodka. It knocks you out and stops you thinking.

A feeling of boundless isolation and a sense of deep injustice gnawing away at his soul. He gets accustomed to his bitter reflections on his miserable state, he even derives a kind of pleasure from them, giving in to them with delight.

I made an outline for a number of etudes.

1. *A passenger train unexpectedly comes to a halt at the station.*

Passengers, wondering why they have stopped, gather by the carriage doors, question each other, some climb down to the platform. The Station-Master watches them with interest, trying to work out who they are, where they are going and why.

After a brief stop the train moves on. The Station-Master is left on the platform alone.

In this etude, the student had to come up with an inner monologue along the lines of: there is nothing he can do to keep any of them here, no one he can talk to, each of them must have such an interesting life he knows nothing about. And now they are speeding away towards big cities full of people and lights, while he is left behind, holding a lamp in the middle of a snow-bound steppe, and no one cares about him.

2. *An ordinary night at the Station-Master's house.*

Alone with his wife. The monotonous tapping of the telegraph keys on the other side of the wall. His wife tries to come up with something to talk about, to entertain him, seeking in his eyes some appreciation of a lovely supper she has made.

These attempts only make him want to hurt her feelings, blame her for all his troubles, give vent to his dissatisfaction with life.

3. *New Year's Eve.*

Husband and wife are laying the table together. Both are delighted that at midnight they will open the two bottles of champagne they put aside the previous autumn. He won this treasure in a bet with a colleague of his, and now they both anticipate the pleasure of drinking it.

The clock's big hand is approaching twelve. The husband starts to uncork the bottle. It slips from his hands and drops to the floor.

His wife tries to conceal her fear, but her thoughts are so disturbed that she cannot overcome it.

Her imagination paints terrible pictures of all sorts of misfortunes, including – worst of all – her husband's death. He tries to calm her, but all is in vain. It ends up in a row, and the husband leaves.

4. *The arrival of his wife's aunt, while he is out.*

The wife does not know how to explain her husband's absence.

The table is laid. The champagne is opened.

He returns. The New Year's Eve celebrations resume, this time with the three of them. Now everything is of interest to him. He wants to talk, laugh, sing.

Having made my outline of the etudes, I checked with Stanislavski if I was on the right track in my analysis of Chekhov's story.

Stanislavski asked me to read 'Champagne' to him.

Having listened to it carefully, he asked:

[Why does your outline of etudes stop with his first meeting with the woman who plays such a big part in the Station-Master's life?

[The student must also come up with what happened after that meeting up until the moment when he turned into the 'rogue' whom the writer makes the mouthpiece of the whole story. Chekhov does not reveal this to us. Chekhov is, as always, succinct. But the actor must earn the right to say, 'I can't remember what happened next ... Everything hurtled downwards, head first, to the devil. I remember a terrifying, violent whirlwind that swirled me around like a feather... From the little station in the steppe it flung me, as you see, onto this dark street...'. To say this, the actor must conjure up so much more in his imagination, build up such a store of mental images that it will become clear to everyone that he does not want to go into the details. He has not forgotten any of it but it is too hard for him to talk about things that are still so vivid and alive in his mind!]

Having checked with Stanislavski if my analysis of facts and actions in the other stories was correct, and if the etudes I planned were accurate, I started my classes.

Conditions for doing this work at the Studio were exceptional. It is not often that Artistic Recitation teachers can count on having the whole group together to work on etudes! The Studio offered that opportunity, and I saw for myself the huge pay-off of this practice.

One of the classes was particularly interesting: after the students had spent a long time working on etudes, studying their roles through physical actions[5] and improvising their own lines, I read the original story to them once again.

They listened to the text with bated breath, eagerly checking their own lived experience of the story and comparing it with what was proposed by the author.

After the second reading the students made notes of the exact sequence of the facts that had to be part of their narrative. They double-checked and absorbed the logic and sequence of the facts silently, as they mentally ran through their own 'film of mental images'.

Once the students found ease and freedom in doing that, we moved on to the next phase of the work – the process of storytelling itself. To start with the students used their own words. The role of the listener in that exercise carried exceptional responsibility! It was not easy to overcome passive listening. But due to Stanislavski's categorical demand that these classes were to be fundamentally an exercise in 'communication', with the listener turning into a storyteller after an hour, we succeeded in eliminating that difficulty, too. It became even clearer to me that it was not possible to begin telling a story without having first grasped the whole picture that I wanted to talk about. I had to know really well what I was telling it for, what I felt about the people and events I was talking about, and what I expected of my partner by telling it to them. Only then could I achieve the creative sense of self in which, 'as if for the first time', I shared with my partner the outcome of what I had seen and lived through. It became crystal clear to me that none of this could be achieved without a partner, without a living communication. By analysing the story through its facts, by assessing these facts, building up a store of mental images and developing the ability to deliver the author's material in our own words, we ploughed up and prepared the soil for the author's words to become essential.

---

5 The method of 'physical actions' is a distinguishing feature of the final period of Stanislavski's creative work. It consists of constructing an unbroken line of the physical actions of the role (ed. note).

So we went back to the text. The lines settled in our minds with ease, effortlessly, the students soaked up the words that expressed better and more precisely than their own the train of thought they had assimilated during their preliminary work.

The question of when and how to move on to the author's exact text, be it in working on the role, or on the spoken word, concerned Stanislavski greatly. He repeatedly emphasised that it was an experimental problem and had to be tested in practice.

Making transition to the purity of the original text demands great sensitivity from the director.

There is a dangerous point when the actor has grown so accustomed to their own improvised text that it appears to them to be more precise and expressive than the author's in conveying their fundamental train of thought.

My own practice leads me to believe that after the rehearsals in which actors speak the text in their own words, we must go back as soon as possible and check the text against the author's original.

This checking encourages the actors to fall in love with the author's words and the way they are used. Even the moment of returning to speaking the original text out loud nourishes them and fills them with joy. Since the actor has already absorbed the logic and sequence of thoughts, they can now develop their understanding of the connections and pathways that have led the author to express their thoughts in this particular way.

Stanislavski showed a lively interest in the progress of each individual piece, watching all of the end of term showings, constantly prompting teachers and students with new ideas, while mapping out ever more precise and subtle ways of working.

It is hard to convey how this great pedagogue would rejoice at the slightest spark of truth in a student's work, how persistently he kindled in us faith in the power of hard work and the need for self-improvement.

An atmosphere of a festive celebration prevailed in his classroom. A sense of inner concentration and responsibility sprung up of its own accord. When the stern 'I don't believe you'[6] rang out, it seemed sometimes that the student would not have the courage to continue. And yet Stanislavski's great pedagogical talent provoked in students such personal rigour that all their false pride and self-consciousness became secondary, and they longed to fulfil at least a fraction of the greater task Stanislavski so passionately bid them do.

The fact that his demanding sternness could quickly give way to an almost childlike joy at the student's slightest success, filled them with an inspiring sense of freedom and self-belief.

---

6 This exclamation of Stanislavski's has become proverbial in the Russian theatre. It can be considered either a motto or a war-cry that unites and brings together all the champions of the 'system' who have always upheld the principle of authenticity in the actor's life on stage (ed. note).

Stanislavski followed the students' creative process with exceptional shrewdness to ensure that their approach was correct, particularly at the point when the student was about to begin their storytelling.

['Examine yourself', he used to say in our classes, knitting his thick grey eyebrows.

[Remember that prior to doing your creative work, you must free your muscles so that your nature can express itself. What does it mean to collect your thoughts? Many people tend to think that in order to concentrate they must withdraw into themselves. This will result in nothing but tension. Have a good look at the audience, find someone you are going to speak to, target your object, then start to speak. But no whispering. If you whisper instead of using your normal voice, you lie. All it means is that you are not sure of what you are speaking for, and that you have not fully assessed the given circumstances. But if you begin by merely speaking loudly, you will simply push and overact. So, you require such given circumstances that will make you, whether you want to or not, speak louder. Then you will be speaking with more power thanks to having an inner task, and a motive. Do not use gestures and facial expressions to paint pictures for us – that's what the words are for! You understand, don't you, that all your little smiles arise out of self-consciousness, of trying to suck up to the audience? Fight against that. Remember, the actor's smile is dishonest. Once you manage to reach the point of being free in your delivery, you will have arrived at a real living conversation. You must get rid of anything superfluous. That's is the most important point. From the outset you must spare no effort to achieve that.]

Stanislavski's demands constantly grew. As soon as one phase of the process was mastered, he would instantly urge both the student and the pedagogue to move on to the next stage of investigation, when the work became even more detailed and thorough.

I remember the class in which one of the students presented Chekhov's 'A Malefactor'.

['Do you feel,' said Stanislavski, once the student reached the end of the story,

[that whenever you see images, you speak truthfully to your target listener. But, when you talk of things you do not see in your mind's eye, you are forced to embellish your words: big, bi-i-ig; small, sma-a-a-ll. As soon as you stop seeing, stop being active, you inevitably start to ham it up, and end up with a cliché. How can we protect ourselves from clichés? *Never allow the film of mental images to break off.* If actors can master this ability, I assure you that we will be able to put on shows in such a short period of time that we couldn't possibly imagine now.]

['And now,' continued Konstantin Sergeievich,

[check if your story's throughaction may be too superficial. Try to deepen it by considering what the author's purpose was in writing the story. Chekhov was never superficial in anything he said, he always exposed the very essence of the event he wrote about. He'd bring something into the open, and out it came, maybe a comedy, or maybe a downright tragedy. Follow this line of thought, look deeply into it, and you might find yourself weeping over this 'malefactor'.]

When he told the story, Stanislavski 'demonstrated' the malefactor, doing it without the author's text, with just a word here and there, a detail, a gesture (he examined something closely, while rubbing his forehead with the back of his hand). The person he embodied in front of us was so unlike Stanislavski himself, yet so full of life, real, and touching in his naïve innocence that we only wished we could keep watching this sketch of genius by the supreme actor-realist.

['How do you perform a story', asked Stanislavski,

[that has several characters? Should you define your task completely from the narrator's point of view, or from the point of view of the other characters? You must share with us the malefactor's thoughts but without demonstrating his way of speaking.! His inflections, or even his gestures, might creep into your inflections since you are already beginning to behave and experience things as he would. But if you stop taking actions and start impersonating him instead, you will get trapped in a cliché. You must enter into the character's given circumstances without imitating them, and convey how you feel about them rather than depicting their inflections.

[Never forget that you have a narrator's *relationship* to the person you are talking about! And however many characters there are in a story, you must have a different *relationship* with each of them – that will make each of them unique.

[A correctly defined supertask is crucial for correctly distributing psychological accents throughout the story. In life, when we talk about an occurrence that has struck us, we constantly use direct quotes from the people involved in the event that affected us, but have you noticed? – in life we never try to impersonate those people. We use their words in order to convey – in diverse ways, more vividly and precisely – the given circumstances we require to tell our story.

[As soon as the actor tries to impersonate the various characters appearing in a story, they will, invariably, get caught up in a false sense of self and lose the fundamental and principal part – themselves – the narrator who holds the basic thread of the story in their hands.

[Remember, when you embark on telling a story you must know exactly what you are doing it for, what thoughts and feelings you want to provoke, and the goal you are striving for.]

Stanislavski was the enemy of any kind of sentimentality. While he demanded that theatre revealed the deepest level of the character's inner world, he called upon the actor to be simple, natural and truthful, without which there could be no authenticity in art. He fought against 'pretty chocolate-box' art in the name of genuine beauty, against teensy-weensy little truth in the name of a great one.

He demanded exactly the same rigour of the classes on Artistic Recitation.

['Take it in a more serious vein, do not go all sickly sweet in your description of beauty.'] Stanislavski urged that teachers forbid their students, once and for all, to speak of nature in sugary tones, or try and depict external aspects of objects.

[Do not assess objects in your story externally, do it from the standpoint of your relationship with them. And do not describe to us a person's appearance by using inflections. Describe the inner essence of the person, and your relationship to them.

[Then you will be able to fight against making linear adaptations.

['I am going to tell you a te-e-errrrible thing!' (but what it is – no one knows!). 'What a glo-o-o-or-riuos moon, what gree-ee-een grass.' You cannot act colours or taste. Convey your relationship to the colour. You cannot put a stress on colours, if nothing else because 'coloured' is an adjective. A colour can only be stressed if it is juxtaposed to something else: 'Over here they are light pink, and over there – red.' If it is a juxtaposition then one should be spoken slower, and the other one – quicker.]

Stanislavski fought vehemently against primitive and linear adaptations in stage speech, regarding them as great sources of clichés. He insisted that if there was an authentic, organic action it would inevitably provoke within the actor that 'wisdom of the heart' which, in order to achieve its goal, would of its own accord seek out varied, diverse devices and adaptations.

In one of his classes at the Studio, Stanislavski said that he had a practical device with which an actor could foster a taste for adaptations.

[Try and recall all the human states you are familiar with: sadness, anger, irony, joy, longing, despair, serenity, agitation, compassion, derision, fault-finding, volatility, contempt, despair, kind-heartedness, doubt, amazement, etc. Then observe them in life. You will see that in life people express their feelings in a surprisingly wide variety of ways. Human beings are cunning, they manage to find diverse colours. Haven't you observed some people speaking angrily of their joy, and with irony of their longing?

[Let's suppose there is an episode in the actor's role, when he arrives and speaks of a wonderful production he has just seen.

[Onstage we often hear: 'What a spleh-en-n-n-did production.' Sugary sweet and unconvincing. But if in real life, when you come back after a show and say the very same words, the subtext tells us, 'It was damn good!' Then we see what you feel about the production, see that you're possibly quite jealous of other actors who have created such a show while at the same time passionately keen to learn how to act as they did. In life, people always bring in their living, emotional attitude to what they are talking about.]

Sometimes during his classes at the Studio, Konstantin Sergeievich, in order to elucidate his thoughts even more precisely, would do a speech himself. I remember one of his classes, when he did Othello's monologue. It was shortly before his death. He entered the room, leaning on his walking stick, as all of us watched him anxiously since it became more noticeable with each passing day that his strength was running out. Only his enormous will-power and conviction that these classes were vital gave him the strength to keep going. But as soon as he sat down in his armchair and said, smiling and taking everyone in, 'Well, let us begin', it was clear, we were witnessing a miracle: Stanislavski's physical frailty yielded to his spiritual might. And when, with an indescribable mastery, in a voice full of power and beauty, he read:

> It gives me wonder great as my content
> To see you here before me. Oh, my soul's joy,
> If after every tempest come such calms,
> May the winds blow till they have wakened death,
> And let the labouring barque climb hills of seas
> Olympus-high, and duck again as low
> As hell's from heaven. If it were now to die
> 'Twere now to be most happy, for I fear
> My soul hath her content so absolute
> That not another comfort like to this
> Succeeds in unknown fate.

None of us could have imagined at that moment that in two months' time Konstantin Sergeievich would leave us for ever ...

Ardent, grateful applause followed as Stanislavski uttered the last lines of the monologue.

But he instantly shifted the students' attention away from himself onto some great all-encompassing questions.

[Just now I have read Othello's monologue for you. What do your think – would anything have changed in my performance, were I to perform it on the stage?

[No doubt, it would.

[In a performance I would have communicated with Desdemona, trying to catch her eye, I would have felt the urge to kneel before her, take her hands in mine, I would have needed gestures as well as words. In short, I would have lived Othello's life in the given circumstances of Shakespeare's tragedy. But just now I read it to *you*, I saw *your* eyes.

[I gave myself a task to make *all of you* understand, as a result of my doing the speech, that Othello was passionately in love with Desdemona. I was not acting, but conveying to you the logic of Othello's thoughts and feelings, I was doing his actions while remaining myself, Stanislavski.

[You heard, I was in no rush, I was waiting to see whether the inner rhythm of it reached you. It is possible to calmly lodge one mental image after another in someone else's mind – you can even do it fast if you will – but lodge them you must, not scatter them randomly. Speaking at speed will not give it rhythm, make a note of that. You must have felt that while speaking Othello's monologue, even when I paused, I never stopped talking to you. The pause was not a stop, a hole, it was a conversation through silence. I never interrupted my communication with you. So do not rush. Serve and deliver the thought. You must love the thought, see its logic.

[Remember that in your spoken word classes you must learn to use the perspective of the speech. By practising on short stories and monologues, you will be able to acquire experience that can be transferred into your stage practice, you will learn to use verbal action when playing a role.

[When Salvini[7] acted, he made no superfluous gestures, he never rushed, delivering the loftiest lines with simplicity, but with significance. And those Salvini's semi-tones in *Othello*! Yet his speech was lyrical.]

The students bombarded Stanislavski with questions: 'How should we approach Shakespeare's monologues?' 'We feel', they said, 'that Othello's monologue cannot be delivered like a piece of prose, but when we try to capture its heightened quality, we unwittingly fall into a false pathos.'

['And what is false pathos?' – interrupted Stanislavski.]

[If you are going to say, 'Go-o-od wea-ea-ea-ther', with the 'heartfelt crooning' you use when saying:

... If it were now to die

'Twere now to be most happy ...

– that's exactly the ill pathos we all loathe. There are important and sublime ideas in Othello's speech. We ought not speak of important things the way we speak of a sausage at breakfast. But there are some who believe that heightened speech requires vocal stunts and a single-minded focus on enunciation. If that's all there is – it will be your ruin!

---

7 Tommaso Salvini (1829–1915), an Italian actor. In his book *My Life in Art*, in the chapter on *Othello*, Stanislavski describes his admiration for and his observations on the famous actor's performance as well as the process of his preparation for a performance (ed. note).

[As soon as I dig deeper into the given circumstances and my thoughts find greater complexity, everything scales up. The style is heightened when the ideas are lofty. Yet anything heightened must also be simple as well as profound and significant, and this requires particularly precise mental images.]

The issue of the heightened and the poetic preoccupied Stanislavski. He used to say that it was hard to perform Pushkin, hard to picture everything on the same scale as Pushkin did. He believed that the poetic quality only emerged in the work when the actors, by delving into the dramatic material, became infected by the sublime content that had given rise to the poetic piece and filled every second of their stage life with the feelings analogous to those of the author's design.

['In the theatre, art can only be authentic,' Stanislavski said to us,

[when simple human feelings and experiences are touched with a spirit of poetry. But this in no way means that you must howl when speaking a heightened text. You cannot rely only on *the manner* of delivery, that's where the false pathos takes root. You must understand that a tragedy is a simple, meaningful and heightened form of art. Enlarging and deepening the given circumstances, and accurately assessing them, is the way that leads us to the tragedy. Speak by following the logic of the action – and the logic of the feelings will follow. Do not rush. Do not think of the tempo, it will come when you make *the difficult familiar, the familiar easy, and the easy beautiful*. Our whole art is in seeing anew what you have seen twenty times before. But today you will see it differently from how you saw it yesterday. And as you see it anew, so try and communicate it.]

Inner monologue

The creation of mental images was one of the most important practical devices in Stanislavski's work with the word.

No less important a device is the so-called 'inner monologue'.

This device is one of the principal ways to achieve a naturally sounding word on stage.

In life people never stop thinking. They think as they look around them and take in their surroundings, think as they grasp an idea that someone has put to them. They argue, refute or agree with others but also with themselves. Their thoughts are always active and specific.

Onstage, actors are able, to some extent, to master thoughts contained in their own lines, but far from everyone is capable of continuing to think while their partner delivers their lines. And yet this aspect of the actor's psycho-technique is decisive in sustaining the uninterrupted organic process that reveals the 'life of the human spirit' of the role.

When we turn to literary examples, we see that writers, in order to reveal a person's inner world, describe their train of thought in the greatest of detail. We see that thoughts spoken out loud are just a fraction of a stream of thoughts bubbling up in someone's mind. Sometimes these thoughts remain as an unspoken monologue; sometimes they may form themselves into a short reserved phrase, or – depending on the given circumstances of the piece – pour out in a passionate speech.

I would like to look at a few literary examples of 'inner monologue'.

Leo Tolstoy, who knew well how to lay bare people's innermost thoughts, provides a vast number of psychological examples of this kind.

Let's take a chapter from Tolstoy's novel *War and Peace*.

Sonya has rejected Dolokhov's proposal of marriage. He knows that she is in love with Nikolai Rostov. On the third day after the above event, Rostov receives a note from Dolokhov.

'As I do not intend to visit your house again for reasons known to you, and am going back to my regiment, tonight I am giving a farewell party for my chums – so come to the Hotel d'Angleterre.'

DOI: 10.4324/9780203125205-25

When Rostov arrives, he finds the card-game in full swing. Dolokhov is the banker. The game focuses exclusively on Rostov. For quite a while the score against him is in excess of twenty thousand roubles.

> Dolokhov was no longer listening or telling stories; he followed every move of Rostov's hands, from time to time glancing briefly over the chalked score against him ... Rostov, leaning his head on both hands, sat at the table, scrawled over in figures, wet with spilled wine, and littered with cards. One torturous impression did not leave him: that those big-boned reddish hands, with hairy wrists visible from under the shirt cuffs, those hands which he loved and hated, held him in their power.
>
> 'Six hundred roubles, ace, a corner, a nine ... impossible to win it back! ... It would be such fun were I at home now ... The knave, double or quits ... it can't be! ... Why is he doing this to me? ...' – Rostov pondered, remembering ...
>
> 'He knows all too well what this loss means to me. Surely he does not want my ruin. He has been my friend. I loved him ... But he is not to blame; what can he do when he is in luck? Nor am I to blame', he said to himself. 'I've done nothing wrong. Have I killed anyone, insulted anyone, or wished anyone ill? Why such terrible misfortune? When did all this begin? Not so long ago I came to this table with the thought of winning a hundred roubles to buy that casket for Mamma's name day, and then going home. I was so happy, so free, so full of joy! I did not realise how happy I was then! When did that end and when did this new, terrible state of things begin? What marked the change? I sat all the time in the same place at this table, choosing and placing my cards the same way, and watched these big-boned agile hands. When did it happen and what has happened? I am well and strong and still the same, and in the same place. No, it can't be! Surely it will come to nothing.'
>
> He was flushed and bathed in sweat, though the room was not hot. His face was terrible and piteous to see, especially from its helpless efforts to appear calm ...[1]

This mental whirlwind rages in Nikolai's mind as he plays cards. The whirlwind of his thoughts is expressed *in a tangible verbal form* but never spoken out loud from the moment Rostov picks up his cards to the point when Dolokhov says: 'You owe forty-three thousand, Count.'

Nikolai Rostov does not utter a word. Thoughts crowd in his head, forming into words and phrases but never leaving his lips.[2]

Unfortunately, the understanding of mental images is badly developed in our practice. We often come across actors who, as they try to visualise something, cut themselves off from, and lose any living contact with, their partners.

1 Leo Tolstoy's *War and Peace*, volume 2, part 1, chapter 14 (ed. note).
2 See Appendix D and H (ed. note).

This happens when the actor, in the course of their preparatory work, has not painted in their mind's eye a vivid and precise enough picture of what they have to talk about. So then, in rehearsal, instead of using their mental images to affect their partner, they are preoccupied with filling in the blanks.

Let's go back to Chatski's monologue in *Woe from Wit* and imagine an actor whose picture of the people he wants to discuss with Sofya is rather vague.

In rehearsals, this kind of actor, as we have said above, having set himself the task of visualising everything he is going to talk about, will put all his effort into achieving that, and cut himself off. He will be in the grip of his own technical tasks, tasks that have nothing to do with Chatski's tasks and actions.

This is what Stanislavski told us in this regard:

[So, you must carry out a huge amount of work on your own to earn the right to 'instil your mental images in your partner', to infect them with the pictures of your imagination. You must collect and put in order all the material to be used in your communications: grasp the essence of what you have to convey, get to know the facts you are going to discuss and the given circumstances you need to keep in mind, and reconstruct the corresponding mental images in your mind's eye.

[When the actor begins to work in this way, actually 'building up the store of mental images' in the course of their preparatory work, they discover that initially the images that emerge are quite hazy. Say, the actor thinks of Pulkheria Andreievna.[3] To start with, he won't be able to say anything coherent about her. But as soon as he asks himself a few specific questions: 'How old is she? What does she look like? What does she wear?', etc. – his imagination, drawing on the full stock of his life experience, will suggest a world of details, and his mental images will crystallise.

[By doing this rather simple work, we subtly engage our feelings in the process, so that the fruits of our imagination become dear to us, and we become keen to go back to them mentally, looking for new, fresher details.

[In this way the object that our imagination is working on, turns into our personal memory, in other words, into the precious 'freight', or material, without which no creative work is possible.]

Let us recall Levin's reflections on the unwholesome, idle and meaningless life he and his family lead, which surface in the novel *Anna Karenina* time and time again. Or the strikingly dramatic journey to Obiralovka, when Anna's ferocious inner torment pours out as a verbal torrent that surges forth from her fevered mind:

My love grows more and more fervent and self-centred, while his keeps fading, and fading, making us grow apart. Yet there is nothing to be done ... If only I could be something else and not just his mistress, passionately

---

3 An aristocratic lady referred to by Chatski in his monologue (trans. note).

in love with him alone – but I cannot and do not want to be anything else … Aren't we all hurled into the world only to hate each other, and because of it torment ourselves and others? … I cannot think of any situation in which life would not be a torture …[4]

In literature, 'inner monologue' is an intrinsically natural phenomenon.

A demand for 'inner monologue' in theatre raises the need for a highly cultivated actor. Often onstage an actor only pretends to think. Most actors do not bother to devise their 'inner monologues'. Not many actors have enough will-power to reflect silently on those unspoken thoughts which propel them into action. Onstage we often fake thinking. Often an actor lacks any genuine thoughts, switching off while their partner delivers the text, and coming back to life only on the cue line, aware that it is now their turn to speak.

Stanislavski suggested that we should scrupulously study the 'inner monologue' process in real life.

When a person listens to someone, an 'inner monologue' inevitably arises in their mind in response to everything they hear. So in life we always carry out an internal *dialogue* with the person we are listening to.

It must be pointed out that 'inner monologue' is entirely linked to the process of *communication*.

For a reciprocal train of thought to arise, the actor must actually comprehend what their partner is saying, must actually learn to be open to the impact of the events occurring onstage. Having a reaction to everything that is seen and heard generates a particular train of thought.

'Inner monologue' is organically linked to the process of assessing everything that goes on, to a heightened awareness of the people around you, to a comparison between your own point of view and the ideas expressed by your partners.

'Inner monologue' is impossible without being genuinely focused and present.

I would like to have a look at another literary example that shows us a process of communication from which we must learn in theatre. What makes this example interesting is that here Tolstoy does not use direct speech for the 'inner monologue' but instead employs a more dramaturgical device and exposes the 'inner monologue' through action.

In this scene from the novel *Anna Karenina* Levin and Kitty declare their love:

'I have long wished to ask you something …'
  'Please do.'
'There', he said, and wrote the following initial letters: w, y, a: i, c, n, b, d, y, m, n, o, t? These letters stood for: 'when you answered: "it cannot be", did you mean never, or then?' It was quite unlikely that she would be

4 *Anna Karenina* by Leo Tolstoy, part 7, chapter 30 (ed. note).

able to make out this complicated sentence; but he looked at her with an expression as if his life depended on her understanding what those letters meant.

… Occasionally she looked up at him, her look asking him: 'Is it what I think?'

'I have understood', she said with a blush.

'What word is this?', he asked pointing to the 'n' which stood for *never*.

'That word is never,' she said, 'but it is not true!'

He quickly rubbed out what he had written, handed her the chalk, and stood up. She wrote: t, I, c, n, a, o.

… Suddenly his face beamed: he had understood. The letters meant 'Then I could not answer otherwise'.

He looked at her questioningly, and timidly.

'Only then?'

'Yes', answered her smile.

'And n… And now?', he asked.

'Well, then read this. I will tell you what I wish. What I very much wish!' And she wrote these initial letters: t, y, m, f, a, f, w, h. This meant, 'that you might forgive and forget what happened'.

He seized the chalk with tense, trembling fingers, broke it, and wrote the initial letters of the following: 'I have nothing to forget or forgive, I never ceased to love you.'

She looked at him with a smile that remained fixed on her lips.

'I understand', she whispered.

He sat down and wrote out a long sentence. She understood it all, and without asking, 'is this right?', she took the chalk, and wrote the answer at once.

For a long time he could not make out what she meant and he often looked up in her eyes. He was dazed with happiness. He could not find the words she meant; but in her lovely eyes, radiant with joy, he saw all that he needed to know. And he wrote down three letters. But before he had finished writing she read it under his hand, finished the sentence herself and wrote the answer: 'Yes.'[5][i]

This example is of utterly exceptional psychological significance for understanding the process of communication.

Guessing each other's thoughts with such precision is possible only in the state of extraordinarily inspired concentration that Kitty and Levin were possessed with in that moment. The example is of particular interest since it was taken from real life. Tolstoy himself declared his love to Sofya Andeievna Bers, his wife-to-be, in this very manner.

---

5 *Anna Karenina* by Leo Tolstoy, part 4, chapter 13 (ed. note).

It is essential to introduce the psycho-technique of 'inner monologue' into rehearsal practice.

In one of his classes at the Studio Stanislavski spoke to a student who was rehearsing the part of Varya in *The Cherry Orchard*.

['You have been complaining', said Konstantin Sergeievich,

[that you find it hard to do Varya's scene with Lopakhin because Chekhov gives Varya lines that not only fail to express her true feelings but also clearly contradict them. Varya is expecting, with her whole being, for Lopakhin to propose to her there and then. But instead he talks of something trivial, looks for something she has mislaid, etc.

[In order to appreciate Chekhov's work, you must first of all understand what a huge part the inner, unspoken monologue plays in his characters' lives.

[You will never be able to achieve truth in your scene with Lopakhin unless you discover for yourself Varya's true train of thought in each and every second of her existence in this scene.

['I am thinking, Konstantin Sergeievich, I really am', said the student in despair. 'But how can my thoughts reach you, if I have no words to express them?'

['That's the source of all our transgressions', replied Stanislavski.

[Actors do not believe that they can reach the audience and captivate them without expressing their thoughts out loud. Believe me, if the actor does have these thoughts, if they actually think, it will be reflected in their eyes, without fail. People in the audience may not know the words you say to yourself, but they will feel the character's inner sense of self, their state of mind and will be gripped by the organic process that creates an uninterrupted line of subtext. Let's try and do an 'inner monologue' exercise. Remind yourself of all the given circumstances leading up to Varya and Lopakhin's scene. Varya loves Lopakhin. Everyone in the house considers the question of their marriage a done deal. But for some reason Lopakhin is putting it off, days and months pass but he says nothing.

[The cherry orchard is sold. Lopakhin has bought it. Ranevskaya and Gayev are leaving. Everything is packed up. Just a few minutes left before they go. Ranevskaya, feeling deeply sorry for Varya, decides to have a word with Lopakhin. It turns out to be quite easy to resolve the situation. Lopakhin is delighted that Ranevskaya brought it up herself and wants to propose to Varya straight away.]

['Excited and happy, Ranevskaya goes to get Varya. What you have been waiting for all this time, is about to take place', Stanislavski is saying to the actress playing Varya.

[Assess everything, get ready to hear his proposal and accept it. I would like you, Lopakhin, to say your lines as they are written, and you, Varya, in addition to the author's text, say everything you are thinking as you listen to your partner out loud. Occasionally, this may overlap with Lopakhin's lines but it should not bother either of you. Speak your own words quieter but so that I can still hear them, otherwise I won't be able to check if your thinking is going in the right direction. Speak your actual lines in your normal voice.]

The students prepared everything they needed, and the rehearsal began.

['Now, right now, it is about to happen, all I've been longing for', the student said quietly as she entered the room where Lopakhin was waiting for her. 'I want to look at him … No, I can't … I am scared …' We watched as she, averting her eyes, began searching through the suitcases for something. Trying to conceal her awkward unsettled smile, she finally said out loud: 'Strange, I cannot find it anywhere …'

'What are you looking for?' asked her Lopakhin.

'Why did I ever start looking for something?' – the student's quiet voice was heard again. 'I am doing it all wrong, he must think that I am indifferent to what is about to happen now, that I am obsessed with all this petty stuff. I will look at him now, and then he will understand everything. No, I can't', continued the student quietly as she rummaged around in the suitcases. 'Packed it all myself but I can't remember where', she said loudly.

'Where will you be going now, Varvara Mikhailovna?' asked her Lopakhin.

'I?' the student said loudly. Then back to her quiet voice. 'Why is he asking me where I will be going? Can he doubt that I will stay here with him? Maybe Lyubov Andreievna made a mistake, and he has not made a decision to marry me? No, no, it's not possible. What he's asking me is where I would be going if the most important thing in my life, the one that's about to happen, did not happen.'

'To the Ragulins', she answered loudly, looking at him with her happy radiant eyes. 'We have made an arrangement that I will look after their house, as a kind of housekeeper.'

'Is it at Yashnevo? About fifty miles from here', said Lopakhin and fell silent.

'Now, now he will tell me that I don't need to go anywhere, that it's meaningless to keep a house for strangers, that he knows I love him, and he will say he loves me, too. Why hasn't he said anything for such a long time?'

'That's that then, the life in this house is over', said Lopakhin finally after a long pause.

'He's said nothing. God, what is this, is it the end, can it be the end?' whispered the student under her breath, and her eyes filled up with tears. 'I mustn't, mustn't cry. He'll see my tears', she continued. 'Oh, yes, I was looking for something, some thing, when I came into the room, wasn't I? So silly of me! I was so happy then … I should look for it again, then he won't see me crying.' And with an effort to hold back her tears, she began to scrutinise all the packed cases. 'Where could it be …' she said loudly. 'Maybe I packed it in the chest … – 'No, I cannot pretend, I cannot', she spoke again quietly, 'what's the point?

How did he put it? – "That's that then, the life in this house is over." – Yes, it is all over.' And giving up her search, she said quite simply:

'Yes, life in this house is over ... It will be no more ...']

['Good on her!', whispered Stanislavski to us, 'do you feel how in this one line she poured out everything that had built up within her throughout the scene?']

['And I am going to Kharkov now ... on the same train. So much work. Leaving Yepikhodov in charge here ... I have hired him', Lopakhin was saying, as Varya repeated under her breath: 'Life in this house is over ... It will be no more ...'

'Last year it was snowing around this time, if you remember', continued Lopakhin, 'and now it is peaceful, sunny. Cold though ... about three degrees below.'

'Why is he saying all this?', said the student quietly. 'Why doesn't he go?'

'I haven't looked', she answered, and, after a moment's silence, added: "Our thermometer is broken anyway ..."

'Yermolai Alekseievich!' someone called Lopakhin from the wings.

'Just a minute', instantly responded Lopakhin, and quickly left.

'That's it then ... The end ...' – whispered the girl and burst into tears.]

['Well done!' – said Stanislavski, pleased.

[You have achieved a lot today. You have grasped from your own experience the organic connection between the inner monologue and the text. Never forget that breaking off this connection inevitably pushes the actor either to ham it up, or to deliver the text in a disengaged manner.

[I am going to ask your teacher to conduct this experiment not only with the actor playing Varya but also with the actor playing Lopakhin. Once you have achieved the required results, I will ask the scene-partners not to say their own text out loud but to speak it internally, without moving their lips at all. This will make your inner speech even richer. Your thoughts, whether you intend it or not, will be reflected in your eyes, will flash across your face. Observe this process in real life, and you will realise that we are aiming to transfer into the sphere of art a deeply organic process intrinsic to the human psyche.]

Stanislavski and Nemirovich-Danchenko constantly spoke of 'inner monologue' being immensely expressive and infectious. They believed that 'inner monologue' arises as a result of heightened concentration, a genuinely creative sense of self, and an acute awareness of how external given circumstances reverberate in the actor's heart and mind.

'Inner monologue' is always emotional.

'In theatre, the human being's constant battle with their "ego" occupies a prominent position', said Stanislavski.

This battle is particularly evident in the 'inner monologue'. It makes the actor couch the character's innermost thoughts and feelings in *their own words*.

It is impossible to deliver 'inner monologue' without knowing the nature of the person you portray, their attitude to the world they live in, their relationship with other people.

'Inner monologue' requires the actor to delve deep into the character's inner world. Most importantly in terms of art, it requires *the actor onstage to be able to think just like the character they portray*.

The connection between 'inner monologue' and the character's throughaction is obvious. Let's take Chichikov from Gogol's *The Dead Souls* as an example.

If we closely follow the manner in which Chichikov manages to charm every single one of the estate owners,[6] we will see that Gogol gave him a phenomenal ability for adaptation, an ability which allows Chichikov in each individual case to find completely different ways of achieving his goal.

In uncovering this faculty in Chichikov's personality, the actor will try and find in his 'inner monologues' – both in rehearsals, and in performance (depending on what he receives from his partner) – an increasingly specific thought process that will bring him closer to this text of genius.

'Inner monologue' requires the actor to have genuine organic sense of freedom which gives rise to a gloriously improvisational sense of self so that at every performance the actor will have the power to infuse the existing verbal form with new, fresh colours.

This profound and complex work suggested by Stanislavski will lead, as he put it, to creating 'the subtext of the role'.

'What is *subtext?* ...', he writes. It is a clear inner sense of '*the life of the human spirit*' of the role that flows continuously underneath the spoken text, constantly justifying and animating it. The subtext contains numerous and diverse inner lines that run through the role and the play ... It is this subtext that compels us to speak the character's words ...

> All these lines are intricately intertwined like the separate threads of a rope, stretching out through the whole play in the direction of the final *supertask*.
> Once the feeling, like an underwater current, starts to permeate the whole of the throughline of the subtext, it produces '*the throughaction of the play and the role*'. It manifests itself both in physical movement and in speech: actions can be performed not only with the body but also with sounds, words.
> What is called *throughaction* in the sphere of action, is called *subtext* in the sphere of speech.[ii]

6 In Gogol's novel, Chichikov, a daring swindler, tries to persuade estate owners to sell him cut-price rights of ownership of the dead serfs. He wants to become their legal owner, if only fictitiously, but still fully acceptable in the eyes of the law (ed. note).

Notes

i   L. Tolstoy, L. & A. Maude, W.G. Jones, *Anna Karenina*. Oxford, OUP (Oxford World's Classics), 1998.

ii   K.S. Stanislavski, *An Actor's Work on Himself*, pp.492–493 (trans. by Irina Brown).

Technique and logic of speech[1]

When we speak of Stanislavski's work on the word, we must not forget the significance he attached to the question of developing vocal technique and priming the vocal apparatus for complex artistic tasks onstage. His insistence on the actors mastering their physical apparatus was enormous. Stanislavski considered classes in diction, voice placement, movement and eurhythmics to be of utmost importance at the Studio.

['Onstage the actor often has deep and subtle feelings, but when they convey this experiencing, their embodiment of it is so crude that it is deformed out of all recognition due to an ill-equipped bodily apparatus', Stanislavski told us, comparing such an actor to a brilliant musician forced to play a broken, out-of-tune instrument.

[The musician tries to produce magical sounds, but the out-of-tune loose strings distort them, causing the artist unbearable suffering. That's why, the more complex *the inner 'life of the human spirit'* of a role, the more subtle, spontaneous and artistically rich must be its *embodiment* by the actor.][2]

Stanislavski places enormous importance on the external techniques: on voice, diction, an ability to mould a word, or a phrase – on the art of speech as a whole, as well as on the plastic arts: movement, gait, etc.

He told his students that they must hone the physical apparatus of embodiment to its natural perfection. They should improve, develop, correct, and attune their bodies, so that their physical apparatus and all its parts were ready for the complex business that nature intended them for: embodying invisible feelings.

---

1 In Russian 'speech' – *retch* – refers to an oral realization of a verbal exchange. As used onstage the notion encompasses qualities of articulation, phonetics and acoustic sound. Sometimes *retch* denotes pronunciation, diction, the art of rhetoric, i.e., certain elements of the acting craft that are taught in Russia within the framework of the 'Stage Speech' course. Stanislavski's and Knebel's approach calls for a wider interpretation (trans. note).

2 The concept of 'embodiment' in reference to the stage realization of the role, is explored by Stanislavski in part 2 of his system entitled *An Actor's Work on Himself in the Creative Process of Embodiment* (ed. note).

DOI: 10.4324/9780203125205-26

He tirelessly repeated that no time limit could be set for the training of the actor's physical apparatus, and that every year actors faced ever greater challenges because they increased the demands on themselves, which meant they had to keep up their voice, diction and movement exercises for the rest of their lives.

Besides, with each new role the actor is confronted with new tasks of embodiment.

But the subject of stage speech takes pride of place in the above list due to both the detail in which it is worked out, and the emphasis which Stanislavski placed on the importance of the problem. He suggests that actors should not accept their speech deficiencies, and stop, once and for all, the habit of using their own bad everyday speech as an excuse to justify even worse speech onstage.

Stanislavski was exceptionally alert to every single defect in the actor's diction and persevered in establishing clear and precise pronunciation, and correcting sound deficiencies and abnormalities.

['The consonants must be expressive, then your speech will be sonorous,' he used to say to us in class. 'The vowels are the river, and the consonants are the banks. Without the banks the river is a swamp.'

['If the beginning of the word is crumpled,' Stanislavski said to us, 'it is like a person with a squashed head. A word with a dropped ending makes me think of a man with his legs cut off. A sound or a syllable that is dropped is just like missing an eye or a tooth, or a similar kind of deformity.']

He attributed as much importance to the correct pronunciation. It was imperative for him to amend regional accents and dialects in accordance with the norms of the Russian standard pronunciation.

'*An actor must know how to speak.*'[3]

That's what Konstantin Sergeievich said to himself after he had suffered his great failure as Salieri in Pushkin's *Mozart and Salieri*.

In his book *My Life in Art* he analyses his own work,[4] and says that despite the fact that there were many who praised his performance, he actually agreed with his worst critics. Stanislavski sees his performance as his greatest failure. But that failure benefited his work to such an extent that it was dearer to him than his greatest successes.

Being severely critical of himself in the book, he strives to identify the reasons that led him to that failure.

---

3 The title of the chapter on *Mozart and Salieri* by Pushkin in Stanislavski's book *My Life in Art*. The production opened at the Moscow Art Theatre in 1915. Directed by Nemirovich-Danchenko, co-directed and designed by Alexandre Benois (trans. note).

4 Stanislavski's performance as Salieri was almost universally panned. Stanislavski was unhappy with his own performance. This compelled him to accept that the system did not quite work, when applied to verse plays. From that moment on Stanislavski began to develop his ideas of '*verbal action*', or '*action through words*' (ed. note).

He ascertains that his true inner life in the role was disrupted as soon as he spoke Pushkin's verse. This led to him being 'out of joint, out of truth, out of tune. I did not recognize the sincerity of my inner feelings in their outer form.'

He becomes convinced that he failed to master Pushkin's verse. Having overloaded each individual word with great psychological meaning, he broke up the integrity of Pushkin's thought. The words became bloated, as it were. Each of them held so much meaning for him that their content overflowed their form, and expanded into silent but deeply significant pauses: a huge gap separated the swollen words from each other. The speech was dragged out to such a degree that by the end of the sentence it was easy to forget how it began.

Stanislavski describes the inner tension as he strained to invest the words with deeper feeling, although he sensed that Pushkin's text sounded leaden in his mouth and failed to carry the poet's thoughts, which made him force even more, leading him 'to puff up, to cramps, to spasms'. In that state he resorted to commonplace actors' tricks and the false actors' pathos.

All this forcing and tension made his voice lose its lustre. The sense of being false, of being 'out of joint', gave rise to the fear of words, and he felt like whispering. It seemed to him that whispering will help him to find the inner truth. All this insecurity and whispering hardly went with Pushkin's tersely forged verses, and made it even more false.

Every actor is familiar with this one-to-one battle with the text, revealed by Stanislavski in this chapter with such ruthless honestly.

'At that torturous time' of feverish reflections in the wake of the production, Stanislavski arrives at the vital conclusions which made him so deeply grateful for his failure in playing the part of Salieri. These conclusions are worded very simply: '*An actor must know how to speak.*'

'Is it not strange,' concludes Stanislavski, 'that you have to live for almost sixty years to understand for yourself, that is, to feel it with your whole being, that simple and well-known truth, one which the majority of actors do not know?'[i]

Reflecting on his *Mozart and Salieri* experience, he writes of it as the time of mental torment, not being able to embody faithfully the beauty he felt so well inside. He compares himself to a pianist, playing on a worn-out, or out-of-tune, instrument hearing how his inner feeling is distorted.

Looking back on his stage career, he comes to the conclusion that many of the basic shortcomings – physical tension, lack of control, overacting, false actorly emotion – often arise from the fact that the actor lacks vocal mastery. That alone can provide what is needed, and express what is happening inside them! Stanislavski speaks of how important it is to feel for yourself the true significance of beautiful and dignified speech as one of the most powerful means of expressing yourself onstage and affecting others. As he worked on improving his own speech, Stanislavski came to realise that the ability to speak simply and beautifully is a science that must have clear laws.

He devoted many years to the study of these laws.

All the actors who worked with him would know how tireless he was in trying to enthral them with the beauty of poetic speech; how he ridiculed those who did not know how to group words properly, and assign logical pauses; how he used to mimic the actors who spoke badly, quizzing them on the true meaning of grammatically incorrect words they used, determined to achieve speech of distinct clarity and understanding.

First, we must set some order for the words to be delivered, group them correctly, or as some say, split them into 'speech bars'. To break speech down into bars requires stops, or in other words, *logical pauses.*

Logical pauses bring words together into groups of words, or speech bars, and divide the groups off from one another. Stanislavski gives a well-known example from Russian history, when the prisoner's life or death depended on the correct positioning of the 'logical pause'.

'Pardon impossible send to Siberia.'

If we put the pause in after the first word: 'Pardon/ Impossible [to] send to Siberia', it means reprieve; if placed after the second word: 'Pardon impossible/ Send to Siberia', it means exile.

As an exercise he constantly reminded us to pick up a book whenever we could and break up what we were reading into speech bars:

['Train your ears, eyes and hands to do it!']

Marking out the text into speech bars is necessary because it makes you analyse the content of each phrase more deeply: it compels you to go deeper and think about the essence of what you are saying onstage, it gives your speech a harmony of form and clarity of expression.

How can we master this?

Having taken the correct grammatical structure of a sentence as the foundation, the actor begins to clarify its main idea to themselves, as they break the sentence up into speech bars.

['Reading by speech bars, has one more major practical advantage', said Stanislavski. '*It helps the actual process of experiencing.*']

Stanislavski describes three types of pauses: logical, psychological pause and *Luftpause.*

Luftpause is the 'air pause', the shortest one of the three, and is simply required for an intake of breath.

More often than not the *Luftpause* is not even a stop, it is just a slight holding back of the tempo of the piece while singing or speaking, without breaking up the continuous line of the sound.

Stanislavski himself liked to employ the *Luftpause* for highlighting individual words, particularly when speaking very fast.

The logical pause helps to clarify the thought in the text.

The psychological pause gives life to that thought, or phrase, as it seeks to convey their *subtext.* Without the logical pause your speech is ungrammatical, without the psychological pause – it is lifeless.

He loved to quote an old orator who had said: 'May your speech be reserved, and your silence eloquent.' It is this eloquent silence that produces the psychological pause.

Stanislavski paid particular attention to stresses, or as he put it – 'accentuation'.[5]

[Stress that is wrongly placed distorts the sense and cripples the phrase instead of helping to create it! Stress is an index finger, marking the key word in a phrase or in a bar! The soul, the inner essence of the subtext, its main points are concealed within the highlighted word.]

Onstage the stresses get scattered all over the text in a disorderly fashion, with the actors forgetting that the prime purpose of words is to convey thoughts, feelings, ideas, concepts, pictures, mental images and not just, as Stanislavski often said, 'to bang the ear-drums with a sound-wave'.

The clearer the actor's idea of what they want to say, the more sparing they are in their use of stresses.

To counterbalance the abuse of stresses, the actor must learn to remove them when they are not needed.

The art of removing excessive stresses, actually, does us a great favour. It is particularly important when delivering a text full of long, heavy sentences. And actors have to deal with this kind of text regularly.

I remember once in his class at the Studio, Stanislavski suggested that we should break down an extract from Gogol's novel *Dead Souls*:

'The visitor was always able to find a way, showing himself as an experienced society man. Whatever the subject of the conversation, he was always able to sustain it ….'"

Stanislavski said:

[The ease with which that swindler, Chichikov, 'was always able to find a way', must be the key to the nature of *inflections* in the delivery of the lines. But use stresses extremely sparingly! Keep asking yourself if the meaning would be clearer, were you to remove a particular stress. Remember, when too many words are stressed, the phrase loses its meaning.]

The students, attempting to get rid of superfluous 'accentuation', tried to speak the linking words at full pelt, hoping they could rattle them off imperceptibly.

['Remember that being fussy with the text weighs your speech down. What lightens it', continued Stanislavski, 'is staying calm and collected.']

5 In the Russian language the tonic stress can fall on a different syllable in each word. This stress plays an important part not only from the point of view of phonetics, but also of semantics. It appears that here Stanislavski examines not only the stress within the word, but also the 'accentuation' of a whole phrase or a sentence (trans. note).

He said that the key words need to be clearly highlighted, and words that only carry the general meaning toned down. In order to achieve that, we should strive to speak unhurriedly, using deliberately colourless inflections, with an almost total absence of stresses, and staying particularly composed and confident, and this would give our speech the required precision and ease.

Stanislavski devoted a lot of time to exploring how to highlight the key words in a complex sentence, as well as those of lesser importance. He said that words could never have equal significance, and should be separated according to how essential they were to the meaning. Once the most important words have been highlighted by a stress, the same thing should be done with words of lesser importance, which nevertheless need to be highlighted, while the 'unhighlighted' words should be toned down.

['Then,' concluded Stanislavski,

[you will end up with a complex scale of stresses: strong, medium and weak. Just as in painting there are tones, semitones, or light and shade, so in stage speech there is a whole range of stresses of various degrees. They should be coordinated in such a way that minor stresses don't detract from, or compete with, the key words but make them stand out more strongly. Everything must work together to construct and communicate a difficult sentence. There must be perspective in the individual sentence and in the speech as a whole.]

In his classes, Stanislavski liked to compare the art of stage speech with painting.

'You know how in painting', he said to us,

artists convey depth of the actual scene, that is, the third dimension. It does not really exist. The artist paints on a flat canvas stretched over a frame. But painting creates the illusion of multiple planes. Some seem to recede into the depth of the canvas itself, but the foreground seems to break out of the frame, off the canvass, towards us.

Such sound–planes exist in our own speech and they lend perspective to the phrase. The key word is highlighted most vividly of all and comes right into the foreground of the sound-plane. The less important words create a series of deeper planes.' [ii]

Stanislavski attributed exceptionally high significance to every possible gradation of stress. He spoke not only of the intensity of a stress but also of its quality, identifying a variety of shades. He spoke of the importance of whether the stress came down from above or up from below, whether it landed heavily or lightly, whether it lingered for a while, or fell down and was instantly removed.

He spoke of combining *inflection* and stresses, making a highlighted word stand out even more by placing it in between two pauses, especially if one of them, and possibly both, were psychological pauses. He spoke of how the key word could be highlighted by removing the stress from all the non-key words so that the stressed word gains strength by comparison.

> *We must discover correlations, gradations of strength, qualities of stress among all the highlighted and unhighlighted words, and create planes and perspectives in sound, that will give the sentence movement and life.*
>
> *This harmonious, balanced relationship between different gradations of stress on individual highlighted words is what we mean when we talk of coordinating words.*
>
> In this way, we create harmony of form and beauty of architecture in a sentence.[iii]
>
> In this way we create in our speech a perspective with various planes.
>
> If they are directed towards the play's Supertask following the line of Subtext and Throughaction, they become critically important for our speech because they help us to achieve what is fundamental in our art, creating the life of the human spirit of a role and a play.[iv]

Everything Stanislavski says about 'accentuation' and coordination of stressed words in a sentence also relates to highlighting individual sentences in a story or a monologue.

Rushed delivery is a fundamental affliction that prevents the actor from truly growing and succeeding on the stage! Stanislavski called those afflicted 'whizz-by actors'.

One of the ways in combating compulsive rushing when speaking was to study how inflection was dictated by punctuation marks.

Stanislavski discovered that all punctuation marks call for specific vocal inflection. The full-stop, the comma, the question and exclamation marks demand their own characteristic vocal shapes.

These inflections have an effect on the listener that requires a particular response from them. A questioning phonic shape requires an answer, an exclamation – a sympathetic response, agreement, or protest; a colon makes you pay attention to what comes next, etc. The inherent phonic quality of a punctuation mark is effective in holding back the 'whizz-by actor' from their excessive rushing.[v]

Interestingly, when speaking about inflection, Stanislavski reveals this concept in a new way.

In describing examples of meaningless inflection, when actors produce whimsical vocal cadences and shapes, he talked of actors singing out individual sounds, or syllables, stretching them out, howling them out with no intention to take actions or express feelings but just to show off their voices, and tickle the ear-drums of their listeners.

'Listening to yourself' is as bad and wrong as the actor's self-adulation and showing off onstage. He fought it ruthlessly.

For Stanislavski, inflections are born out of knowing the laws of speech, and from striving to communicate the content of the play in action.

He was adamant in his demands, obliging actors to study the laws of speech, and learn how to put them into practice. When he introduced exercises on mastering the shape of the inflection of the question mark, he would start it with the simplest of questions. For example: 'What's the time now?'. Or, 'Where are you going after the rehearsal?'. He did not let you answer until he heard the real question.

['Can you hear a question mark?' he asked the class, with the smile to start with, but after multiple repetitions, with displeasure. 'I do not hear it. I hear a full-stop, a dot dot dot, a semi-colon, anything at all but the question mark! And since you do not ask me the question, I do not feel like giving you the answer.']

['Fall in love with a comma,' Stanislavski cajoled us, 'it is the comma that will make others listen to you.']

Telling us about the nature of the comma's inflection, he compared it to a hand raised in warning, forcing the listener to wait patiently for the unfinished sentence to continue.

['It is crucial for you to trust', he elaborated,

[that following an upward inflection on a comma the listener is bound to wait patiently for you to continue and complete the phrase you have started, so there is no need for you to rush. That should not only calm you, the actor, down, but force you to sincerely fall in love with the comma and all its innate attributes.]

Stanislavski not only considered these classes to be essential, he also loved doing them. Having gone through immense self-development in this field and having mastered his speech to perfection, he demonstrated brilliantly his skill of operating according to the laws of speech. He spoke of the satisfaction, when telling a long story or speaking a long phrase, of curving the inflection upwards before the comma, and then waiting confidently, knowing for certain that no one will interrupt or rush you.

As he elaborated his demands on developing a wealth of inflections in speech, he was emphatic that for the actor to master the shape of any inflection, they must first master their voice. He pointed out that the actor often does not hear their own patterns of intonation, making them sound like a broken gramophone record, turning round and round, repeating the same melody over and over again .

['You can observe that in life you never come across two syllables spoken on one and the same note', he often repeated. 'Actors, however, more often than not, seek vocal power in physical tension.']

He called this use of tension to produce power, in the acting jargon, 'to play up the voltage', saying that this approach limits the vocal range and leads only to hoarseness and shouting.

He describes a lesson in which he suggests that the student, the narrator of *An Actor's Work on Himself*, should test for himself the meaninglessness of his efforts to find vocal power in muscular tension.

He asks the student to deliver the line 'I can endure it no longer!!' with as much physical force as he can summon.

The student carries out the task.

> 'No, more power!' Tortsov ordered.
>
> I tried again, increasing the power as much as I could.
>
> 'More power, more power', Tortsov urged me. 'Don't expand the vocal range!'
>
> I obeyed. Physical tension turned into a spasm. My throat constricted, my range was limited to thirds and I still couldn't achieve an impression of power.
>
> Having used up every resource, I had once more, when pressed by Tortsov, to resort to mere shouting.
>
> It was awful. I sounded as though I were being strangled.[vi]

Tortsov then offers the student an opposite approach of completely relaxing the muscles of the vocal apparatus, which removes all the tension. He suggests substituting the force with *vocal range*.

'"… now speak the same sentence for me calmly with the maximum vocal range and *properly justified inflexions. To do that, imagine Given Circumstances which excite you.*"'[vii]

Once the student gets rid of his tension, he succeeds in doing the exercise. But Tortsov asks him to do it again, each time expanding his vocal *tessitura* (the vocal range), until he has reached a full octave. With each repetition Stanislavski rigorously reminds the student to devise new and even more exciting given circumstances in his imagination.

Stanislavski comes to a conclusion:

> 'It came out powerfully, not loudly and with no pushing. That's what the movement of sounds up and down in, so to speak, a vertical line can do. Without the "high-voltage", without the thrust along a horizontal line, as it happened last time. When you need power in the future, use a wide variety of upward and downward inflexions, like a piece of chalk making shapes on a blackboard.'[viii]

The cited example is typical of Stanislavski the pedagogue.

He often said that students assimilated the correct approach best, if they practically tested the damaging effect of widely spread bad methods for themselves.

He would make the students tense their muscles up multiple times, and then let them instantly release them to test for themselves the difference in their onstage sense of self.

Most often he resorted to such pedagogical devices in his voice classes. He must have considered stage speech to be the most complicated part of dramatic art.

Interestingly, in the above example the students seemingly are given a specific technical exercise, but Stanislavski is emphatic that they can only succeed in doing it if they have devised given circumstances that excite them.

Stanislavski considered the art of speaking to be no less complicated than the art of singing. Not surprisingly, he often said: 'A well spoken word – is already singing, and a well sung phrase – is already speech.' In his notes to theatre actors he often cites examples from the art of singing, and attaches great significance to vocal mastery.

['You see,' he used to say,

> [when you lack vocal control, and are not able to deliver the thought clearly, loudly, and distinctly, when you are unable to project the sound that reaches the listener, then you try to cover up these deficiencies with vocal gimmicks. You may be full of pathos but instead of letting the sound fly, you have been spitting it out and it fails to land.]

Even more often he battled with the actors who looked for their 'power of speech' in pushing the volume up.

' "*Forte*" isn't a fixed quantity like a metre or a kilogram!'

In the chapter 'Stage speech'[ix] Stanislavski suggests that we should study examples of great singers to see the powerful impact produced by the gradual increase of the sound volume:

> Let's suppose you begin the speech very quietly. If you speak slightly louder after the first line, that won't be the *piano* you started with.
>
> You say the next line louder still so that it will be even less *piano* than the previous line, etc. until you reach *forte*. If you increase power step by step you will ultimately reach the highest level of loudness, which can only be described as *forte-fortissimo*. It is a gradual transformation of sound from *piano-pianissimo* to *forte-fortissimo* that constitutes the increase in relative loudness.[x]

Although he introduces the actors to this method of gradually increasing their vocal power, he instantly warns them against the dangers of employing it mechanically.

He speaks of singers who consider it chic to produce sharp dynamic contrasts between quietness and loudness, with no concern for the content.

He gives an example. If they sing the opening line of Tchaikovsky's *Don Juan's Serenade*[6] very loudly ('Night falls on distant Alpujarras' ...'), and the next

---

6 'Night falls on distant Alpujarras' golden lands ...' are the opening lines of *Don Juan's Serenade* by Tchaikovsky based on Leo Tolstoy's poem (ed. note).

line '… golden lands' very quietly (*piano-pianissimo*), and then go back to *forte fortissimo* in the line that follows, etc. – the meaning of what they sing is completely lost, and all that's left is clichéd vulgarity.

'The same thing happens in drama theatre. There is exaggerated shouting and whispering in tragic moments, regardless of inner meaning and common sense.'

When the actor becomes a virtuoso in their use of inflection to create the perspective and planes of sound in the speech, their delivery has irresistible power. Only such speech can express all the nuances of thought of a genuine work of art.

Stanislavski did not just fight slipshod delivery of the text. He wanted to foster in actors the idea that stage speech is an art, which requires daily practice; that they must study 'secrets of vocal technique', that it was high time to put an end to the amateurish attitudes of those actors who covered up their illiteracy on the subject with a hackneyed response: 'It is unseemly for the school of acting based on 'experiencing' to concern itself with the external aspects of speech.'

Stanislavski often said that studying the laws of creativity could dull the spark of inspiration in a mediocre actor, but would blow it into a great blaze in a genuine artist. He believed that only through daily and systematic work could the actor master the laws of speech to the point where they became second nature. Tireless creative work is the foundation of Stanislavski's requirement that the actor must 'make that which is difficult familiar; make the familiar easy; make the easy magnificent'.

For Stanislavski the questions of the perspective of speech occupy a place of great importance.

Usually, when people refer to the 'perspective of speech', they have the so-called logical perspective in mind.

Stanislavski broadens the set of issues related to this problem. He writes:

1. the perspective of the thought to be conveyed (the logical perspective)
2. the perspective of conveying a complex feeling
3. the artistic perspective which skilfully distributes the colours [to illuminate the story, narrative or speech in the various planes].[xi]

By addressing the issue in this particular way, Stanislavski is drawing attention to the fact that the artist's creative nature cannot express itself merely through the logic of the thought to be conveyed.

In the process of mastering the logical perspective, the actor naturally draws on a whole combination of creative tasks that enables them to embody the artistic idea. The logic of thought when relating a story or a monologue will be lifeless unless the actor, by using their psycho-technique, conveys the emotional essence of the piece, and discovers diverse colours and adaptations.

But we must always remember that neither the perspective of conveying a complex feeling, nor the perspective of artistic distribution of expressive means can emerge organically unless the actor has grasped the sequence of unfolding their thoughts, the logic of which must unfailingly strive towards the main goal.

The actor who fails to study the syntax of the author's text, will miss the writer's guidelines that it contains.

But the key to mastering the perspective of a thought to be conveyed is being able to *carry its main idea all the way through via the chain of sentences that make it up.*

Just as Stanislavski fought against the actor trying to play isolated episodes in their role that had no perspective on the further development of the action, so he fought their inability to feel the perspective of their speech.

['Why have you put a full-stop here? Is it really the end of the thought?' he cut the student short angrily.

['Konstantin Sergeievich', responded the student apprehensively, 'there's a full-stop in the text.'

['But have you forgotten the law of gradation? Why would you think that it has nothing to do with punctuation?']

Then, having reminded us of G.B. Shaw's well-known paradox that the art of writing, despite being so grammatically elaborate, is incapable of conveying inflections, since there are fifty ways of saying 'yes', and five hundred ways of saying 'no', but only one way of writing it down, Stanislavski asked:

[Is there only one way to express a full-stop?

[Why did the author put a full-stop here rather than a semi-colon or a dot dot dot? Perhaps, they want to highlight this particular thought, or perhaps, they need to highlight the next thought, and are setting it up.

[You must know well the phonic shapes of punctuation marks, and use them to express *the thought as a whole.* Once you have thought through and analysed the fragment as a whole, the distant, beautiful and enticing perspective will reveal itself to you and then the speech will become, so to speak, *long-sighted*[7] rather than short-sighted, as it is now.

[Then instead of uttering isolated words or phrases, you'll be able to express *the thought as a whole.*

[Imagine that you are reading a book for the first time. You don't know how the writer is going to develop their thought. There is no perspective in such reading. You only perceive the words and sentences right in front of your eyes. The writer reveals their perspective to you gradually.

[Onstage the actor cannot do without the perspective, without the ultimate goal, without the supertask. Otherwise, how can you make others listen to you? If you finish the thought with every single phrase, there will be no perspective of speech to talk of! But once you have completed your thought, then go for the full-stop, and make it such a one, that I understand that you have really completed your thought.

[Picture in your mind's eye the kind of full-stop at the end of a whole chain of thoughts that I am talking about. Imagine that we have climbed

7 The Russian word literally means ability of 'seeing long-distance' (ed. note).

up to the top of the highest cliff above an abyss, picked up a heavy stone and hurled it down, to the very bottom of it.

[That's what you must learn to do when putting a full-stop as you *complete your thought.*][8]

Let's take as an example a remarkable scene from Alexander Ostrovsky's *The Storm*: Katerina's monologue in Act 5.

Act 4 finishes with Katerina's 'repentance'. The storm is raging. The scared townsfolk chatter, convinced that such a storm must end badly, and that someone will get killed ... The rich Old Lady appears and addresses Katerina, prophesising, 'Why try and hide, silly? There's no escaping God! You will all burn up in unquenchable fire!'. Highly agitated, Katerina gets confused and bewildered: the sense of her guilt and depravity in the face of her husband, overwhelms her and pours out as an impassioned monologue, full of repentance.

'Ah! I am dying! ... Ah! Hell! Hell! The fire unquenchable! ... My heart's in shreds! I can bear it no longer! Mother! Tikhon! I have sinned against God and against you! Did I not swear to you I would not set eyes on anyone when you were away?! You remember, don't you?! And do you know what I did, a wanton sinner, when you were gone? I left the house on the very first night ... And every single night after that ... all ten nights I spent with ... With Boris Grigorievich.'[9]

At the beginning of Act 5 Tikhon confides in Kuligin that he is afraid that Katerina 'may be driven in her misery to lay hands upon herself! She grieves and grieves so, ohhh so!'

And then ... '*Katerina enters and slowly crosses the stage.*'

In his stage direction Ostrovsky writes: '*Throughout her monologue and in the following scenes she speaks stretching out and repeating words, lost in thought, as if half-conscious.*'

Ostrovsky is precise both in specifying Katerina's physical state ('*as if half-conscious*'), and in proposing an amazingly subtle verbal characterization ('*... lost in thought ... stretching out and repeating words...*').

His writer's talent discovers distinctive words to express Katerina's boundless anguish, but what's amazing is that – *he hears* the way she speaks, hears her intonation. It is thanks to this that the syntax of the monologue is so expressive, the punctuations marks so compelling, and the perspective so amazingly vivid.

The actor playing Katerina must not only work out the character's given circumstances, events and actions leading to this particular onstage moment, not only understand Katerina's all-consuming love for Boris, and grasp the nature of her pangs of conscience, and her extreme loneliness in the midst of

---

8 See Appendix I (ed. note).
9 *The Storm* by Alexander Ostrovsky, Act 4, sc. 6 (ed. note).

those around her, she also must discover for herself what it means to be '*as if half-conscious*'. Ostrovsky structures the monologue in such a way that all of Katerina's inner strength is focused on one thing only: to see Boris one more time, to say goodbye to him, then even death will no longer be so terrifying.

The actor playing Katerina must understand why the writer heard Katerina speak '*stretching out and repeating words*', '*lost in thought*'. For this she must study not only the *content* but also the *character of inflection* so brilliantly used by Ostrovsky, who had the ability to give each of his characters an individual voice, while also using a word, a punctuation mark, a pause or a repeat to convey the subtlest stirrings in their heart.

Let's look at Katerina's monologue.

> KATERINA (*alone*): No, nowhere to be seen! What's he doing now, my poor boy? All I want is to say goodbye to him, and then ... and then I might as well die. Why did I lead him into trouble? Made it no better for me! I alone should have suffered! But I have ruined myself, ruined him, brought dishonour on myself, – perpetual disgrace on him! Yes! Dishonour on myself, – perpetual disgrace on him. (*Silence.*) If I could only remember ... what was it he said? How did he take pity on me? What were the words he said? (*Clutches at her head*). I can't remember, I have forgotten everything. The nights, the nights are the hardest for me! All go to bed, and so do I; nothing in it for others, but for me it's like lying in a grave. So scary in the darkness! Strange noises, and the singing as if at a burial; but so soft, almost out of hearing, far away, far from me ... How one longs for the light! But I can't bear to get up, the same people again, the same talk, the same torture. Why do they look at me so? Why is it that nowadays they do not kill us? Why don't they do that? In the olden days, I heard, they used to kill. If they picked me up, and threw me into the Volga; I would be glad. 'If we executed you', they say, 'you would be relieved of your sin, but you must live and suffer for your sin.' But I have suffered for it enough! How much longer am I to suffer? ... What have I to live for now, what for? I care for nothing, nothing is dear to me, not even the light of day! – and still death does not come. I call for it, but it comes not. Whatever I look upon, whatever I hear, there is nothing but aching here (*touching her heart*). If I could be with him, there, perhaps, might still be some joy for me ... Yes: it's all the same now, my soul is lost already. How I long for him! Ah, how I long for him! If I cannot see thee, at least hear me from far away. Wild winds, bear my grief, my longing to him! Good heavens, I'm so wretched, so wretched! (*Goes to the edge of the river bank and cries loudly at the top of her voice*) My joy! my life, my soul, I love you! Answer me! (*She weeps*).'[10]

10 *The Storm* by Alexander Ostrovsky, Act 5, sc. 2 (ed. note).

When we, if only out of curiosity, take a closer look at the nature of punctuation marks in this monologue, we will notice the prevalence of *exclamation marks*. It is used here by Ostrovsky *seventeen times*! Can this be overlooked? We cannot fail to see that such a quantity of exclamation marks obliges us, on the one hand, to a certain level of inner intensity, and on the other, to studying the *gradual increase* in the expressive quality of the exclamation mark's inflection, to studying the laws of the artistic perspective.

Let us compare the exclamation mark after Katerina's first line: 'No, nowhere to be seen!' It implies that she has given up looking for Boris, bitterly aware of her loneliness, with the exclamation marks in the monologue's final lines: 'How I long for him! Ah, how I long for him! Wild winds, bear my grief, my longing to him! Good heavens, I'm so wretched, so wretched! My joy! my life, my soul, I love you! Answer me!'

Is there even a drop of resignation in these latter exclamation marks? None at all. It is a protest, a mutiny by someone who has not been defeated!

The question marks are also of great interest in this monologue. There are *ten* of them. All these questions Katerina asks of herself, as she tries to find some answers. The questions make her restless, but they are not equally probing.

The first group of questions refers to Boris: 'What's he doing now, my poor boy? ... Why did I lead him into trouble? ... If I could only remember ... what was it he said? How did he take pity on me? What were the words he said?'

And the more insistent her questions, the more terrifying the answer: 'I can't remember, I have forgotten everything.'

The only thing left in life is: '... the same people again, the same talk, the same torture'.

The second group of questions comes up: 'Why do they look at me so? Why is it that nowadays they do not kill us? Why don't they do that? ... How much longer am I to suffer? ... What have I to live for now, what for?'

She has found the answer, but '... still death does not come'.

There are no more question marks in the monologue. Full-stops, ellipses, exclamation marks ... A coincidence? No!

I would like to stress that the performers must be alerted to the technical problems of speech at the very beginning of their work on the role, during the stage of 'active analysis'. This is the time when the actor who plays Katerina is still in the initial period of her work, while she is creating her film of mental images, her illustrated subtext, and is still using her own words in etudes!

After an etude, when we go back to the text to check how specific the actors have been in dealing with a particular theme, how correct they have been in their relationship to the play's ideas and facts, I always draw the actors' attention to the stylistic peculiarities of the author's vocabulary. Exclamation marks in Katerina's monologue are, for example, yet another helpful device to uncover the essence of the piece.

In the final stages of our work we are duty-bound to learn and speak the author's text exactly as written. Disregarding punctuation marks, or rearranging words around in a sentence – it is like thinking that we could deliver Pushkin's verse as prose!

Every year Stanislavski grew more and more insistent in his demands on studying the laws of speech, on keeping up constant voice and speech training and specialized text-work.

But Konstantin Sergeievich also firmly reminded us of the essence of the verbal action. The words are dead unless they are fired by the performer's inner feeling. He repeated tirelessly that every actor should always remember: at the point when we are creating onstage, the words come from the writer, the sub-text – from the actor. Otherwise, no one would bother going to the theatre and see a show, but would rather stay at home and read the play.

Stanislavski wrote:

> Actors must set the text of the play to the music of their own feelings and learn to sing that music of feelings through the words of their character. Only when we listen to the melody of the living heart, can we fully appreciate the worth and beauty of the text and what it contains.[xii]

Notes

i   K.S. Stanislavski, *My Life in Art.* Moscow, Iskusstvo, 1948, p.503 (trans. by Irina Brown).

ii   K.S. Stanislavski, *Rabota aktera nad soboj, Sobranie Sochinenij*, vol.2, chapter 4. Moscow, Iskusstvo. (*An Actor's Work*, p.435.)

iii   K.S. Stanislavski, *Rabota aktera nad soboj, Sobranie Sochinenij*, vol.2, chapter 4, Moscow, Iskusstvo. (*An Actor's Work*, trans. by Jean Benedetti, p.436. Adapted by Irina Brown.)

iv   K.S. Stanislavski, *Sobranie Sochinenij*, vol.3. Moscow, Iskusstvo, 1955, p.125. (*An Actor's Work*, trans. by Jean Benedetti, pp.436–437. Adapted by Irina Brown.)

v   For more information see *An Actor's Work*, trans. by Jean Benedetti, p.414.

vi   K.S. Stanislavski, *Sobranie Sochinenij*, vol.3. Moscow, Iskusstvo, 1955, p.109. (*An Actor's Work*, trans. by Jean Benedetti, p.423.)

vii   Ibid., p.109 (Maria Knebel's italics).

viii   Ibid., p.110 (*An Actor's Work*, trans. by Jean Benedetti, p.424).

ix   See *An Actor's Work on Himself in the Creative Process of Embodiment*, chapter 3. The chapter's title has changed. In the 1955 edition it was called 'Voice and speech', divided into subsections: '1. Singing and diction' and '2. Speech and its laws' (*An Actor's Work*, trans. by Jean Benedetti, p.381).

x   *An Actor's Work*, trans. by Jean Benedetti, p.424.

xi   K.S. Stanislavski, *Sobranie Sochinenij*, vol.3. Moscow, Iskusstvo, 1955, p.343. (*An Actor's Work*, trans. by Jean Benedetti, p.453. Adapted by Irina Brown.)

xii   *An Actor's Work*, trans. by Jean Benedetti, p.403. Adapted by Irina Brown.

Psychological pause

When explaining the nature of psychological pause, Stanislavski gave this example in one of his lessons:.

['Suppose', he said,

> that tomorrow I will be playing Famusov[1] again after quite a long break. So I will invite your whole year to come and see tomorrow's performance, apart from two of you: the students I am not happy with because they have broken the rules, will not be invited to the show. You won't be coming,

he said sternly addressing the worst offender in the matters of discipline. 'Nor –', he spoke to a very gifted student, who was recently late for his class for the first time in his life, '– will you!]

['Did you notice', Stanislavski asked the second student,

> that I made a pause after the conjunction 'nor'? As you know this is a violation of the laws of speech, since 'nor' does not tolerate such stops. But this *psychological pause* occurred as I spoke in order to soften the blow about to be inflicted on you. I do believe that what you did will never happen again, and I wanted to show you that, even whilst punishing you.

['Remember, psychological pause is an extremely important weapon of communication!' continued Stanislavski.]

He believed that a genuine verbal action occurs when the actor, having mastered the primary stage in the art of speech, i.e., the logic of speech, learns to lay bare and reveal the subtext through psychological pauses. But he warned of a hidden danger in using psychological pauses to excess, a danger which sets in as soon as a productive action is stopped by a pause.

There have been cases when a talented actor, having rightly sensed the need for a psychological pause, starts to abuse it. Well aware of their sway over the

---

1 Stanislavski played the character of Famusov in Griboyedov's comedy *Woe from Wit* in a number of different productions (ed. note).

DOI: 10.4324/9780203125205-27

audience, they let the audience languish as it were, before moving on to the next line. In this way they contrive to pull the audience's attention away from the play's action to themself, and their own 'artistry'.

In 'such cases' the pause degenerates from being truly psychological to being a mere actor's 'hold-up', and that creates a confusion on the stage – a pause for the sake of pausing. This kind of stop in the action is a hole in the artistic fabric of the play.

On the other hand a psychological pause that is justified, is a vital element of stage speech.

['The psychological pause can sometimes lead to the creation of a whole scene, what we call in our theatre parlance, "the star pause",[2] Stanislavski said.

[The 'star pause' is only possible when the actor has stored up enough material through working on all the given circumstances, when the throughline of action is totally clear to them, when they closely relate to the character's state of mind and have mastered both its inner and outer tempo–rhythm.

[The 'star pause' is a mighty tool of the actor's psycho-technique. Many of the greatest Russian actors expressed their characters most subtle feelings by using 'star pauses'.]

Alexander Lensky's[3] celebrated pause as Benedick in Act 2 of *Much Ado about Nothing* is well-known. Lensky (Benedick) eavesdrops on the scene that his friends play for his sake as a joke, and learns that Beatrice is deeply in love with him. As soon as the instigators of the ruse leave, Benedick (Lensky) emerges from his hiding place. He has been shaken by the news that Beatrice is madly in love with him, but she hides her feelings to avoid mockery. Benedick has a spectacular monologue here, but Lensky was in no hurry to go to Shakespeare's text. He needed time to sort out the thoughts jostling against each other in his head.

Here is an eyewitness account of Lensky's pause:

... Benedick stands there for a long time, staring directly at the audience, his face transfixed, stunned. Suddenly, somewhere in the corner of his lip, under his moustache, a little vein quivers. Watch him carefully now: Benedick's fixed eyes are frozen but from under his moustache, imperceptibly, gradually sneaks out a triumphantly-happy smile. The actor has not uttered a single word as yet but you can feel with your whole being the hot wave of joy unstoppably rising from the bottom of Benedick's heart. Its momentum is such that the cheeks' muscles pick up the laughter of the lips, and the unchecked smile spreads all over the

---

2 *Gastrolle* (German) *means* a 'guest appearance' by a famous performer, hence *gastrol'naya pausa* in Russian, which means 'a visiting star's pause', or 'a star pause' (trans. note).

3 Alexander Lensky (1847–1908), a member of the Moscow Maly Theatre Company, an actor, teacher and director. Known for his performances in Shakespeare and Ibsen as well as Ostrovsky, Griboyedov, etc. (ed. note).

quivering face. Suddenly this unconscious sense of joy is pierced by a thought, and like a final chord of this silent scale, a blazing joy ignites his eyes until now fixed in amazement. Now Benedick's whole body bursts with wild happiness, the audience explodes with applause although the actor has not yet uttered a word, and only now begins his monologue …

Vladimir Davydov[4] was also famed for his masterfully developed 'star pauses' (in Gogol's *Marriage*, Sukhovo-Kobylin's *Krechinsky's Wedding*, in Ostrosky's *The Ardent Heart*). Konstantin Varlamov's[5] 'star pauses' became part of the Russian theatre chronicles. We know that 'star pauses' were equally used in comedies as well as tragedies.

Stanislavski maintained: since the 'star pause' is the outcome of the psychological pause, our ability to express a wide range of thoughts and feelings through a pause is totally dependent on the intensity of our inner monologue, on having a continuous train of thoughts born out of our assessment of the given circumstances.

From the very beginning of rehearsals actors must train themselves in this ability to think continuously as their character, expanding the author's text. Then as they rehearse, they will feel the need to embody in a pause thoughts and feelings they have stored up.

I remember Stanislavski working with Leonid Leonidov[6] on the part of Othello. He often spoke to him about consciously allocating 'temper' points, and urged Leonidov to make use of psychological pauses.

['Remember', advised Konstantin Sergeievich,

> that in a pause the actor *is mentally catching up with all the images* of things he has been talking about! Such a pause sets up and heightens the emotional intensity and rhythm, while preventing the actor from an overtly emotional display, which must not be used to excess. An overt display of strong emotions should be assigned to a few particular isolated moments in the role, which can be compared to a tenor's high C. If there were too many high C's in the vocal score, the singer would be in danger of losing his voice.
>
> [In this role there are quite a number of striking moments that seem to be pushing the actor to openly splash out the feelings that have been building up inside him, but he must try to hold himself back, dismissing linear choices that more often than not lead to shouting, and look for diverse ways of expressing his feelings through the psychological pause.]

---

4 Vladimir Davydov (1849–1925), an actor who performed in the provinces as well as Moscow, most importantly at the Alexandrinski Theatre in St Petersburg. His repertoire consisted primarily of Russian plays (ed. note).

5 Konstantin Varlamov (1848–1915) – a comic actor from St Petersburg (ed. note).

6 Leonid Leonidov (1873–1941), a Moscow Art Theatre actor. In 1910 he played Mitya in *Brothers Karamazov*, in 1930 – Othello (ed. note).

When rehearsing Leonidov in Act 3 and dissecting the nature of Othello's sense of self in that tragic scene, Stanislavski suggested that the bit that comes straight after Iago has planted the poisonous thought of Desdemona's infidelity in Othello's imagination is decisive for his character. For the first time this terrifying thought has crept into Othello's mind, instantly shattering his happiness. He does not yet know what to do about it; the excruciating pain clouds his mind, he needs time to understand what has just happened. Actors rarely convey the immense happiness Othello feels prior to the severe doubts instilled in him by Iago's speech. But that is vital, since the tragedy of the scene is in Othello *bidding farewell* to any likelihood of returning to the supreme happiness he had been feeling, the reality of which was ingrained in his life.

What can he do now, how can he live without the happiness that had filled him to the brim?

Having lost his happiness, Othello appreciates it even more, and comparing it to the future that appears to him immeasurably desolate, he suffers deeply.

['You must', said Stanislavski to Leonidov,

go deep inside yourself to remember the past and see the bitter future. This is the moment of deep self-absorption. Othello does not notice what's going on around him, and when he comes face to face with reality, he can't help but pour out the accumulated bitterness and pain.]

In one of the rehearsals, when Leonidov, with an indescribable sense of tragedy worked through his monologue and the scene with Iago, Stanislavski, pleased and happy, suggested to him:

[And now try and do this scene with no words. Think what a person would do if they were suffering from an excruciating inner pain, unsettled, agonized, striking the most improbable poses to alleviate the pain, with their fingers making mechanical movements, some senseless scratching that expresses the inner rhythm of this suffering.]

An actor passionate in thought and temperament, Leonidov played the scene in such a way, that for me it has remained as one of the most powerful impressions of my life.

['Now go back to the text', said Konstantin Sergeievich, as he hugged and kissed Leonidov.

[Remember that to carry out any task the actor, first and foremost, requires the author's words, thoughts, text. The actor must, above all, operate with *the word*, and that is often forgotten. But now develop the scene, and with the help of pauses expand it in such a way that the audience will see the enormity of the inner torment we have just witnessed.]

Stanislavski marked all possible pauses in the text. He warned Leonidov to treat these pauses not as mandatory but as possible. He suggested that Leonidov should mark his own pauses throughout his part, so that by the end of rehearsals two or three of them could be developed as 'star pauses'.

OTHELLO[7] I had been happy, if the general camp,
Pioneers and all, had tasted her sweet body,
So I had nothing known. *(PAUSE)*[8] O, now, for ever
Farewell the tranquil mind! farewell content! *(PAUSE)*
Farewell the plumed troop, and the big wars,
That make ambition virtue! O, farewell! *(PAUSE)*
Farewell the neighing steed, and the shrill trump,
The spirit-stirring drum, the ear-piercing fife,
The royal banner, *(PAUSE)* and all quality,
Pride, pomp and circumstance of glorious war!
And, O you mortal engines, whose rude throats
The immortal Jove's dead clamours counterfeit,
Farewell! Othello's occupation's gone! *(PAUSE)*

Leonidov's pauses grew out of one thought that completely absorbed Othello, as he tried to crack an insoluble problem. The thought of Desdemona drove him to the insanity of suffering, he thrashed about from side to side, moaned as from a physical pain, and at a loss of what to do with himself, finally threw himself at Iago, to vent his anger at him.

The 'star pause' is impossible to create without the inner monologue that expands the author's text and reveals the inner workings of action. It is the inner monologue that provokes the actor to express their feelings in a pause.

Stanislavski said that apart from pauses there are other technical devices to aid actors in holding themselves back from acting out 'naked temperament'.

He often recalled Salvini's Othello. He was amazed at how the celebrated tragic actor structured his role in line with his own inner and outer expressive creative capabilities, allowing him to allocate correctly and use sensibly the material he had internally stored for the part.

['Salvini', said Stanislavski,

[always kept *the throughline of the perspective* in his mind, from the moment when he first entered, in love like a passionate youth, all the way to the end, when he is consumed by the boundless hatred of a jealous murderer. Throughout the role, with mathematical precision and inexorable logic, moment by moment, he revealed the development of his feelings as they ripened within him.]

---

7 Shakespeare, *Othello*, Act 3, scene 3 (ed. note).
8 In Russian most of Stanislavski's pauses are marked at the end of lines since the lines in translation are longer (trans. note).

Adaptations[1]

To elucidate his ideas Stanislavski liked to borrow his examples from the world of fine arts. He looked closely into this 'adjacent' art form for the means of expressing creative laws that related to the art of theatre .

He was drawn to the giant figure of Repin,[2] the might of his talent. He wanted to understand what painterly techniques allowed Repin to arrive at such psychological depth in portraying the subject matter of his paintings, how Repin managed to reveal the subject's inner world and convey the most subtle nuances of their feelings and thoughts. What means did Repin use to compel us to hear the very timbre of Ivan the Terrible's voice as he screamed in horror?[3] How did he manage to convey in a painting those things which seemed previously to have been out of the reach of the fine arts?

An art historian, specializing in Repin's work, Igor Grabar[4] states:

> Repin's creative work expanded the confines of all the visual means of expression that he had found in the fine arts. He proved that what once was considered out of bounds for painting, and was only to be expressed in literature, was now fully in the power of and within the means of figurative arts!

Here's Kramskoi's letter to Suvorin,[5] written immediately after Kramskoi had seen an unfinished painting of *Ivan the Terrible and his Son Ivan* at the Repin's Studio.

---

1 *'Adaptations' or 'adjustments' allow the actor to 'adapt' to their role, enhancing it with different shades of colour produced through their own observations and inventiveness.* 'The word "adaptation" is the one we shall use in the future to designate the ingenuity, both mental and physical, people use to adjust their behaviour and so influence other people, their object.' *An Actor's Work*, p.259, translated by Jean Benedetti (trans. note).

2 Ilya Repin (1844–1930) was a leading realist Russian painter. The painting *Ivan the Terrible and his Son Ivan, November 16th 1581* was painted in 1885, the Tretyakov Gallery, Moscow (ed. note).

3 See Appendix K, Fig. A2 (trans. note).

4 Igor Grabar (1871–1960), a painter, restorer and art historian (ed. note).

5 Ivan Kramskoi (1837–1887), one of the leading Russian painters, famed for his portraits. One of the founders of the Peredvizhniks (Itinerant Art Exhibitions movement). Alexei Suvorin (1834–1912), a famous journalist and publisher, passionate about theatre (ed. note).

DOI: 10.4324/9780203125205-28

Shaken to the core, Kramskoi writes:

... First of all I had a feeling of complete satisfaction on Repin's behalf. There it is, the object equal to his talent. Judge for yourself. Expressively, in sharp relief, pushed to the foreground – murder by accident! That's the most phenomenal part of it, extremely hard to do but solved here with just two figures. The father has struck his son in the temple with the staff, and he did it with such force that the son instantly collapsed, bleeding. A moment ... then the father screams in horror, rushes to his son, grabs hold of him, goes down on the floor, lifts the son onto his lap, and with one hand presses hard, so hard, the wound on his temple (with the blood gushing out in between his fingers), while clutching him across the waist with the other hand, and clasping him tightly to himself, kisses hard, so hard, the head of his poor, exceptionally endearing son, as he himself bawls in horror (bawls at the top of his voice), helpless. When he hurled himself forward, grabbing his head, the father smeared half of his face (the top half) with blood. A comic detail worthy of Shakespeare. This brute of a father, howling in terror, and his dear sweet son, meekly fading away, with that eye, with his strikingly attractive mouth, his noisy breathing, his helpless hands! Oh, my God, can't we hurry up, hurry up and help him! It does not matter that there is already a big puddle of blood where the son had hit his temple, it does not matter that he will still lose much more blood – that's just one of those things! A mortally wounded person, naturally, will lose a lot of blood, that's not what's so upsetting! But the way it is painted, good God, the way it's painted!

Really, just imagine, there is a huge amount of blood in the painting but you don't think of it, and it does not affect you, because there is this terrifying, noisily expressed father's grief, his deafening scream with his son in his arms, the son he had killed, and the son ... no longer able to control his eye, breathing heavily, he feels his father's grief, his terror, hears him screaming, lamenting, and tries, like a child, to smile at him as if to say: 'Nothing to be afraid of, Daddy!' Oh, my God! It is imperative that you see it!!![i]

Stanislavski liked to quote Leo Tolstoy's letter to Repin regarding this painting: '... good, very good ... Moreover, it is so masterful that the mastery is invisible ...'.[ii]

This 'imperceptible' form of mastery referred to by Tolstoy was the ideal Stanislavski strived for when he challenged the actors to develop their technique to the highest degree.

Stanislavski was exhilarated by Repin's ability to express the most complex psychological motive through the use of colour, composition and a variety of other artistic means related to painting.

He spoke of the 'patches of colour', as he drew our attention to the way the artist conveyed emotion using colours to express the essential qualities of the story. Extraordinarily diverse shades of red: dark scarlet, crimson, garnet, burgundy, purple and many others used to depict the carpet, blood on Tsarev-ich's face, his pink coat, green boots and dark blue trousers; Tsar Ivan's black coat, the bloodstain on the carpet – a whole symphony of colours merging together to produce the overall sense of the tragedy of this accidental murder in the picture *Ivan the Terrible and his Son Ivan.*

['The very unexpectedness of colour change is powerfully affecting! In our own business', Stanislavski added,

> [we use adaptations as our colours. The richer the palette of adaptations, the more diverse and unexpected our psychological moves and their inter-nal justification, the greater and more vivid the feelings expressed in those moments when we go for the full *forte-fortissimo.*]

Adaptations, as both internal and external forms of communication with others, are the psychological manoeuvres we employ to communicate with each other, they show our ingenuity in how we manage to affect one another. From Stanislavski's point of view, adaptation is one of the most important ele-ments in the actor's craftsmanship.

He maintains, that to be able to penetrate into someone else's heart and mind, to get a sense of their inner life, we need adaptations. Equally, in other cases, we need adaptations to hide our own feelings.

In life, adaptations emerge on the spur of the moment. A natural living communication is bound to stir a person to make a series of psychological manoeuvres, allowing them to carry out their actions. On stage, sponta-neous adaptations occur only when the actor strives for a genuine organic communication.

Stanislavski says that the quality of adaptations is significant: how vivid, col-ourful and subtle they are.

He believes that some actors are splendidly imaginative at adaptations in serious emotional drama, but lack the aptitude for it in comedy, or, vice versa, are startlingly resourceful in comedic adaptations, but lose all their vibrancy in serious drama.

'But there are a number of actors, on whom fate has not smiled, who have poor, monotonous, vague yet accurate adaptations. These people will never make it to the front ranks.'[iii]

So Stanislavski insists that the actor's talent is most vividly revealed *in the qual-ity* of their adaptations, and that the most interesting adaptations emerge only when feelings 'run high'.

He speaks of the audience's joy when they witness brave and audacious adaptations born on stage. Won over, stunned with the unexpected truth of it, infected by the originality of the character's emotional responses, the audience believes that this is the only possible interpretation.

Stanislavski tirelessly reiterated that the biggest danger for an actor was to get carried away by a description or a story of spectacular adaptations discovered by other actors, and then to try to borrow them. That leads to clichés.

Although he did everything possible to bring the actor close up to the organic sense of self that laid the ground for independent adaptations, Stanislavski admitted that in some cases it was permissible to make use of adaptations prompted by others. But, as he put it, 'Adaptations of this kind must be treated with caution and wisdom'.

['We should also do this in those cases', said Stanislavski,

[when someone observes adaptations typical of their role in real life, and feels like making use of them for their character. In this case, too, we must avoid replicating them. This always pushes us into overacting and the use of stock-in-trade techniques.]

Notes

i   I.N. Kramskoi, *Pis'ma*. Moscow, Izogiz, 1937, vol.II, p.324.
ii   *I.E. Repin*. Moscow, Izogiz, 1937, volume 1, p.262.
iii   K.S. Stanislavski, *Rabota aktera nad soboj. Sobranie Sochinenij*, vol.3, part 2. Moscow, Iskusstvo, p.301 (*An Actor's Work*, trans. by Jean Benedetti, p.261. Adapted by Irina Brown).

Tempo-rhythm

'Tempo-rhythm' is a crucial part of the system but it still has not been developed in enough detail.

In the final years of his life Stanislavski devoted a lot of attention to this issue. He told us that he had made a vital discovery of tempo-rhythm being inseparably linked to feelings, and vice-versa, feelings – to tempo-rhythm.

'Probe deeper into what I've been saying and appreciate the full value of our discovery. It is extremely important', writes Stanislavski in the chapter 'Tempo-rhythm'.

> We are talking about the *immediate, frequently automatic effect the outer Tempo-rhythm has on wilful, arbitrary, disobedient and apprehensive feelings, which won't take orders, which shy away at the least hint of being forced and hide away where they can't be got at.*[1] *Hitherto we've only been able to affect them indirectly, using 'lures', but now we have a technique for direct access!!!*
>
> This is indeed a great discovery![i]

Many years before Stanislavski wrote the above, we, the new generation of actors at the Art Theatre, as well as the magnificent 'old folk' led by Moskvin, Kachalov, Knipper-Chekhova, Leonodov[2] and others, were divided into groups of ten or fifteen people, and Stanislavski conducted systematic sessions in experimenting with exercises on tempo-rhythm.

We all remember enthralling classes with a few different metronomes set to mark time at different tempi.

Stanislavski made up for not having enough metronomes by tapping out the missing ticks on the table with his keys at various speeds. It turned into a whole orchestra of ticks and taps.

---

1 In the original, Stanislavski writes: '... which shy away at the least hint of being forced and hide away in the deep recesses [of the psyche], where they can't be got at' (trans. note).
In talking of his system Stanislavski often refers to the 'secret recesses' of the unconscious (or subconscious). See *An Actor's Work on Himself in the Creative Process of Experiencing*, chapter 2 (ed. note).
2 In the 1920s and 1930s the Art Theatre company was comprised of several generations of actors. The 'old folk' referred to in the list above were part of the generation that founded the theatre in 1898.

DOI: 10.4324/9780203125205-29

He made us perform a wide range of exercises, starting with clapping our hands in unison at different tempi, with accents on different beats in a bar – now on the first one, then on another – while speeding up, or slowing down the tempi of the metronomes.

The sessions were full of fun and joy. He sharply switched tempo-rhythms, and we had to change over at the speed of lightning.

['See, what a wizard I am', Konstantin Sergeievich used to say. 'I can not only control your muscles but your feelings, and your moods, too! I can, at will, lull you to sleep, or drive you into exhilaration.']

The clapping out of bars and beats was only the beginning. We then moved on to much more complex exercises. The point was to learn in practice that any situation in life, any action was always linked to a corresponding 'tempo-rhythm'.

'Where there is *life* there is *action*, where there is *action* there is *movement*, and where there is *movement*, there is *tempo*, and where there is *tempo*, there is *rhythm!*'[ii]

[Conduct for me the tempo-rhythm of a person who is packing their suitcase an hour before the departure of their train. And now conduct the tempo-rhythm of a person unpacking their suitcase on the arrival at a health spa. Now imagine that you are at the hospital, waiting for the doctor to come out and let you know the results of your mother's operation. Go on [Stanislavski insisted], conduct your own tempo-rhythm for this.]

He was tireless in coming up with new exercises to make us understand through our own experience that tempo-rhythm could not be recalled or experienced without creating mental images, picturing given circumstances and conjuring up all sorts of tasks and actions to go with it.

Later working as a pedagogue at the Studio led by Stanislavski, I was amazed by the enormous importance he attached to working with tempo-rhythm, and the scope and depth to which he had developed this part of the actor's psycho-technique.

He frequently talked of tempo-rhythm being extremely beneficial to the performance as a whole: often a brilliant play, seemingly well staged and well acted, is not well received due to the failure to establish the right tempo-rhythm.

If only we had at our disposal psycho-techniques to determine an effective and appropriate tempo-rhythm for a play or a role, it would be of great help.

'But we have no psycho-technique in this area,' Stanislavski told us, 'and this is what happens in reality, in practice.'

Mostly, finding the Tempo-rhythm of a performance is a matter of pure *chance*. If the actors, for some reason, feel the play and the role as they should, if they are in a good mood, if the audience is responsive, then the right kind of experiencing and, therefore, the right Tempo-rhythm happen spontaneously. But when that doesn't happen, we are helpless.[iii]

Comparing theatre actors with opera and ballet performers, Stanislavski exclaims: 'How lucky musicians, singers and dancers are! They have metronomes, conductors, chorus-masters, ballet masters!'

'For them the problem of Tempo-rhythm has been resolved, and its importance in creative work recognized.'[iv]

Music sets the rhythm required for their performance, and the conductor controls its tempi and metre. The situation faced by theatre actors is much worse. They have neither the score nor the conductor.

'That is why the same play can be performed in different tempi and different rhythms on different days.

'We, theatre actors, have no one to turn to for help with our tempo-rhythm onstage. Yet we need it badly!'

He was concerned that actors often transferred the tempo-rhythm of their own daily life to their performance, irrespective of whether it suited the play or their characters.

The actor's own tempo-rhythm is in a constant flux under the influence of different everyday circumstances. When the actor arrives at the theatre before the show, they may be excited, or depressed by what goes on in their personal life. So they carry their own tempo-rhythm onto the stage like daily litter. 'The performance thus depends on the accidents of daily life, not on our psychotechnique',[v] writes Stanislavski.

Often the actor is pleased with themselves, oblivious to their error. It happens not only because there are still very few actors trained in tempo-rhythm, but due to total lack of awareness of how crucial both tempo and rhythm are for dramatic writing.

Stanislavski constantly and scrupulously studied performances by great actors. He writes of how our great predecessors: Shchepkin, Sadovsky, Samarin[3] and many others stood in the wings for a long time before their own entrance, closely following what was happening onstage.

It was not merely their conscientiousness that prompted them to arrive so early. They needed to tune in to the tempo-rhythm of the performance.

Accounts of productions, theatrical anecdotes about the great actors' practice as well as Stanislavski's personal observations led him to the realisation that

> … consciously or unconsciously they were sensitive to Tempo-rhythm and knew what it was. Evidently they could recall the speed, the slowness, the metre of the action in every scene and in the play as a whole … They got into the right Tempo-rhythm intuitively or, perhaps, using certain devices of their own …[vi]

Stanislavski sees in this awareness one of the reasons why our predecessors carried life and truth onto the stage with them.

---

3 Mikhail Shchepkin (1788–1863) and Prov Sadovsky (1818–1872) – see above. Yuri Samarin (1817–1885), a Maly Theatre actor, Shchepkin's student, acted in Griboyedov, Shakespeare and French melodramas (ed. note).

He speaks of tempo-rhythm as being an amazing facet of the psycho-technique which, on the one hand, allows actors to penetrate the essence of a play and a role, and on the other, guarantees that our discoveries in long-running productions can be maintained!

What is the psycho-technique for establishing the Tempo-rhythm of a play or a role based on?

Stanislavski answers:

> The Tempo-rhythm of the play as a whole is the *Tempo-rhythm* of its *Throughaction* and *Subtext*. And you know that when dealing with the Throughaction you need *a double perspective* on the whole play – the actor's and the character's. Just as painters lay out their colours in their pictures and try to achieve a proper balance among them, so actors try to lay out the Tempo-rhythm alongside the whole of the play's Throughaction.[vii]

How can we make sense of Stanislavski's statement that 'the Tempo-rhythm of the play as a whole is the Tempo-rhythm of its Throughaction and Subtext'?

Let's start with its basic premise. Tempo-rhythm arises from how we assess a particular event depending on the play's given circumstances.

The moment any event in the play is viewed in isolation from its supertask, or with no connection to the play's given circumstances, the director and the actors involved will inevitably encounter huge difficulties that often lead to serious errors.

We must not overlook the fact that this process is totally reliant on the general conclusions the artist has derived from the play.

Different interpretations of one and the same dramatic situation lead to a different assessment of events, and sometimes call for a diametrically opposed tempo-rhythm.

I shall try and analyse this proposition by using the finale of Act 3 of Griboyedov's *Woe from Wit* as an example.

The production of this comedy was revived by Stanislavski and Nemirovich-Danchenko a number of times, and they left behind their remarkable analysis of the play in the directing logbooks of the productions. [4] Interestingly enough, in all the three stage versions they note a particular challenge in the final scene of Act 3.

Despite the great mastery of the directors and the actors, and the huge success of the production with the audiences, Nemirovich-Danchenko believed that they 'couldn't quite pull off' the Act 3 finale.

Both Stanislavski and Nemirovich-Danchenko were ambivalent about the lack of psychological justification for the transition to dancing once Famusov's guests became convinced that Chatski was insane.

---

4 Alexander Griboyedov's play was directed by Stanislavski and Nemirovich-Danchenko in 1906, revived in 1914 and then again in 1924. Stanislavski played the part of Famusov in all the three versions of it. The production stayed in the Art Theatre's repertoire until 1938 (ed. note).

Referring to historical documents, a literary scholar M.V. Nechkina in her book *A.S. Griboyedov and the Decembrists* disputes MAT's interpretation:

> In theatre productions (including that at the MAT) the rumour of Chatski's insanity is interpreted as information on the true state of affairs, as in: yes, indeed, all the guests, all these old men and women, Khlestova and Famusov, all of them must be sincerely convinced that Chatski has lost his mind.

This interpretation reduces the intensity of the situation and fails to reflect the true meaning of the play. In *Woe from Wit* we are not dealing with Famusov's and his guests' erroneous belief that Chatski has lost his mind, but with a case of deliberate *slander* consciously *casting aspersions on Chatski.*

The author compellingly proves that it was an accepted reality of Russian life in the 20s and 30s of the 19th century to proclaim your opponent to be insane. Famusov's world, the world of the metropolis, already condemned by history but still hugely powerful, uses this tactic as a weapon to fight dissenters. In support of this interpretation, the author quotes a wonderful letter from Griboyedov to his friend P. Katenin, in which he gives detailed explanation of his view of the situation in the play. Expounding the idea of the play to Katenin, and highlighting Chatski's conflict with 'a cunning ... sinister ... absurd' society, Griboyedov writes: 'Out of spite, someone makes it up that he is insane, no one falls for it but everyone keeps repeating it, and the voice of the general malice reaches him in the end.'

Let's analyse the comedy one more time, examining in detail how Griboyedov embodies his idea step-by-step. Having learnt in Act 4 that he was declared insane, Chatski assesses this operative fact as an act of deliberate slander against him.

> What's that? I can't believe my ears!
> It's not a jest, it's pure spite ...

Chatski admits that some of those spreading the rumour of his insanity are 'dimwits' who believe the gossip to be true. What appals him is not the stupidity of the 'ungainly bright sparks, crafty simpletons, evil old women and old men' but their malice and spite. Bitterly, he exclaims:

> Oh! What if I saw inside these people:
> What part of them is worse? the mind or the tongue?
> Who made them up?!

Consistently, Griboyedov conveys the through-thought that Chatski is being deliberately slandered by Famusov, Khlestova and other guests. What kind of arguments do they have to offer to prove Chatski's supposed madness?

> I'm quite puzzled that he hasn't been
> straitjacketed as yet!

Try mentioning the government to him,
He then spews forth such nonsense!
Or if you were to take a slightly deeper bow,
Be it to the sovereign, or someone else,
He labels you a scoundrel! ...

An interpretation based on a thorough and active study of Griboyedov's dramatic intention will demonstrate that all these characters – 'the tormentors' pack' – understand all too well that Chatski's advice to Natalya Dmitrievna's husband to go and live in the country, or his suggestion to Molchalin not to join the Moscow Archives Department, are in no way signs of madness! The treacherous accusations show very clearly that these 'inventors' are set on getting rid of Chatski, on maligning him, and incapacitating his new way of thinking. Famusov diagnoses the cause of Chatski's 'madness' precisely:

Learning's the plague; knowledge – the cause
That nowadays there are many more
than ever before
Men, acts, opinions – all deranged.

Zealously intent on eradicating the burgeoning progressive ideas that attract ever more young people, Famusov exclaims:

... to nip this evil in the bud,
I'd take all books away, and burn them.

At last, in the Act 4 finale, in the guests' departure scene, the Princess conclusively vents her spite:

It's time to lock him up...
I think he's nothing but a Jacobite,
This Chatski of yours!!!

These words reveal the true cause behind the slander!

M.V. Nechkina argues with the critics who wrote about a number of 'shortcomings' in the Act 3 finale.

The critics objected that Famusov, being the master of the house, did not take measures to get rid of the madman as soon as possible, but instead, unconcerned, was having a lengthy argument with Khlestova about the number of serfs (souls) owned by Chatski. They objected to the author not providing any stage directions to interrupt Chatski's long monologue in order to control the crowd-behaviour. How was it possible, they said, that the scared and startled guests, instead of staying on to the end of the monologue to hear about the Frenchmen from Bordeaux, moved on to the dancing and playing cards?

The interpretation of the scene in the Art Theatre's production corresponded to the comedy's traditional interpretation by the literary criticism of yesteryear. Naturally, the Art Theatre 'couldn't quite pull off' – as Nemirovich-Danchenko put it – the transition to the dancing and cards after everybody was petrified by Chatski's insanity. But as soon as we accept the modern interpretation of what spurs the whole of Famusov's Moscow society to denounce Chatski as a madman, without actually thinking he is mad, we get a very different understanding of the guests' behaviour at the ball.

Having spread the rumour of his insanity, they feel deeply satisfied: they, the fierce guardians of the old, are revenged on him for trying to oppose them with his new ideas. He who has been ridiculing them, gets his comeuppance, while his enemies are vindicated and extolled.

Such an interpretation justifies and makes sense of the argument between Famusov and Khlestova regarding the number of serfs (souls) owned by Chatski, despite the presence of the 'madman' next door. In this case, both the action and the tempo-rhythm of the guests moving on to dancing and cards in the middle of Chatski's monologue, are completely logical. The guests dance 'with the greatest zeal', leaving all alone the one person who dared to rebel.

This example demonstrates the significance of a precise analysis of the play's given circumstances in our creative work, and the crucial importance of having a clear understanding of how each particular event, and the character's behaviour are linked to the play's supertask.

In the process of embodiment, the character's assessment of an event, and the tempo-rhythm that ensues as a result of it, are wholly linked to the interpretation of that event.

If it is decided that for Famusov's guests the main event is that Chatski has actually gone mad, then it is only right to demand that the behaviour and tempo-rhythm of actors will be of people facing a lunatic across the room, whose actions are fraught with danger for everyone present.[5]

But if the production accepts Griboyedov's own interpretation that the main event of the scene is not *madness but slander*, enthusiastically taken up by the reactionary crowd of Famusov's guests, then the scene's spirit and its tempo-rhythm will be entirely different.

The guests' main action will be driven by their desire to get even with the 'Jacobite' in their midst and punish him, so they withdraw in scornful silence before he finishes his 'crazy' speech, and move on to dancing and cards, back to the fun and games they came to Famusov's for in the first place.

In this interpretation their behaviour and tempo-rhythm will be diametrically opposite to the traditional interpretation, and will have, from my point of view, an organic connection with the play's throughaction: the battle of two hostile camps.

---

5   In *An Actor's Work on Himself in the Creative Process of Experiencing*, chapter 3, book 1 deals with the given circumstances. Tortsov proposes that his students do an etude, where they have to defend themselves from a madman who is threatening them from behind the closed door (ed. note).

So whether we assess the play's events, or the scene's tempo-rhythm, rightly or wrongly is a matter of principle to us, and one which has a decisive effect on the correct development of the play's action, and on the artistic discovery of its meaning.

Stanislavski demands that the actor consciously trains in himself a particular tempo-rhythm that is in accord with the active analysis of a scene and the play as a whole.

Stanislavski suggested that we observed ourselves in different given circumstances, advised us to recall as often as possible various events from our own life so that we could picture the tempo-rhythm that went with a particular moment:

[Remember, by searching for tempo-rhythm, you unlock feelings inside yourself. Our sense of tempo-rhythm is always right here, within us, close at hand, so to speak. We can always, more or less, recall a general idea of every moment we have lived through. Recollecting that tempo-rhythm brings back to life details that have escaped our memory, and consequently, is both the means and the cause of eliciting the inner emotional material required for our creative work.]

As he questioned the students and pedagogues: 'What is the tempo-rhythm of the Mayor's arrival at Khlestakov's inn?',[6] 'What is Katerina's tempo-rhythm when she arrives for her date with Boris?',[7] 'What is the tempo-rhythm of the guests leaving Famusov's house?',[8] Stanislavski made sure we could conduct these different rhythms. He was tough and critical in his assessment of the conducted rhythms. He demanded that we told him of the tiniest details of the given circumstances, specified the events and assessed them, disclosed actions and tasks. He constantly repeated that if we got the right tempo-rhythm, then the right feeling and experiencing occurred naturally, of their own accord. But if the tempo-rhythm was wrong, the wrong feeling would emerge. It was only possible to correct this by altering the tempo-rhythm to go with the right feeling.

Training and drilling within yourself the one and only true tempo-rhythm is a challenging but necessary task in the actor's work.

Let's try and analyse tempo-rhythm one more time with reference to one of the characters in Gorky's play *Philistines*.[9]

To start with, finding a characteristic tempo-rhythm for the master of the house Bessemenov is not an easy task. Old Bessemenov always led a measured and steady life. But for some time now he has been in a highly agitated state due to the growing awareness that both his home and his world are collapsing.[10]

6 *The Government Inspector* by Nikolai Gogol. Act 2, scene 8 (ed. note).
7 *The Storm* by Alexander Ostrovsky. Act 5, scene 2 (ed. note).
8 *Woe from Wit* by Alexander Griboyedov. Act 4 (ed. note).
9 Maxim Gorky's *Philistines* was directed by Stanislavski at the Art Theatre in 1902 (ed. note).
10 See Appendix J (ed. note).

In a wonderful letter to Stanislavski regarding the production of *Philistines* at the Art Theatre, Gorky writes about Bessemenov:

> The old man is in an absurd situation that exasperates him. Devil knows how long he has been working day and night, swindling if need be to get bigger returns – and all of a sudden, he discovers that it was for all for nothing! It wasn't worth it, it seems! Not for anyone. His children – definitely a failure. And his life's meaning, that makes no sense to him, starts to fill him with horror. When talking, he cuts the air with the palm of his hand, as if it were a knife: he lifts his hand to his face, and without bending at the elbow, straight from his nose, with just one movement of his wrist – he cuts through the air. His movements are slow.[viii]

The actor has to cultivate in himself the measured slow movements, find Bessemenov's characteristic manner of expounding his thoughts unhurriedly and wordily despite the ever-present irritation that gnaws at him, making him prick up his ears when others talk, as he tries to catch the faintest signs of change in those around him, being constantly on his guard.

These are all prerequisites to the inner and outer tempo-rhythms of Bessemenov's character.

Bessemenov's true-to-life and authentic tempo-rhythm will introduce the actor as well as us into the atmosphere of Bessemenov's everyday existence.

But however deeply and accurately we were to elaborate on the tempo-rhythm, it will remain a dead weight unless the actor is able to apply it to his *speech*.

There still is a persistent view that Konstantin Sergeievich paid no attention to the form and technique of stage speech. Underestimating this exceptional part of Stanislavski's system, as well as some other serious reasons, has resulted in the fact that stage speech is the part of the actor's psycho-technique that lags well behind.

As a rule young actors stop working on their diction and breath as soon as they get their theatre school diploma. While the older generation of actors, having devised 'the survival minimum' that stops audiences complaining about the actors not being heard, settle down into a humdrum routine. Rarely do they concern themselves with the multifaceted and challenging tasks they face regarding speech due to the uniqueness of the playwright's vocabulary. Rarely do they turn to the experience offered by the teachers in the science of speech.

Speech rhythms of a whole generation of actors are mixed up. The change of rhythm happens accidentally, without any internal lead-up to it. Sometimes the rhythm changes within a single phrase. Often half a sentence is spoken deliberately slowly, the other half – almost like a tongue-twister. In some cases we even encounter a mixed-up rhythm in individual words, for example, when the actor speaks half the word rapidly, and then stretches out the other half to give it extra significance.

'Many actors', writes Stanislavski, 'with their slapdash use of language and disregard for words, start by dropping word endings and end up, due to the mindless rushed delivery, with complete words and phrases unfinished or broken off.'[ix]

Need I say that a purely technical comment 'Don't rush!' hardly gets the required results from an actor or a student?

Of course, not. It would be rather naïve to think that there are directors or pedagogues who fail to remind a young actor every single time not to rush! The thing is, teaching voice and speech for the stage requires exceptionally highly qualified pedagogues. And another thing: there is still a gap between methods of teaching stage speech and those of teaching acting. We must be able to demonstrate, in accord with the Stanislavski system, the internal and organic interconnection of all the aspects of psycho-technique.

Stanislavski's comments on how inaccuracies of tempo–rhythm in a phrase, which cripple the contents of a speech, go against his demand that every single letter should be seen as a part of a harmonious whole. When working, for example, on Othello's monologue, Konstantin Sergeievich would point out his students' technical mistakes with amazing lucidity. He expected the students to know the monologue's throughaction, the place this particular monologue occupies along the throughline of the whole role, Othello's inner tempo–rhythm as he delivers it, and whether there could be two tempo–rhythms in Othello's heart and mind at that point: the inner and the outer ones. The inner one that conveys Othello's true feelings, and the outer – externally calm, which hides his agitation.

In the light of these questions the lack of technical skill seemed shameful and embarrassing, so both students and pedagogues grew keen to master all the challenges. It was clear that without genuine technical skills it was impossible to communicate artistically the enormous tasks set to us by Stanislavski.

He often said that stylistic qualities of each individual writer call for a particularly sensitive attention.

'Our problem is that many actors haven't developed two important aspects of speech. On the one hand there is *smoothness, slow, resonant flow* and on the other *speed, light, clear, clean* articulation',[x] writes Stanislavski in the chapter on tempo-rhythm.

With sadness Stanislavski notes that more often than not pauses onstage are unnaturally long, and the words between them are rattled off at speed. Yet what we must strive for is an uninterrupted *cantilena*[11] of sound that is sustained in a singing line. Only then will we achieve expressive flow of slow speech. It is even rarer for the actors to be masters of good rapid delivery, with a crisp and clear diction, and correct pronunciation, capable, most crucially, of communicating ideas.

In his practical classes Konstantin Sergeievich made the students read very slowly, getting them to achieve a 'confluence' of the words within the verbal bars, insisting that they always found internal justification for the slow pace of speaking. He said that the actor had no right to go onstage unless they had developed a slow and fluid way of speaking.

---

11 *Cantilena* is the part carrying the melody in a composition (from Italian/Latin 'song').

For developing their rapid delivery, Stanislavski suggested practising to speak exceedingly slowly with exaggerated precision:

> By repeating the same words over and over you can train the organs of articulation until you can say them very fast. That requires regular exercises and you must do them because stage speech cannot do without pace.[xi]

Stanislavski, by attracting our attention to a particular element of the system, said again and again as we worked that none of the elements were important in and of themselves: they were only conductors to lead us to our organic nature. But we should not be like a child who, having planted a flower seed, dug it out every half an hour to look at it! No such flower will grow.

Stanislavski was losing his physical strength, and by the summer of 1938 he hardly ever got out of bed. The doctors categorically forbade him to do any more classes with his students. But he could not stop thinking about the Studio. So he called now one, now another pedagogue to come and see him, and asked them endless questions, and talked ...

I will never forget my last meeting with Konstantin Sergeievich.

Large dark circles around his eyes, still sparkling with deep thought.

['What's happening at the Studio? How are the classes going?', he asked me.

> [Have the students started to feel an organic need for working with the physical action? Have they mastered the process of mental images? Do they understand that communication is the prelude to action? Are they using words as action? Have you noticed if they are interested in developing characterisation organically? And most importantly, do they understand that they have to give themselves to art completely, and for this they must have a supertask in their own life: that the supertask cannot be discovered unless we have a profound and wide knowledge and understanding of the tasks set before us by life itself. So the problem of ethics is the foundation of a life in art.]

These were the last words I heard Konstantin Sergeyevich saying to me.

How can we carry throughout our life the seed of the magnitude and light he tried to plant in us? When I think about Stanislavski, I remember one of the actors of the Art Theatre, Leonid Leonidov, once telling me:

> The worst possible thing in life is the force of habit. But there have been two phenomena in my life that I could never get accustomed to. They constantly amazed me. Please, Maniasha,[12] do not laugh at me! They were: the sun and Konstantin Sergeievich.

---

12 'Maniasha' was Maria Knebel's nickname/term of endearment: from Maria/Masha/Maniasha (ed. note).

Notes

i   K.S. Stanislavski, *Rabota aktera nad soboj v tvorheskom processe voploshcheniya*, chapter 5 (*An Actor's Work*, trans. by Jean Benedetti, p.502).

ii   Ibid., chapter 5 (*An Actor's Work*, trans. by Jean Benedetti, p.473).

iii   Ibid., p.576 (p.484).

iv   Ibid., p.576 (p.484).

v   Ibid., p.577 (p.484).

vi   Ibid., p.579 (p.486).

vii   Ibid., pp.579–580, chapter 4 (trans. by Jean Benedetti, p.486. Adapted by Irina Brown).

viii   Maxim Gorky, *Sobranie Sochinenij*. Moscow, GIKHL, 1950, vol.6, p.545.

ix   K.S. Stanislavski. *Sobranie Sochinenij*, vol.3, part 2. Moscow, Iskusstvo, 1955, p.173.

x   Ibid., pp.173–174 (*An Actor's Work*, trans. by Jean Benedetti, p.491).

xi   Ibid., p.174 (*An Actor's Work*, trans. by Jean Benedetti, p.492).

Conclusion

We have arrived at the conclusion that Stanislavski and Nemirovich-Danchenko proposed to us, theatre pedagogues, directors and actors, that we pursue a dialectical approach in resolving the issue at the heart of the art of theatre, that of the art of the word. While they accepted the author's word to be both the starting point of creative work as well as its crowning glory, they warned us against the dangers hidden in a 'linear' approach to working with text.

When we consider the existing practice of theatre rehearsals, we have to point out that in many cases the primitive approach to text is still alive and well. Despite the fact that the Stanislavski system has become part and parcel of the theatre's daily life, its acceptance and acknowledgement have not led to real changes in most theatres' rehearsal practice.

Breaking down traditions formed over many a decade is, naturally, extremely complicated.

Conservatism and the stuck-in-a-rut rehearsal formats, often prevent smart and talented people from drastically changing their rehearsal practice, although they can see the actor's living feelings perish when fettered to the mechanical assimilation of the text. This happens even though there is not a single director or actor who doubts the general precept of the realistic school that the actor must make someone else's alien words, i.e., the author's, their own.

And yet Stanislavski showed us a radical way of how this could be done!

Stanislavski's theoretical thesis can and must become a reality, but for this to happen it is necessary to seriously examine the changes he proposed to the practice of rehearsal.

Each year as he widened and deepened his teaching on actions, Stanislavski made ever greater demands on actors in terms of conscious creativity. Conscious creative work above all implies that the actor has mastered the full complement of images, ideas and thoughts contained in the text, that they are able to 'think on the line', and to affect others by their thought, expressed in living and active words.

The founding fathers of the method[1] bequeathed us an enormous amount of material that we are obliged to consider. Using their discoveries as the basis

---

1 In the Russian theatrical tradition Stanislavski's teaching is usually called 'system', 'method' or 'school' (ed. note).

DOI: 10.4324/9780203125205-30

for extensive experimental work, we could introduce into our own practice everything that will undoubtedly revitalise our art.

The basic idea of Stanislavski's pedagogical approach lies in making an indissoluble connection between the text and the character's thoughts, tasks and actions from the very start of rehearsals.

Memorising the text mechanically destroys the workings of the imagination. Once the actor gets shackled by a text they have not fully understood, they will never be able to achieve true harmony in their onstage sense of self.

Stanislavski suggests that the actor should first of all scrupulously work through the events and given circumstances of the play, so that they can get a clear grasp of the throughline of their behaviour.

It is not possible to understand the throughline of behaviour unless you know your interrelationship with every single character in the play.

Having outlined their throughaction and settled on the goal they are striving for in their actions, the actor, to an extent, begins to discover the play's internal structure – its skeleton. Such an awareness of the logic and sequence of behaviour throughout the play gives the actor great advantages. From the moment of they start to get familiar with their role, they learn to grasp it as a whole.

By breaking the play down into major events, the actor learns to identify the place each particular event occupies in their character's life. Considering that the play's events always provoke a variety of reactions in different characters. The actor becomes aware that in response to these attitudes, they themself undertake actions that in turn lead to a new sequence of events, etc., etc. In the process of work the actors get accustomed to thinking concretely from the very beginning, seeing the play's events as a cause or a motive for a particular behaviour. In other words, actors learn to take each moment onstage not in isolation but as indissolubly linked with the behaviour of all the characters.

This period of gaining conscious awareness of the internal structure of the play is of crucial significance.

Stanislavski writes in the chapter on the 'Supertask' and 'Throughaction':[i]

> Everything that happens in a play, all its individual Tasks, major or minor, all the actor's creative ideas and actions, which are analogous to the role, strive to fulfil the play's Supertask. Their common link with it, and the sway it holds over everything that happens in the play, is so great that even the most trivial detail, if it is irrelevant to the Supertask, becomes harmful, superfluous, drawing one's attention away from the essential meaning of the work.
>
> This pursuit of Supertask must be continuous, unbroken throughout the whole play and the role.

Were we to ask actors to give an honest answer regarding the extent to which they use in their own practice the cornerstone of the Stanislavski's teachings – his teaching on the Supertask – I am convinced that most of them will speak of how much time they spend being in the dark. It starts when an actor, with no clear idea of the overall connections between different aspects of the play, rehearses the play from scene to scene, trying to find colours and inflections in a text which is still unfamiliar to them. In such a case, trying to produce something, the actor forgets that the simplest action they decide on must come as a result of them having a sense of the whole, which will make their work incomparably easier and more productive.

Stanislavski insisted that premature rehearsals, with the text memorised but as yet not consciously processed, are a waste of time. Such rehearsals only produce clichéd results.

By looking closely at the text, getting a clear understanding of the play's storyline, and establishing the sequence of events, the actor gets into the habit of taking conscious note of their character's actions and behaviour, becoming aware of the role's inner development, of the changes it goes through. Once the actor has 'anatomised' the play, as Stanislavski called it, only then – armed with the understanding of the piece as a whole and their place within it – do they have the right to move on to the author's text.

Stanislavski maintains that getting to know and understand the play is incomparably more effective when it is done in action.

Since he bases his new approach to rehearsals on the unity of mind and body, Stanislavski states that this approach evokes 'a sensory experience of the role' by creating the physical 'life of the human body' of a role. He proposes starting with the 'life of the human body' of a role from the very first days of rehearsals.

By analysing the role through action, and creating its 'life of the human body', the actor gradually discovers the truth of their own onstage existence, discovers faith in the authenticity of the stage actions proposed by the playwright, and, without forcing themself, they start to experience feelings. Stanislavski used to say: 'In our art-form to understand means to feel.' And it really is so. His thoroughly considered approach leads imperceptibly to the enticing of genuine and passionate feelings from the actor, without which, there is no creativity.

In describing the process of his work on *Othello,* Stanislavski comes to the following decisive conclusions. At the beginning of rehearsals he took away from the actors their playtexts and made them use their own words. So they, like in life, selected the words that most helped them to fulfil their intended task. As a result their speech was dynamic, active. He kept the actors working in that way until the correct throughline of tasks, actions and thoughts had matured. Only after having laid the ground in this way through etudes, was the printed text given back to the actors. They hardly ever needed to memorise the lines, since Stanislavski had been long prompting them with Shakespeare's text when the actors sought it to fulfil a particular verbal task. The actors grasped Shakespeare's text hungrily, since the playwright's lines expressed the meaning or the action performed so much better than their own. They retained Shakespeare's lines, fell in love with them, and those words became indispensable to them.

Through etudes, once alien words became ingrained in the performers naturally, unforced, and thanks to that their most vital characteristic was retained: the words remained active.

'Consider it well, and tell me', writes Stanislavski,

> do you suppose that if you started your work on the role by learning your lines by rote, as is most often done in theatres the world over, you would have achieved the same result as you have done by using my new approach?
>
> I can tell you straight away: no, no way would you have achieved the results you were after. You would have crammed the sounds of the words and lines of the text into your mechanical memory, onto the muscles of your vocal apparatus. That would have dissolved the thoughts behind the speech, and the lines would have been isolated from your tasks and actions.

Some people in the arts mistakenly claim that this kind of Stanislavski work requires too much time, and that a number of theatres that produce a lot of new shows have no capability, moreover no right, to experiment.

A profoundly incorrect point of view! Don't forget Stanislavski's words: 'Only that which is inorganic is hard to do, everything that is organic is easy'.

These words contain a profound truth. The actor who creates their role following the method proposed by Stanislavski, protects themself from an inorganic process. Once they have set off on the journey that is organic, it is easier for them to discover themself and their creative potential. They become free and conscious creators.

I try to use Stanislavski's new methodology to the best of my ability both as a director and pedagogue. I am deeply convinced that this way of working allows us to create a production in the shortest possible time, because it is structured in accordance with the demands that the particulars should be resolved in relationship to the essential elements, and that the work on the physical and psychological life of a role should be linked together into a single process; it demands that the character's thinking should follow the common laws of human thinking.

These demands offer the actor conditions for working productively, conditions which must inevitably be reflected in both the organisation of the production process and in the quality of its outcome.

Stanislavski was deeply convinced by the practical significance of, as he often put it, his 'discovery'.

In one of the conversations with his students to celebrate the 40th anniversary of the Moscow Art Theatre, he said:

> If those who run the theatre believe that they have once and for all understood its direction, if they do not move forward to the rhythm of present-day life ... they cannot create a theatre to serve their country, a theatre

of a century-long significance, a theatre of its era, a theatre is that part of creating every aspect of life in today's world.[ii]

Notes

i   K.S. Stanislavski, *Rabota aktera nad soboj, Sobranie Sochinenij*, chapter 15 (*An Actor's Work*, trans. by Jean Benedetti, p.307).

ii   *Besedy K.S. Stanislavskogo.* Notated by K.E. Antarova. Moscow, Iskusstvo, 1952, p.35.

I am Mikhail Chekhov's Student

Chapter Two from
My Whole Life by
Maria Knebel

Chapter Two from *My Whole Life* by Maria Knebel

The school matriculation exams were drawing near. I made a decision to go and study mathematics at the University. The grown-ups prevailed upon me. They were, probably, right – you should study something you are good at. The idea of theatre suddenly seemed to be just a childish dream.

But life turns everything around in the most unexpected way (the unexpected must have its own logic). One day, just before the exams, I was working at my father's desk, with the bright sun shining straight into my eyes. I went up to the window to draw the curtains and spotted my classmate, Lyda Gurevitch, on the opposite side of the road.

'Lyda!' I called her sticking my head out of the window, 'Come up!'

'I can't, I don't want to be late for the Studio!'

'What Studio?'

'I am studying at Mikhail Chekhov's Studio![1] I'm going to be an actress!' she shouted for all the street to hear.

Somehow I managed to persuade her to come up, and in five minutes she told me, choking with excitement, haste and pride that she was studying with Chekhov, the one who was playing Caleb in *The Cricket on the Hearth*,[2] spoke of the existence of the Stanislavski system and of Chekhov teaching his students the 'elements' from it, that she could not tell me about it all in detail now because she was in a rush, and that everything that took place at the Studio was extraordinarily interesting.[3]

---

1 'Mikhail Aleksandrovich "Michael" Chekhov (1891–1955) was a Russian-American actor, director, author and theatre practitioner. He was a nephew of the playwright Anton Chekhov and a student of Konstantin Stanislavski. Stanislavski referred to him as his most brilliant student' (https://en.wikipedia.org/wiki/Michael_Chekhov).

2 *The Cricket on the Hearth: A Fairy Tale of Home* (1845) by Charles Dickens was produced as *Sverchok na Pechi* at the First Studio of Moscow Art Theatre (1914), and later made into a silent film (1915).

3 Inspired by the example set by an experimental Studio created in 1905 by Stanislavski and Meyerhold within the Moscow Art Theatre, studios started to emerge all over Russia from the mid-1910s. In his book *My Life in Art* Stanislavski defines an experimental studio in a way that can suit all such set-ups: 'It is neither a theatre set to produce work, nor a school for beginners, but an experimental

DOI: 10.4324/9780203125205-32

I don't know what happened to me but I, uncharacteristically, became so persistent in persuading her to take me with her to her class that she agreed. We ran in silence all the way to the Gazetny Lane, where Chekhov lived. Then she asked me to wait in the courtyard while she went up to get the Studio's head student. Several minutes later she came back with a pretty girl, Natasha Tsvetkova, the head student.

'She has agreed to let you join the class', Lyda said. 'We shall enter the room after everyone else, and share two chairs between the three of us. There is a lecture today. No practical work, so no one will notice you.'

When we entered the hallway the students were already on their way into the room. Natasha Tsvetkova, energetically and demonstratively, started to sort everything out by setting down all the chairs, while they hid me in the corner of the entrance hall. Finally, having seated everyone, Natasha looked out into the hall, cheerfully winked at me, and the three of us instantly settled on the two chairs pre-set for us. I was so thoroughly squeezed in, it was virtually impossible to suspect my presence there.

Then Mikhail Aleksandrovich Chekhov entered. Everyone got to their feet, apart from me, squashed as I was and unable to move.

My first impression of Chekhov was unusually intense. He came in awkwardly, pulling up his trousers, unprepossessing, plain-looking. Then immediately I saw his eyes – his gaze fastened somewhere, not looking at anyone in particular – as if expecting an answer of some kind. I was so struck by these bright unfathomable eyes, full of pain, loneliness and some kind of silent question, that I forgot all about myself.

Everyone was standing still. Chekhov stopped half-way to the armchair set up for him.

'I am not able to talk to you about Konstantin Sergeievich today', he said. 'I am really sick. Maybe it is best for you all to go away? Let's meet another time …'

No one moved or said a word.

'You know what, maybe don't go', Chekhov said suddenly, having apparently sensed the general mood. 'Let's try and do a group etude. Imagine that this room is a psychiatric hospital. You are all locked up here. I will be the doctor, you, the patients. Each of you will have your own idée fixe, your own obsession.' Then quickly, without a second's hesitation, he started to allocate ailments to each of the students.

Chekhov moved softly and swiftly between the students. Once he had given someone their task, he moved them to one side. The group of those without a task was growing smaller. In vain was I trying to get either to the door, or to my two friends, who had totally forgotten about me by now. Then suddenly Chekhov lightly touched my shoulder, and looking past me, said:

---

laboratory for the actors who have more or less completed their training.' Mikhail Chekhov opened his Studio in January 1918 (ed. note).

'You've got it into your head that you are … made of glass, you're scared to be smashed to pieces …'

I rushed over to Lyda and Natasha. 'Help me get out', I whispered to them, terrified.

'Don't you dare, you'll get us into trouble', they answered, no less terrified. 'There are lots of us, he won't notice you …'

'But how can I act being made of glass?' I would not let go of them, scared to death.

'No need to act anything, just imagine that you are made of glass … For God's sake, leave us alone, he might see you! …'

Every escape route was cut off. I turned around and saw a peculiar sight. Everyone's eyes had lost their normal expression. Each one seemed to be looking inside themselves, trying to get to grips with something. One young man climbed up on the chair, looking at something as if trying to hear it. It was I.M. Kudryavtsev, a would-be MAT actor. Chekhov told him that he was the god Janus and had two pairs of eyes, one pair on his face, the other at the back of his head. I could not take my eyes off him. He made a gesture with his arms, which seemed to be directed at me, and I suddenly remembered that I was made of glass.

I was literally seized with the dread of being smashed to pieces. No idea what happened, but I forgot about everything. Forgot that I was at the Studio illegally or that Mikhail Chekhov himself was present. I cautiously walked around every single person trying to step lightly and softly. I still remember the joy of having complete belief in what was taking place, and a sense of complete freedom of doing things. In search of a place that would be safe for me, I climbed up on the window sill. Chekhov invited me to get back down, but with confidence and lack of inhibition I spoke to him as if he were incapable of understanding how dangerous it was for me to get down. Chekhov kept insisting that he understood it well, so I gave in. With great care he helped me to climb down, led me across the room, and sat me down on the sofa. He led me as if I were made of glass, going around everyone. En route he talked to others, asking something here, comforting someone there, but I saw that not for a second did he forget about me. He played the doctor's part, and everyone turned to him trustingly.

Suddenly he clapped his hands – and the clap meant that the etude was over. For me it also meant the beginning of the repayment for the happy moment of creativity, to which at that point I had no right.

Chekhov sat down in the armchair reserved for him, everyone else went to their seats. I was again stowed away behind everybody. Chekhov was analysing the etude, giving notes, reproaching some for lack of concentration, praising others for being 'in the circle'. I did not understand what it meant to be 'in the circle', but did not dare ask my friends. I was trying not to breathe.

'Now, where's the girl made of glass?' Chekhov asked suddenly.

I could not answer since I had burst into tears, sobbing, my face tucked into the back of the girl sitting in front of me. My friends also burst into tears. They wept, realising that they had done something dishonourable and were scared they would now be kicked out of the Studio. I sobbed desperately because I had incidentally come into contact with something mysterious, and now that inexplicable happiness was to be taken away from me; and ahead of me was a strictly mapped-out life, with no theatre and no happiness in it ...

Chekhov said goodbye to the students, keeping behind only the two guilty girls and myself. He was not angry. Our tears amused him, and he demanded that we explained to him more clearly what I was there for if, according to me, I had no intention of joining the Studio. I made a long muddled speech about my determination to go and study mathematics at the University because I was no beauty, and my parents would never allow me to study at the Studio anyway.

My monologue regarding the Department of Mathematics, broken up by outbursts of sobs and tears, apparently did not affect him in the least. He let the girls go home, and when they left, said to me sternly:

'Calm down, stop crying. I will now give you another etude to do', and he called over the boy who was putting away the chairs. 'Konjus, please stay a moment, I will need you.'

I no longer remember Konjus, or when and why he later left the Studio, but the etude we did together has stayed with me for the rest of my life.

'You are husband and wife', said Chekhov. 'He is leaving you. You can do and say whatever you want.'

I remember experiencing such acute longing and loneliness during it, such complex feelings which at eighteen I, naturally, had never experienced in my life before, and had only a very vague idea of. Overwhelmed by emotion, I never said a single word, although I really wanted to stop him going. Konjus didn't speak either as he went on packing his things ...

'Have you ever experienced something similar in your own life?' Chekhov asked me.

'No', I answered sincerely.

'Never forget what you have just been through. Art is an exceptionally complicated thing. You have not had a life experience, but your imagination is like a bee, it has been collecting honey from everything you've ever perceived, heard, read, seen, and has now revealed itself in a creative act. As soon as you start training in the art of acting, your spontaneity, innocence, faith will go. But only for a time, later they will return in a new capacity.'

I stayed at Chekhov's for several hours. He talked to me about theatre, about himself. Told me that his wife had left him, taking his daughter away with her; that his life was hard, but he believed that he would be saved by art. He spoke of his desire to create a studio, where he could employ all his knowledge.

Then Chekhov's mother came into the room, and he said to her:

'Mama, let me introduce you – this is my new student ...'

Everything in my life took off, as they say, head first. As I walked home, I saw neither the streets, nor houses, nor people. 'Chekhov's student! Chekhov's student!' my heart sang. For the first time, being at home was hard. Everything remained the same there, but I had a secret. I knew there was no point in telling anyone at home about what had happened. No one would have understood me, anyway.

But what was to be done about enrolling at the Department of Mathematics? I went back to my textbooks. A few days passed. I did not go to the Studio but I was drawn to it irresistibly. I decided to go and tell Chekhov about my hesitation.

He met me warmly, joyfully, as if he had known me from childhood. He settled on the sofa, cross-legged, sat me next to him, and spoke to me, using a familiar form of address: 'You must tell me everything, everything …' He had a slight lisp. On stage he knew how to transform his speech defect into the most diverse characterisations, while in life it gave him a sort of childish naïvety.

I told him about my parents, about my father, about an instance when Tcharin suggested that I should go on the stage, and the conversation that had followed with my father, who convinced me that with my looks and crippling shyness I had to let go of my dreams of the theatre.

I also told him that despite not being able to think of anything but his words – 'this is my new student' – I still went on as before, and everyone still thought that I was applying to study at the Department of Mathematics.

'You know what,' said Chekhov, having listened to me very carefully, 'of course, you must not upset you parents. For example, no one is more dear to me than my mother. But the Department of Mathematics – it is, in my opinion, the most staggering nonsense! Of course, I cannot promise that you will become an actress. Your looks do not worry me – it is so much more interesting to play character parts. You did two good etudes. Quite possibly it happened by chance, maybe because you had sneaked secretly into the Studio, you reached a particular level of nervous concentration. Either way, you are capable of concentration and attention, and you have imagination. I believe that your idea of doing math – that's just due to overtaxing yourself …'

I listened and believed his every word. I remembered all the fine arts, literature, music and theatre that filled my whole childhood, and felt that I wanted to do nothing else.

'Do you know what's most important?' said Chekhov finally. 'Will you fall in love with theatre so that you give it your all, all of you? Stanislavski says that you should not love yourself in art, but love art in yourself. That's very hard. If you are not afraid of this challenge, go on, try it out. When I was studying in St Petersburg, a student had once told Pevtsov during an exam that he would only want to go on the stage if he had real talent. Pevtsov's response was that if that was the student's idea of theatre, he'd be better off not joining a theatre since he would quickly become redundant there. Theatre only needs those who love it so much that they will be happy to be prompters, follow-spot operators – do whatever is necessary, so long as they could live in the theatre and for the theatre.'

We decided that I would come to the evening classes at the Studio, and enrol in the Art History rather than Mathematics Department. And in a year's time Chekhov would tell me whether it was worth my coming to study at the Studio.

'I promise you to be very demanding', he said as we were saying goodbye.

… Mikhail Chekhov – my first teacher of theatre, who gave me so much that to this day I still feel a sense of gratitude to him. It is not easy to write about him.

I remember how during the rehearsals of *The Government Inspector* Stanislavski, without taking his eyes off the stage, threateningly lifted his hand up to stop someone rustling the pages of a script in the auditorium, afraid that this rustling might disrupt Chekhov's creative process.[4] I remember Stanislavski saying to us, the new intake into the company:

'Study the system by observing Misha[5] Chekhov. Everything I am teaching you, is encapsulated in his creative personality. He is a mighty talent. There isn't a single creative task that he would not be able to execute onstage …'

The Studio came into being at a challenging period in Chekhov's life. Time and again, his mental problems prompted him to make up his mind to give up theatre for good.[6] He began considering other ways of making a living. At the time he never left the house. He started by carving wooden chess-pieces for sale, learnt book-binding. Then one of his friends persuaded him to open a studio. He got excited by the idea, drawn to working with young people. Everyone who got accepted into the Studio was told that there would be a fee to pay, but he never took any money from any of us. From the very first lessons the Studio became the most important part of his life. Later he would say that he got well only thanks to working with us. I believe that's exactly how it was. He craved contact with young healthy people, in love with his creative personality.

He revealed himself to us with such absolute candour that it gives me the right to say that neither his audiences nor his long-term theatre colleagues knew him to the extent that we did. We knew Chekhov in all his complex contradictions – his weaknesses, breakdowns, inspired quests, self-doubts, disappointments and discoveries. There was no logical order to his lessons that was presumably required for our systematic development. But those lessons made me realise once and for all that the creative personality of the pedagogue is a powerful formative force.

He was teaching us not for our sake but for his own. If any of us showed signs, even to the smallest degree, of grasping his creative quest, that person became indispensable to Chekhov. As soon as someone started to lag behind

---

4 Chekhov played the part of Khlestakov in *The Government Inspector.* It premiered in October 1922 (ed. note).

5 In Russian, 'Misha' is a nickname for 'Mikhail' (trans. note).

6 By 1917 Chekhov pulled out from the *Seagull* rehearsals at MAT. In his letter to Stanislavski he explained that he had left due to the mental problems he, as he put it, 'had suffered from for two-and-a-half years' (ed. note).

or demanded special attention, they became a hindrance, and Chekhov gazed right through them, without seeing, hearing or noticing them. He did not teach us but he gave us an opportunity to take part in his own search, and for that I am eternally grateful to him.

Now, so many years later, having got to know the Stanislavski system not only through Chekhov, but having had the happiness of also calling Stanislavski and Nemirovich-Danchenko my teachers, I realise that at the time when his Studio was emerging, Chekhov was *the genuine disciple of Stanislavski*. Leafing through my diary from the time, through the notes of lectures, etudes and exercises, I am full of admiration at the depth of his understanding of Stanislavski's ideas! And my diaries of the later period reveal how gradually, almost imperceptibly the definitions were changing, and Chekhov started to depart and turn his back on Stanislavski. Until finally it led to one of Stanislavski's best students finding himself on the opposite side from his teacher's civic and aesthetic position ...[7]

Our classes at the Studio were mostly dedicated to the 'elements' of the system and to finding the creative sense of self through etudes, in other words, the first section of the Stanislavski system. I cannot recall us doing work of any interest on scenes or a play – that kind of work was outside Chekhov's sphere of interests. The problems of concentration and attention, imagination, improvisation, the 'seed', atmosphere, etc. mostly interested him as an aspect of what Stanislavski called 'the actor's work on himself'. He was excited to be developing the actor's psycho-technique *in preparation* for working on their roles. He realised that in that particular area we could be his small-scale creative laboratory.

Chekhov's interest in the questions relating to creative technique was that of a great *actor*. Unfortunately, it happens rather rarely in the arts. It is mostly directors who are interested in the actor's psycho-technique, since they naturally consider it their duty to develop the actor. But actors rarely address the questions of self-development. On those rare occasions, when I happened to observe an actor agonising as they themselves sought to get to the secrets of their profession, they were usually all exceptional and creative personalities.

Chekhov, just like Stanislavski, believed that on the whole actors fail to raise the level of their profession to that of great art, still clinging to outdated, long extinct forms. Secretly those actors love amateurism, mistaking it for freedom, while Chekhov's dream was to arrive at an even more subtle insight into the creative process, an increased precision of the psycho-technique. That is why he was so enthusiastic about creating his Studio and doing all the exercises and etudes together with us.

---

7 After emigrating in 1928, Mikhail Chekhov became *persona non grata* in the Soviet Union. He remained as such in 1967 when Knebel's *My Whole Life* was published. See Adolf Shapiro's introduction to this edition where he tells of Maria Knebel's continual battle to have him exonerated (ed. note).

Most of us, of course, did not understand this at the time. Nearby Vakhtangov[8] was building his own Studio, creating his theatre, but Chekhov wilted in front of your eyes if asked about the Studio's repertoire. We were being proactive, had a great number of ideas for productions, but they quickly vanished into thin air, and nothing ever went beyond the casting stage.

Admittedly, sometimes Chekhov got the urge to start working on something big. For example, he dreamt of *Faustus*, so we read it out loud, analysed it. Once he told us that Vakhtangov dreamt of adapting the New Testament for the stage. He talked of it the way he always talked to us about Vakhtangov, with interest and curiosity, as if trying to guess what was hidden behind Vakhtangov's words. Suddenly he asked us:

'Do you think Vakhtangov might want me to play Christ?'

From that moment, he got excited about doing a production of the New Testament at the Studio. He cast it. We were trying to decide which bits of the New Testament were most dramatically viable. Then suddenly an unexpected hurdle arose. One of the students confessed to her friend that she did not believe in Jesus Christ. In the next class the friend, who found herself harbouring 'sedition', got up and announced in a tragic voice:

'Misha (Chekhov demanded that we called him by his name, using a familiar form of address), Misha, you know, Ella does not believe in Jesus Christ!'

All fearfully, questioningly turned to the apostate. Chekhov looked at her with great severity and asked, if that was true. Ella Stein, white as a sheet, courageously asserted that it was true and she did not believe in Christ. A sombre silence set in. Then Chekhov looked away, lost in thought.

'Do you believe in Hamlet? In King Lear? What about Faustus? I was hoping that we would be looking for ways of fulfilling Vakhtangov's dream at the Studio, but now …'

Mikhail Aleksandrovich left the room, while we stayed behind devastated and totally confused. Some attacked the daring student, the others vaguely sensed that having a belief in Lear or Faustus was not quite the same as having 'faith in Christ' that Chekhov had talked to us about. But we were far too young and far too in love with our teacher to argue with him. In our next class Chekhov suggested that we should carefully consider how serious we were about adapting the New Testament for the stage. No longer did he bear any grudge against the 'rebel'. Then he improvised a few scenes for us. It seems to me now that what he was looking for in the character of Christ was similar to what Kramskoi[9] sought in him, i.e., a profound thought, deep concentration and humanity.

---

8 Yevgeny Vakhtangov (1883–1922), one of Stanislavski's disciples. An actor, pedagogue and director of great renown in Russia, Vakhtangov created the so-called 'fantastic realism', and created a number of productions that left an indelible mark in the history of theatre. Mikhail Chekov and Vakhtangov knew each other well as a result of long-standing collaborators at MAT's First Studio. Chekhov played the leads in a number of Vakhtangov's productions (ed. note).

9 Ivan Kramskoi (1837–1887), a painter. He created a famous painting *Christ in the Desert*, with Jesus presented absorbed in a deep mystical thought, as if stripped of the customary divine attributes (ed. note).

He suggested that we examined the image of Christ created by great painters, and bring back to him whatever each of us would have found most affecting.

After many discussions, most of us chose the image of Christ in Leonardo da Vinci's *The Last Supper*. I recall we even 'acted out' that painting. Chekhov played Christ. The point of the etude was to find an inner justification for the pose of one of the figures in the picture. While working on this etude, Chekhov unravelled Leonardo's work for us, its composition, rhythm and the shape of each of the figures. Most memorable for me was the expression on Chekhov/Christ's face, the way he looked at his disciples intently and attentively.

But soon Chekhov went off the idea of adapting the New Testament for the stage. He was preoccupied with new thoughts, as always concerned with perfecting the actor's psycho-technique. He was interested in the actor embodying various genres, interested in fantasy, and in stage hyperbole, in tragicomedy and, most of all, an improvisational sense of self that he considered to be the foundation and the pinnacle of the actor's craft. Perhaps, there was no other actor at the Moscow Art Theatre who was so powerfully and passionately absorbed by Stanislavski's dream of improvisation.

Just like Stanislavski, Chekhov believed that an improvisational sense of self must never become anarchic, must never lead to the actors indulging in a free-for-all. The text, the precisely defined relationships, even the mise-en-scène, these are the bedrock, the basis for the actor's improvisations.

Where does the actor's own freedom of expression lie? First of all, in adaptations, in colours, in subtext. Chekhov said over and over again that if actors assimilate the psychology of the creative improviser, they would find who they are as artists. So actors must be, first and foremost, trained as artists of improvisation. Most of the etudes and exercises at the Studio were devoted to that problem.

Goethe said that 'out of all the knowledge that enriches a person throughout their life, they only remember that which has been experienced'.[1] I have forgotten much of what happened at the Studio but some of it has stayed with me as if it happened yesterday. So, I recall the diverse ways Chekhov used to develop our improvisational sense of self.

Taking creative risks was the primary requirement without which no etude or exercise could be carried out. I understand now that Chekhov was looking for unnecessarily overt means of getting to the subconscious, and consequently many of us found the exercises he gave us hard to do, and the amount of etudes that we failed at was great. But he did teach us to 'jump into the icy water head first'. Chekhov loved etudes on 'self-exposure', that is, etudes where the unexpected occurred, leaving no time for reflection. These exercises, which he had learnt from Stanislavski, appealed to him greatly since he himself was an enormously spontaneous actor.

He used to set us such exercises in a rather particular way, never revealing the etude as a whole but continually feeding us our next actions as prompts. If anyone got distracted listening to his prompts, he instantly stopped the exercise. He believed that the primary step towards mastering the art of acting was in learning to live for the sake of the task in hand so that the pedagogue's prompts – and further down the line, the director's – never interfered with carrying out your task, but assisted it. Chekhov fed his prompts with the extraordinary sensitivity of an actor, as he co-experienced whatever was going on, almost always at some point joining in as a participant of the etude.

'You enter the lift', he told me on one of my very first days at the Studio. (I entered.) 'Shut the door.' (I shut it.) 'You are going up to see Stanislavski. He wants to hear you recite something. Go over the poems in your head. You are nervous, but excited – you are about to see Konstantin Sergeievich.[10] You are carrying a bouquet of roses. Pick it up – you have dropped a rose, careful, don't get pricked by it. Go over your poems again. Now, press the button … 6th Floor.' (I made a move to press the button but instantly heard Chekhov's alarmed voice.) 'There's no button panel. What's happened? Where could it be? On the opposite side? You are inside a lift shaft with no lift!' (Although I had no idea what was happening, I grew anxious.) 'What's to be done?' he suddenly said in horror. 'The lift is above you! And it is coming down! Get out, get out, fast!' (But as soon as I made a move, Chekhov was next to me, trying to open the door.) He said: 'Try and stay calm, we will save you. The door's locked. You closed the door that had no key in it. Why're you sitting there?' he lashed out at the other students. 'Save her! Run upstairs! Stop the lift. Maybe there is someone up there. Lie down, lie down on the floor …' (There was no point in saying anything to me any more. Terrified, I fainted.)

'Why did you faint?' Chekhov asked me bewildered, when I came round. 'This is naturalism, crude naturalism', he said, displeased. 'None of your feelings had anything to do with art. It was your hysteria and the primitive tensing of your muscles that made you faint. Set me the most "horror-filled" etude to do right now, and you will see that I will experience nothing but pure creative joy from doing it …'

Each of us was keen to come up with an etude for him to do, but as the 'victim' I was apparently keener than others. I had an idea for the etude, but admitted that I was not brave enough to 'conduct' Chekhov to his goal.

'No need to do that. Just tell me what it is about, the theme. The reason I introduce you into your etudes gradually, is for you to learn to hear the prompt. What's more – you are not aware of it as yet – but the most beautiful thing in art is anticipation, a foretaste of the whole.'

That day he told us for the first time that Stanislavski attaches great significance to the concept that he called the 'seed'. The 'seed' is the essence, the fundamental, the key from which the future work of art will spring. Just as the would-be plant is concealed in a seed, so the would-be productions or characters are concealed in the artistic 'seed'. Stanislavski called the 'seed' the soul of

---

10 Michael Chekhov found himself in a similar situation, when he went to see Stanislavski for his audition. He was asked to perform an extract from *Tsar Feodor*. As a result of this Chekhov was accepted into the Moscow Art Theatre Company (ed. note).

the role, and sometimes, 'the raisin in a glass of kvass'. Chekhov shared with us that as an actor his understanding of the 'seed' was that of 'a sense of the future as a whole', and when he did not get that sense, all the many details and particulars fell apart into a thousand tiny pieces, and he experienced nothing but chaos. He said that many actors start concocting a character, forcing it out of themselves far too early, inventing character traits and weaving them artificially into the character's lines, rather than paying heed to 'a sense of the whole' and trusting that sense completely.

'And now – set me an etude', Chekhov interrupted himself.

In my etude Chekhov was to pick fruit off a tree, when suddenly he was to discover a poisonous snake. He asked if any of the students wanted to do the etude before he did. Everyone was keen to have a go. (We had quickly learnt from Chekhov to throw ourselves into doing every single exercise with great zeal. He treated those who used to 'hang back' with such coldness and contempt that each of us, without any concern for the success or failure of the exercise, bravely charged forth to do it.) Someone brought over a stool from the kitchen, got up onto it, and started to pull off imaginary fruit. There was suddenly a violent scream: trying to 'save himself from the snake', a student rushed into the next room as fast as he could. A few seconds later, looking somewhat embarrassed, he returned. One after another everyone climbed up onto the kitchen stool, having, in their mind, firmly established the tree in the exact same spot where it had been placed by the first student. The only difference was that some of them were bitten by the snake and they, rather artificially, instantly died, while some managed to save themselves from the snake either with a loud scream, or – for some reason – tiptoeing away.

Chekhov mocked everyone. But most of all those who tiptoed away from the snake.

'You're eighteen! Where did you get such clichéd ideas?' he asked, horrified. 'Konstantin Sergeievich is right when he says that clichés are sucked in with a mother's milk! And such a dearth of imagination!' He was unable to calm down. 'The first person came up with the most banal situation, and then one after another, everyone clutched on to it. Well, of course, the true pearl was trying to get away to safety by tiptoeing. Pity no one said to the snake, "Do please forgive me, I am in a rush!"' He roared with laughter.

We knew that we did the etude rather badly, but thought it was due to our own lack of skill. In reality, as I see it now, Chekhov made a pedagogical miscalculation. He demanded that we produce big passionate feelings straight away, which could only lead to hysteria and hamming it up. He did not know how to put himself into our shoes. When he tested the task on himself, he felt that he could handle it brilliantly.

Chekhov did a few different versions of the 'Snake' etude. I shall recount the two that I noted down.

'I shall do this etude as a fairy-tale', he said. (He generally believed that fairy-tales contained an enormous potential for developing the actor's ability. They are good for developing imagination; tragedy and humour are often

intertwined within them, they instil a sense of style and call for the precision of
form. At the Studio, we did a lot of work on fairy-tales. For example, we had
the 'Flying Carpet' etude that we did day in, day out. It gradually grew bigger
and bigger, with the addition of new events, details and characters. 'The Snake'
was the first fairy-tale that Chekhov acted for us and with us.) 'First of all, get
rid of this kitchen stool. Secondly, stay attentive and alert. I may need your
intervention – don't delay for a second.'

We sat by the wall to let him have as much space as possible.

He went out into the entrance hall, and soon returned as a very, very ancient
man. He leaned on a stick and appeared to be deadly tired. He could hardly
shift his feet, the bright light making him squint. He was hot, short of breath.
As he entered, he looked around, searching for some shade. He thought of set-
tling down first under one tree, then under another, constantly checking which
canopy provided a more substantial shade. He was about to put his stick down
on the ground, when the thought that there might be more shade elsewhere
made him straighten up and shuffle off to yet another tree. He softly chuckled
at his own indecisiveness, as some barely perceptible sounds came from his
dry lips, either a titter, or a word. Finally, he settled down. By the way he lay
down, relaxed all his muscles, stretched out his legs and closed his eyes, you
could tell what a long journey the old man had made, and how good he felt
at that moment.

He lay perfectly still, and seemed to have fallen asleep. Suddenly we saw that
without opening his eyes or making a single move, he became alert, listening.
Then he pressed one ear a little closer to the ground. 'Nope,' he said blissfully, 'I
imagined it!' He snuggled down again and tried to go to sleep, but the rustling
noise he imagined had scared off his sleep. He got fully engrossed by the apples
densely covering the branches above his head. 'What a load of apples', he whispered in a child-like excitement. His exhausted body did not stir, only his eyes
and dry lips longed for the fresh fruit. At long last he picked up his stick and
tried, from where he was sitting, to reach a branch and pull it towards himself.
A great variety of manoeuvres ensued. Now the branch was getting closer and
closer, and he was about to get hold of his apple, when suddenly it escaped him
and bounced back up, then he looked for a more pliable branch, trying to hook
it and – with the utmost caution – pull it down towards himself. Suddenly
there it was, an apple, right above him, and the old man, feeling mischievous,
decided not to pick it off by hand but bite it with his toothless mouth. Finally,
it seemed he would quench his thirst.

Suddenly he recoiled, looked around and asked in consternation: 'Who has
said these are magic apples, and no one is allowed to touch them?'

'I have', said Natasha Tsvetkova.

Chekhov turned to her. 'Who are you?'

'Don't question me', she answered.

'Stay, don't leave me', Chekhov reached out after her with sadness and
longing, but the student guessed it would be best not to go on but to leave
him alone. Chekhov followed her with a long look, as if she were slowly

disappearing somewhere. Then his attention was again drawn to the apples. 'I am thirsty, I am very thirsty!' he whispered barely audibly, fighting the temptation. The branches whipped his face – that was made clear because of the way he pushed away the apples that were trying to get into his mouth with his head and hands. It was touching and funny all at once. His desire to have an apple was driven to such a degree that it seemed no force could stop him. But just a split second before picking off an apple, he glanced meekly, like an old man-child, in the direction of the voice he had heard. Since no one, apparently, was there, he stretched out his hand, smiling cunningly, towards the apple, but the dread of the terrible injunction forced him to look around again and again.

Now trying to outwit her, who he feared would stop him again from touching the apples, he quickly glanced around and made his way through the thicket of trees to the far-off corner where, hidden from everyone, he could pick his apple.

'Where are you off to?' An unexpected sound of another student's voice stopped him in his tracks. It was an imperious, firm call. It stopped Chekhov dead. We expected him to get scared and give in, but suddenly the old man became irate. He stamped his feet, threateningly waving his stick, muttering some indistinguishable words. First he turned to where the severe voice had come from, then to the other side, where the original ban had issued from.

'I will eat it, yes I will', he repeated over and over, 'I will eat it, yes I will!' Such determination in this tiny, slight, helpless creature, such mischievous courage! We could not help wishing that he would disobey everyone, and finally pick off his apple and quench his thirst.

And he did. He ate it greedily, quickly and joyfully, hastily wiping off the juice running down his chin. While he did that, he must have discovered that he had a beard, because from then on there was an old man with a funny little beard before us. Having devoured the apple, he must have felt such an overwhelming sense of bliss that he even began to do a little dance, but suddenly got frightened again and listened hard to something inside himself. His eyes opened wide and stopped. All of a sudden he opened his mouth as his eyes swiftly followed something, and, before we could recover, he grabbed the snake that was crawling out of his wide-open mouth with one of his hands. In one sweeping movement, he coiled it around his arm, while squeezing its head with the other hand. Then he flung the snake far off. It was all done with such a wonderful sense of humour, with such physical precision that we burst into applause. But it turned out the etude was not over yet.

'My stick! Where's my stick?' he cried to us without taking his eyes off the snake. One of us, with lightning speed, gave him his stick. 'The snake is about to grow bigger. There is a battle afoot. Stand by. Not a move until you hear my command', the old man ordered us, despite his frailty displaying courage and authority.

The battle began. Chekhov used his stick with sophisticated inventiveness. Now he drew a circle to prevent the snake from getting out, then twirling the stick above his head, produced some extraordinary sound through his tightly held lips, then he lured the snake onto the stick and whirled it around in the air.

Suddenly we heard his tragic voice, 'Look, it's growing bigger and bigger, I can no longer control it. What darkness! Nothing but the snake's sparkling eyes. It is advancing towards us', he said while continuing to wrestle with the huge snake. We could guess that the snake had grown enormous by the unusually expansive movements of the stick.

'It's raised itself up, and is out of our reach', he exclaimed. 'I have no more strength left. Save me!' That call was enough for us all to rush to his rescue. Chekhov found himself on the shoulders of the tallest student. 'Now we are all one,' Chekhov's voice sounded young and confident, 'and together we must behead it.' We all moved in the direction of the snake. 'Look,' we heard Chekhov's happy voice, 'it's slithering away ...'

I saw many an old man played by Chekhov. In *The Case*[11] he was a remarkable Muromsky and in *Petersburg*, Ableukhov.[12] But, quite possibly due to the fact that our old man emerged 'out of nowhere', neither from a play nor from an idea by a playwright, but was given birth there and then by the actor's imagination, it produced the strongest impression on me.

'Now I shall perform it as vaudeville', continued Chekhov. 'Of course, vaudeville requires song and dance, so it will be hard to do it without music. But I want to make you understand – the entirety of vaudeville's inner and outer make-up is very particular ...'

He picked up the same walking-stick but now it had turned in his hands into a light cane. Whistling softly, he kept glancing around, clearly waiting for someone. His mindlessly happy eyes skimmed over the surroundings as if trying to determine where *she* might come from. But since *she* was still nowhere to be seen, he checked himself: he tied his cravat into a big bow (Chekhov was a virtuoso at performing actions with imaginary objects), made a middle parting in his hair, then began to mentally fantasise how he was going to greet her. He adopted a variety of poses. Now he rushed towards her with a happy smile, lifting his non-existing hat, while twirling his cane with ease. Now he noticed that his shoelaces were undone, and started to do them up.

His cane was in the way, but it never occurred to him to put it down on the ground. He kept coming up with increasingly incredible ways of holding it to avoid it being a handicap. He shifted it from one hand to another, so that the hand, which at that point was holding both the cane and the shoelace, let go of either the cane or the shoelace. He squeezed it between his legs, but then it stopped him bending down. Tried to force his head under the cane and, looking astonishingly stupid yet utterly earnest, found himself unable to work out which of the two crossed-over legs was the right one and which was the

---

11 A Sukhovo-Kobylin play that Chekhov performed in for the Maly Theatre Company in 1927 (ed. note).

12 An adaptation of the novel by Andrei Bely that was premiered in November 1925 (ed. note).

left. At the same time, he was getting more anxious that he would end up in front of *her* with one shoelace undone. The rhythm of his actions kept changing all the time as he either lost all hope of doing his laces up, or tried to do it with extreme speed. Finally, he stopped. He was struck by a brilliant idea. He lay down on the ground, put his cane under his head, lifted his leg, and holding it virtually above his head, did his shoelace up. Having finished it with an elegant little bow, without changing the position of his arms and legs, he sharply turned over onto his side and looked around in alarm, but soon calmed down – *she* did not see him, *she* had not yet arrived.

Satisfied, he quickly checked himself out, looked at his watch and suddenly … looked hurt. He would meet her in the guise of a hurt man. Placing his stick behind, with his feet wide apart for support, he perched on its handle, crossed his arms and threw his head back. After sitting like this for a few seconds, he saw an apple. With one quick movement of his hand, he pulled the branch down, sunk his teeth into the apple, and chewed it all up in a split second. He chomped on it frenziedly. Having finished the apple, Chekhov spat out the core. While doing this, he was already pulling down another branch, and tearing off another apple with his teeth. Then his arm resumed its previous 'Napoleonic' position. His movements precise, fast, dexterous, while his body remained totally still and relaxed. The cane seemed to be screwed firmly into the floor with the actor perching on it casually, with utter ease.

Yet despite the clowning which seemed to overtake each individual episode for its own sake, not for one second did he forget that his every action was linked to *her*, the one he was here to meet. So the colouring of all the actions was psychologically extremely varied. Now Chekhov appeared mortally offended, now triumphantly indifferent, now carefree and jolly.

Suddenly he saw the snake. He saw it as his hand was reaching out to get another branch. He remained in the same position, following its fast movements only with his eyes. It was slithering away. He did not feel any fear, just a growing sense of curiosity. He decided to catch up with it. Made a few steps forward, but the snake was disappearing without noticing him. Suddenly he froze, the snake must have coiled itself up. Then he pulled off an apple and cautiously started to roll it towards the snake. Eventually, it noticed him. Chekhov was jubilant. He started to tease it with his hat, then with the cane as he sang something jolly to himself.

Suddenly he shook all over. 'Do not bite me, don't you dare', he was almost hissing, having lost his voice in terror. He kicked away the snake with his foot, then unexpectedly caught it in his hat, as if it were a butterfly net, threw the hat down on the ground, and sat down on top of it. He'd won! After all he had been through, he readjusted his bow, smoothed down his hair and started to look around again, whistling lightly and awaiting the arrival of his beloved. He sat on top of his imaginary hat with such grace, his eyes shining with naïve self-satisfaction, that we could not help laughing, we cried with laughter ….

By comparing our etudes with Chekhov's, we could see that what hindered us most was that both our intention and its realisation were simplistic. We did not know how to go beyond the plot in our imagination. We just followed the logical outline of the action that led naturally to schematic feelings. Whereas when Chekhov heard the task, it was as if he pushed it into the background. At the forefront were the given circumstances with which the imagination enveloped the plot of the etude.

'Pulling apples off a tree, and then seeing a snake – these are just empty words', he analysed the outcome of the etude. 'Without getting "a sense of the whole", I would not have been able to do a thing. I must have a sense of the etude's beginning and end; choose its style, the genre in which the given plot will be developed. And so, I decided to do it as a fairy-tale in the first instance and a vaudeville in the second. But what I needed most was to get a sense of *who* it was that saw the snake. All that produced the character's 'seed', his characterisation. And I, no longer bound by the plot but instead fertilised by the theme that revealed its essence, got on with my improvisation with confidence.'

Chekhov said that was how he approached not only etudes but every one of his roles. It was precisely what Stanislavski, Nemirovich-Danchenko and Vakhtangov demanded of him, and that was what he wanted to train us to do. Each role had to be treated as material requiring enormous work of the imagination. That's why actors had to undergo a lengthy 'schooling in improvisation', learning to use the plot to find the freedom to express their creative individuality. Only then, playing the role over and over again, does the actor discover further nuances.

Every second the actor spends on the stage he should feel that he is the author's *co-creator*.

'You must experience the play or etude as *your own creation*. How can you achieve that? Stanislavski's gives us the answer: "The crucial thing is our imagination, the mighty 'if' without which creative work is impossible. There is not a single day when the actor can be permitted not to work on developing their imagination."'

Chekhov was convinced that actors have to master devices of inner and outer techniques to such an extent that they turn into the *new capabilities of their soul*. This is achieved by doing constant exercises and improvisations.

Note

i   Johann Peter Eckermann, *Razgovory s Goethe*. Moscow/Leningrad, Academia, 1934, p.233 (*Gespräche mit Goethe*).

Appendices

Appendix A to page 52

Surikov's *Boyarynya Morozova*[1]

Figure A.1[i]

Let's take as an example a Russian painting. Everyone, of course, knows the painting by Vasily Surikov *Boyarynya Morozova*. It portrays the courage of a Russian woman, who is ready to endure any torture and die for her truth. Its far-reaching meaning still affects the viewer despite its obsolete plot.

Thrown onto a pile of hay, chained, taken away to face horrendous tortures, Boyarynya Morozova has not resigned herself, has not yielded. Her eyes are glaring, she looks pale, driven, inspired: her right hand raised up high, two fingers together in the Old Believer's sign of the cross. Her every movement, every impulse comes down to the one throughaction: 'I assert my faith, and I want to convince the common people around of the truth of it.'

Surikov, a painter of genius, conveys this throughaction with an amazing feeling and intensity.

---

1 *Boyarynya Morozova* (1887, Tretyakov Gallery) by Vasily Surikov (1848–1916).

DOI: 10.4324/9780203125205-34

Now let's imagine that the throughaction referred to above will be substituted by another one. For example: 'I am going to be martyred and want to say farewell to Moscow and its people'; or: 'I want to see my enemy – the Tsar Alexei Mikhailovich who is peeping out through the grille in a small church window', or … we can imagine many more actions, but none of them could take the place of the profound and precise throughaction discovered by Surikov.

And I believe that even the least sophisticated of people looking at the painting would know that, however remarkable the depiction of the people, 17th-century Moscow, and the snow may be, the painting would fail to produce such a powerful impression on them, if its supertask had been breached.

Appendix B to page 54

Kremlin Chimes by Nikolai Pogodin[1]

Let's take as an example Nikolai Pogodin's play *Kremlin Chimes* and analyse the role-throughline of Engineer Zabelin.

Engineer Zabelin is one of the main characters in the play. His storyline concerns one of the crucial problems faced by Soviet power in the early days after the Revolution of 1917 – the problem of getting honest decent Old Regime specialists to change sides and serve the young Soviet state.

The actor must realise how much a personal encounter with Lenin[2] affects Zabelin and changes his state of mind. The impact of this encounter is such that Zabelin finds himself going back to work.

Zabelin, a prominent engineer, an energy specialist, believes that the victory of the Revolution heralds the end of civilisation, science and culture.

A strong and talented man, Zabelin loves his country 'in his own way', but the ground has slipped from under his feet with the Revolution, and now he accepts nothing that has come in its wake.

The collision between the two worlds is the theme of the opening scene 'By the Iversky Chapel' in the production of *Kremlin Chimes*. Engineer Zabelin, dismissive of Soviet power, goes to the flea market by the Iversky Chapel to trade in matches as a sign of protest.

Here, in a huge marketplace by the Iversky Chapel, where the flotsam and jetsam of history cluster together, the collision of the two worlds is shown through the people and the facts. Here, amongst black marketeers, hustlers and petty thieves, Zabelin declares himself to be 'Prometheus, who brings fire to the people', while selling matches as a form of protest against the powers that be.

But here, among the dregs of society, he is also alone. Convinced that the Revolution is the death of Russia, Zabelin sees his own fate bound up with the apparent collapse of the country.

---

1 Nikolai Pogodin (1900–1962), a Soviet playwright. *Kremlin Chimes* written in 1940 (trans. note).
2 Vladimir I. Lenin (1870–1924) was the head of government in Soviet Russia (1917–1924) (trans. note).

DOI: 10.4324/9780203125205-35

He perceives the silence of the Kremlin chimes – 'the prime clock of the state' – as the symbol of Russia's ruin. Speaking to one of the black marketeers, Zabelin asks him:

Zabelin: Listen, you grain-dealer!

Dealer: Yes, your honour!

Zabelin: If the chimes of Westminster Abbey in London grew silent, what would the English-man say?

Dealer: I cannot say, your honour!

Zabelin: The Englishman would say that England is done for.

Dealer: That's liberty for you, liberty!

Zabelin: That's a cardiac arrest, grain-dealer!

For Zabelin there is chaos everywhere, and Russia is at the centre of world chaos. He, Engineer Zabelin, is no longer needed, and that's his personal tragedy.

In one of the following scenes he says:

Savages have captured the ship of the civilisation, killed all the passengers, thrown the crew overboard, and gorged themselves on every last bit of the provisions ... There you have it ... And now what? You must know how to steer the ship but they haven't got a clue. They have promised socialism, but getting there? – no one knows how.

This is Zabelin's perception of the new Russia, the new power.

On top of the social 'collapse' this, for him, is also a moral collapse. He is incapable of accepting anything new. His beloved daughter Masha is dating a Red[3] sailor. She has just gone to the Metropol Hotel, the Headquarters of the Second House of the Soviets. Zabelin sees it all in a different light. He talks it over with his wife, when she arrives at the steps of the Iversky Chapel to pick him up.

Mrs Zabelin: Anton Ivanovich! You should go back home!

Zabelin: I live on the streets now.

Mrs Zabelin: Who makes you live on the streets? Who has kicked you out? No one.

Zabelin: The Soviet power has.

Mrs Zabelin: It's beyond my comprehension.

Zabelin: Let's talk again when your comprehension grows greater. Anyway, I think you'd better keep an eye on your daughter ... I don't need a guardian.

Mrs Zabelin: Masha is no longer a child. She is on the cusp of living her own life.

Zabelin: Yes, that's true. I wouldn't be surprised, if she became a streetwalker any day now.

---

3 The Red sailor means the Soviet sailor. (The Red Army was formed after the Russian Revolution in 1917) (trans. note).

Mrs Zabelin:	Anton Ivanovich, beware of the Almighty! How can you say this of Masha?
Zabelin:	An hour ago your daughter went to the Metropol Hotel with a man …
Mrs Zabelin:	The Metropol is no longer a hotel … They set up the Second House of the Soviets there.
Zabelin:	I have no idea of what the House of the Soviets means. The Metropol is a hotel. And our daughter went there to meet a man in his room …

A few lines later Zabelin says: 'If this gentleman does not come and see us within three days, I will have to take measures …'

Let's consider the characters of Masha, Zabelin's daughter, and the sailor Rybakov, who is in love with her. This is vital for understanding the role of Zabelin.

Masha is an educated young girl, with an unshakable passionate faith in the Revolution and its righteousness, while at the same time attached to the other world, that of her father, Engineer Zabelin. She loves her father with all her heart, and tries, in every way possible, to introduce him to her new truth and she is worried about him, but is not prepared to forgive him anything.

Rybakov, the sailor, a hero from the *Aurora*, now throws himself into vanquishing the heights of world culture with the same passion he showed not long ago in storming the enemy trenches. Rybakov is our new man: he came to the Revolution from the lowest level of society, and now he is reading *A Hero of our Time*[4] for the first time, and dreaming of the electrification of Russia. Pogodin, with his great knowledge of life and precise sense of the period, creates a vivid and unique character of Rybakov. Rybakov and Zabelin belong to two different worlds, and their collision reveals one of the fundamental conflicts of the play.

In Scene 7 we meet Zabelin again. At Zabelin's house there is a get-together of all the neighbours from the same apartment block. This is Zabelin's world. These people belong to another time. For them, as for Zabelin himself, the Revolution means only chaos, the end of civilisation. But while Zabelin, industrious by nature, feels the futility of his life due to the collapse of his activities, and while he passionately loves his people and his country, the characters of his guests are synonymous with philistinism, crassness and narrow-mindedness.

Surrounded by them, Zabelin has a familiar sense of his intellectual superiority.

The complexity of Zabelin's inner drama is that he has no understanding of who carried out the Revolution, and has no desire to find out who they are. He imagines these new, unknown people to belong to a much lower level of evolution than the people that he has known all his life.

But then Masha, at her mother's insistence, brings Rybakov home. She introduces him to Zabelin and his guests. Meeting a Communist for the first time in his life, the man from another world, is an important stage in Zabelin's life.

---

4 *A Hero of our Time* is a novel by Mikhail Lermontov (1814–1841), published in 1840. One of the most important classics of Russian literature (ed. note).

With a sense of righteousness and superiority, Zabelin argues with Rybakov. The two men clash in a verbal duel. Who will win? It is a battle that reveals to Zabelin completely unexpected sensibilities and perceptions of the man from the other world, with his, as Zabelin puts it, 'naïve self-confidence'.

In the dialogue between Zabelin and Rybakov, Zabelin tries to prove to Rybakov that he, a specialist, an expert, has been thrown overboard from the ship of life, that neither his knowledge, nor his work are any longer of any use to anyone. Rybakov parries Zabelin's attack, accusing him of having only himself to blame for making himself redundant.

During the bitter altercation Zabelin says:

Zabelin:	Hold on! The fact that I am unemployed – is that not true?
Rybakov:	Not true!
Zabelin:	The fact that I have been thrown away like an old boot by you lot – is that not true?
Rybakov:	Not true!
Zabelin:	Then, you know what … then, sir, get out of here! I don't know you and I don't want to know you!
Rybakov:	I am not leaving.
Zabelin:	Oh, I see … I forgot that you can requisition my apartment!
Rybakov:	I am not here to requisition –
Zabelin	Then you stay! I will go!
Rybakov:	I won't let you. You make me laugh, raging at everything like this. I think you are a savage!
Zabelin:	A savage?
Rybakov:	A savage.
Zabelin:	And you have turned up here to enlighten me?
Rybakov:	What else? Of course!
Zabelin:	*(roaring with laughter)* Bad luck … Ladies and gentlemen, he has won me over with his naïve self-confidence! Just look at him! He wants to enlighten me! I am all ears, comrade missionary! Enlighten me!

Zabelin experiences rather complex emotions. He wants to kick Rybakov out, yet he is drawn to him. He observes Rybakov with curiosity. He even gets excited by his shouting match with Rybakov, since he wants to understand the nature of these power-usurping 'savages'. Who are these people to whom he is nothing but a reactionary, a counter-revolutionary, he, Zabelin, who has spent his whole life working for his country.

This is followed by Zabelin's fake arrest, which for him is a long-awaited and inevitable end to his life. He even has a bundle with a few of his things waiting by the door.

In the next scene we see Zabelin at Lenin's, where he has been invited as one of the greatest experts in electrification of the country.

Zabelin's meeting with Lenin is a decisive scene in the throughline of Zabelin's behaviour.

From the very first moment, Zabelin sees the magnitude of the task he is charged with. At the same time, he still feels the furious inner resistance of the man who has got accustomed to the role of scientist, builder and expert, kicked out by the Bolsheviks, since they have no need for his knowledge, expertise or talent.

An intense struggle takes place in Zabelin's heart. He does not want to make peace but he can't help getting more and more excited by the problems presented to him by Lenin. He is tormented, tortured by the thought that if he now refuses the offer, turns down the work he has dreamt of all his life, he will cut himself off from it for ever, and condemn himself to total inactivity. He understands Lenin's anger all too well when, on learning that Zabelin trades in matches at the market, he tosses off the remark, 'Feel free to go back to selling matches'. Lenin loses interest in Zabelin, and moves on to some other business that awaits him, and Zabelin's vanity is deeply wounded.

'I am not sure if I am capable of doing it', says Zabelin, unwilling to capitulate straight away. And yet he has a strong feeling that there is no going back to the Iverski Market, that there is no point in him flaunting his discontent. No one is interested in it, least of all himself.

So Zabelin goes home after his meeting with Lenin. He longs to share the enormity of what has just happened to him. When his wife comments that he has been out for three whole hours, he responds, 'Not for three hours, for three whole years'. That's how mammoth the scale and significance of what occurred in his meeting with Lenin appear to him.

Zabelin wants to get rid of the guests as soon as possible. He needs to speak to his daughter privately.

In his conversation with Masha, Zabelin, affected by his encounter with Lenin, reviews all that has happened to him up to that meeting, his whole life over the tumultuous years that the country has gone through since the Revolution. Deep in his heart he feels that Masha believes in him, and he is no longer afraid to set off on his new path.

Zabelin:　　Mashka, this old Russia of ours ... with its steaming samovars, its parochial attitudes ... they're leaving it behind ... Just imagine ...

He feels a need to do something straight away, using this new energy that fills him to the brim. In his excitement, he starts to clear his writing desk of matches, cigarettes and other useless objects. It is an outlet for his joy in coming back to life, to science, to being active again.

The logical continuation of his scene with Lenin is the scene in an abandoned mansion allocated to him for his work.

He wanders amidst the wreckage and litter, drags into the room a huge Gothic-looking armchair, puts on airs for his own benefit as he delivers furious monologues about this deserted ballroom, full of rats strolling about with the insolence of street profiteers, more fit for acting out the mad scene from *King Lear* than for developing the country's electrification plans.

Yet in everything he does there is an excitement and life-affirming joy of a person who is absorbed in his work, having regained his old self, as he, Zabelin, did after his meeting with Lenin.

Mischievously he accepts Rybakov's assistance, who declares himself, to Zabelin's utmost pleasure, to be the academic secretary of the research institution.

'The sailor and I are now at the wheel!', exclaims Zabelin. The association that once seemed improbable to him, is now joyous and straightforward.

Eventually, in the finale, Zabelin meets Lenin for the second time. This is a meeting of working associates, walking along the wide road side by side.

That's the throughline of Engineer Zabelin in Pogodin's play *Kremlin Chimes*.

The vital thing, in doing the 'mental reconnaissance' we have just done, is not getting to know the play 'in general' but getting to the bottom of it through events, actions and behaviour. This allows the company to understand the play's main points, and to grasp the play's fundamental idea, that is, to realise its main point: the play's supertask.

By grasping the supertask, we grasp the writer's intention. Every actor must strive to achieve that. Every actor playing Zabelin must understand and study all the material contained in the play.

However, there will be as many different Zabelins as there are actors playing the part.

As a director, I have worked with five Zabelins. Each of them was a celebrated Moscow Art Theatre actor: Tarkhanov, Khmelev, Bolduman, Livanov and Amtman-Briedit (in Riga). Zabelin, as created by each of these actors, followed many a complex path the playwright led him towards, and yet the individuality of those actors made each Zabelin different from all the others. Each actor created his own Zabelin, emphasising the character traits that were closer to each of them personally. That's how the unique phenomenon that Stanislavski calls 'the actor-role' comes into being.

Appendix C to page 58

Pages of a Life by Viktor Rozov and *Kremlin Chimes* by Nikolai Pogodin

I believe it would be appropriate to cite here the analysis of some extracts from the plays by Soviet playwrights, and examples of the etudes based on them. Let's take two well-known plays, firmly established in the repertoire of our theatres: Viktor Rozov's *Pages of a Life* and Nikolai Pogodin's *Kremlin Chimes*.

Etude forces the actor, as they embody a series of particular actions, to pick out those which are most typical for the character-in-the-making; it provokes the actor to discover distinctive individual character traits and teaches them to express the character's sense of self in a concrete form within the particular circumstances of the moment.

Here's an example of how an etude should be set up. Let's take the night scene from Scene 4 of Rozov's *Pages of a Life*.

In terms of the text, it is not a long scene. Kostia comes to see Boris, wants to stay the night, then he falls out with his friend, and leaves. These are the bare facts. But in order to do an etude, that's not enough. We must get to the heart of their quarrel, understand the intricacies of their interaction in the rehearsed episode.

Earlier that day, at the factory, there occurred an important event which put an end to all of Kostia's aspirations: he discovered that the invention he came up with had already been invented. And perhaps for the first time in his life he felt his lack of knowledge, realising that his level of education was not enough to achieve much. Deep down he acknowledges that Boris, who studies every single night, is doing the right thing. At the factory, while throwing the model of his 'invention' into the fire, Kostia badly burnt his hand. After his wound was dressed, he ran away from the hospital, defying the doctor's orders. He wandered around the streets, mulling over what had happened, and over his life. Feeling drained and desolate, he went back home, but found no peace there, either. He was desperate to speak to his friend, so overcoming his pride, he put out of his mind his earlier falling-out with Boris and left home, telling them that he would stay the night at his friend's. Once he got there, he approached the door a few times but did not dare ring the bell, until finally, timidly, he knocked on the window.

That's the complex web of experiences the actor must conjure up before starting the etude.

DOI: 10.4324/9780203125205-36

What happens next? A few initial awkward moments, then a joyous sense of closeness and mutual understanding, as his friend's concern for him returns. It seems to Kostia that his burnt hand no longer hurts so much, and the heaviness has lifted from his heart. He makes himself comfortable on the sofa, lying there with a cigarette, watching his friend leaning over his textbooks. But he cannot sleep, his thoughts are racing as he keeps going over, in his mind, the earlier events at the factory: he wants to know what his comrades thought of him, whether they judged him harshly, or ridiculed his failed invention. He turns to Boris for answers, secretly hoping to get words of comfort, to have his pain alleviated.

But true friendship is blunt and pulls no punches. Boris feels sorry for Kostia, but at the same time is compelled to tell him that he is wrong, that he has made a big mistake with his life. Kostia is on the verge of realising this himself, but today he is not ready to hear the hard truth; the truth right now is too painful. The deep-seated disagreement that has so long caused the split between them flares up with redoubled intensity. Kostia, his coat thrown over his shoulders, walks out into the night, a lonely figure, as Boris, torn by conflicting emotions, watches as he goes. It seems, at any minute now he will rush out of the door and urge his friend back, apologising for his bluntness. But in his heart, he feels it was the right thing to do, and the tough lesson that Kostia needed. After a moment's hesitation, Boris stubbornly goes back to his books, and reads the problem specifications aloud in a monotonous voice: '... the plane loops the loop ...'.

This is a rather condensed summary of what happens during the scene. The actor, whether he likes to or not, will have to take it all on, as a whole, without – as far as possible – missing a thing. Otherwise, there will be nothing for him to bring to the etude, or the etude simply won't work, there will be no scene as such, since it is comprised entirely of one internal shift after another.

There are no more questions left. The performers seem to be clear about it all. They have analysed the scene with enthusiasm and excitement. Time to start the etude. The actors get up from the table, and begin to get ready.

But what's up with them? They look confused, bewildered, self-conscious, physically tense. The would-be Kostia says something to Boris, who nods his head, as if to say, 'Got it!', while it is quite obvious that he has not heard a word.

What's bothering the actors?

'What if I forget the sequence of events, or enter too early and disrupt the scene, or skip a vital section?' But more importantly – the text. 'What am I going to say? In my own words? It will be ridiculous. Do we really have to do it? Everything is clear as it is ...'

Yes, we do. We must. It's essential. And the etude begins.

Boris studies, bent over his textbook. Nadia – asleep in the next room. It's quiet. Only Boris is heard, whispering the specifications of the problem under his breath. A loud whistle comes from outside the window. What's that ...? The actors did not agree this in advance. The actor lifts his head, thinking. It is an easy guess what's on his mind: 'It will probably come across as fake, if I instantly believe that it's Kostia.' So he leans over his books again. Another whistle, more insistent. 'Now it is quite clear – it's Kostia.' Something else is also clear: the actor's behaviour is that of a performer, the etude's author, and not that of Boris. A new situation has arisen: Kostia is now wandering around the street, rather than, as is assumed, entering the room straight away, or ringing the front-door bell. Boris runs to the window, and peers through the frozen pane of glass. He spots Kostia, signals to him and rushes to open the front door. That's good. All these details are executed with great precision. But they are not pre-planned or considered in advance, they have emerged of their own accord, just now. Particularly true was the way Boris signalled to Kostia. From the outside, Kostia could not see Boris through the frozen window, but only his shadow. So Boris, raising his arms up high, waved them around, indicating to Kostia that he is going to open the door for him.

What a quick transformation that was. Just a moment earlier there was this timid, concerned person on the stage, and all of a sudden – the complete opposite: there is Boris, full of life and energy. And although there was neither a street, nor a frozen pane of glass, the actor behaved in such a way as if they existed. Why? What helped him to get such confidence? He stopped trying to devise the etude, he was compelled to take action.

What will the meeting of the two friends be like?

Kostia enters the room first. He is gloomy. His crumpled hat is pushed low over his forehead. The hurt arm is in a sling. Without taking off his coat, he crosses the room. Boris watches him silently: 'How well my scene-partner has managed his transformation! And the bandaged arm looks so realistic.' This fleeting thought distracts him from the scene, but instantly something stirs in the actor's – Boris's – heart: maybe it is a sense of how serious this moment is, or his compassion for Kostia. A pause ... How will they start the scene? Boris remembers that Kostia will have to ask him about what happened at the factory, and what the other lads were saying about it. But Kostia is silent.

'Sit down', says Boris, moving a chair closer.

Kostia, glances at the chair, but seems to have decided against it. Carefully, supporting the hurt arm, he starts pacing up and down.

'How are you?', asks Boris, trying to get the scene going.

Kostia does not answer. He keeps wandering around the room. That's how he must have been wandering the streets, unable to make up his mind to come here.

'Does the arm hurt badly?', asks Boris after a short pause.

But Kostia is silent. He has casually thrown his hat down on the table, finally sits down, as though he owns the space, deep in contemplation. Boris is puzzled. Why is Kostia silent? Why doesn't he start the scene ...? But Kostia's actions are absolutely correct: he just cannot bring himself to start the conversation. He feels that in the heat of the moment he behaved rashly at the factory. The whole business must have looked ridiculous to others, and this makes him feel wretched.

'Hey, play the guitar, why don't you?' he orders rather than asks Boris in desperation.

'What ...? What's the guitar got to do with it?' Boris, taken aback, freezes. 'We've skipped a whole chunk!'

'Play something, do! It isn't too much to ask, is it?' pleads Kostia.

But Boris is totally at a loss. He believes they have 'made a complete hash' of the etude. Any minute now he will stop the etude and have it out with his scene-partner. For one moment he had felt the truth of what was happening, but it is now fading away. His only concern now is to correct the situation. Then, suddenly, unexpectedly, even to himself, he begins to comfort Kostia.

'Forget it. Who cares, it's all nonsense. You were unlucky, that's all. Well, what's to be done now – hang yourself? It'll all pass, it'll all be forgotten. No need to despair!'

'No one's despairing! Stop whining! All this snivelling! I am fed up as it is', Kostia cuts him short. He has quite rightly picked up on Boris's mistake. Boris would never have been so insensitive in the circumstances. That's not what their friendship, their relationship, is like.

Boris stops short. He also feels that he has made a mistake, but pretends that he is hurt by Kostia's rudeness. A pause ... The partners are putting their feelers out again to see if it is possible to kick-start the scene again under present circumstances.

Kostia gets up and starts pacing up and down the room again. The actor is trying to recover that feeling, which had previously helped him to find the key to Kostia's true sense of self. What was it? The true life of his body! A few seconds later the actor recovers it.

'Well, what happened there ... after I'd gone?', starts Kostia cautiously. 'How did they all respond ...?'

But Boris has not been wasting his time, either. He is hurt, isn't he? So why is he staring at Kostia? That's wrong! So, the actor turns his back on Kostia, drumming the desk with his fingers. The drumming rhythm is getting more and more nervous.

'Has the cat got your tongue?' Kostia is trying to spur him on.

'What are you snapping at me for? Why are you here? What are you playing at?' It is hard to understand whether it is Boris speaking, or whether it is the performer expressing his dissatisfaction with his partner.

'All right, all right ... Don't flash your eyes at me.' Kostia has recalled one of his character's lines, although it is from another scene and refers to another character. 'So, what then? They must have jeered at me, gloated ...'

'That they did', Boris teases him.

'They didn't really ridicule me, did they?' This bothers Kostia more than anything else.

'You can be sure they did.'

'Who did?'

'Everyone did.'

'You, too?'

'Me too.'

'You're lying!'

'Well, if you don't believe me – don't', says Boris in an exaggeratedly grave way.

'I see', Kostia is seriously concerned. 'What about Nurka?'

'Nurka? She started it ...'

'No way! Even Nurka? It cannot be!' Kostia has got muddled up. In the play, his attitude to Nurka is ironic, and rather negative. But now the impression he gives is that she is his true friend, and he values her opinion. 'What did she say?'

'Nurka?' Boris is considering it, as if trying to remember the insulting and cruel words uttered by Nurka, but out of the corner of his eye he sees that Kostia has realised that he is pulling his leg. Their eyes meet, and ... they burst out laughing.

Nothing can stop the etude now. Necessary words come up with ease. The words may be clumsy or unrefined in a literary sense, but in their essence – they are spot on.

They have been sitting next to each for a while now. Boris astride a chair. Kostia comfortably settled in the armchair, with the hurt arm on the arm-rest. He dragged that armchair over at some point in the conversation. No one even noticed how, or when. At the same time Boris got cigarettes and matches from Kostia's jacket pocket, placed one cigarette in Kostia's mouth, and lit it. Neither of them is play-acting, they firmly believe that Kostia could not do it himself because of his arm.

'Hey, Boris, do play the guitar! Do ... Please.'

'I can't, Nadia's asleep. And besides, I must get back to my books.'

'Get back, do, study. I'll stay the night, if that's OK? It feels too depressing to go back home.'

'You can sleep on the sofa. I am not going to bed, anyway.'

Another thought pops up for a second, interfering with the etude: 'I must make Kostia's bed. But I didn't think of setting a pillow and blanket before the etude!' The actor looks helplessly around the room. Again, he is ready to stop the etude. But a moment later he discovers that the bedding is set and ready behind the screen. He is transformed again. Trying not to wake Nadia, he tiptoes quietly across the room to get the pillow and the blanket. The more cautiously he steps, the louder the creaking of the parquet floor, which makes them both irrepressibly jolly.

While Boris is making the bed, Kostia is rummaging around in the sideboard for something to eat.

Both feel natural, free and at ease. They are in no rush. Their imagination offers them unexpected adaptations.

Swapping wisecracks, teasing each other, trying not to make any noise, they are each doing their own thing. Kostia is going to bed, at all times careful of his bandaged arm as he lies down, Boris goes back to his books. But ahead of them is one more event, the main event in this scene, Kostia's unexpected departure. Again, there is confusion in the actors' eyes. They are both trying to remember how the end sequence of the scene works in the play. Kostia is the first to remember.

'OK, joking apart, tell me what they were saying about me at the factory.'

Boris is silent.

'Have you lied to me saying that no one blamed me?' continues Kostia warily.

'I have', Boris says sternly. 'Go to sleep. Let me work.'

'Tell me what they said. Do you hear me?'

'You know yourself what they said, you're not a baby. Stop interrupting my work!'

A long silence.

Kostia takes a long drag on the cigarette. He wonders what to do. Then he carefully sits up. He pulls the chair with an ash-tray towards himself, and stubs out his cigarette. He glances at Boris. But Boris does not react to the noise of the chair. 'I see', thinks Kostia, and sadly shakes his head. 'He no longer thinks he has to hide from me the fact that everyone at the factory blames me. At first, he took pity on me, but now …! Away, I must get away from here!'

Kostia decides to leave, but to leave in a way that Boris does not notice. And he achieves it, taking amazing precautions. He gets up very quietly, puts his boots back on, picks up his jacket hanging on the back of the chair, puts it on, puts the cigarette packet and matches into his pocket … It is not easy, since one of his arms is in a sling. But the more careful his movements are, the more we feel that his inner conviction of having been unjustly hurt grows stronger and stronger. He no longer wants any help from Boris.

He puts on his coat and picks up his hat, left right next to where Boris is working; he moves so quietly that Boris *actually* hears nothing.

At that point the actor playing Kostia comes out of the etude for a split second. What should he do now? In the play Boris tries to stop Kostia from leaving!

From this came one of the most successful moments in the whole etude. The actor felt that Kostia, despite doing everything he could to leave without being noticed, in his heart of hearts, wanted to see how Boris would respond when he saw him leaving. That feeling arose intuitively, rooted in the truth of Kostia's physical behaviour, but it revealed to the actor playing him the essential quality of his character.

Kostia stands still, thinking, then as quietly as before he moves towards the door but … *as if by chance* he brushes against the chair. The chair does not fall over, but hearing a rustling noise behind his back, Boris turns around and sees Kostia in his overcoat, ready to leave.

'Where are you going? What's happened?'

'Going back to my place. You're surrounded by scientists, engineers … And what am I? Nothing but a little worm … an extra', he adds, and leaves.

Boris, confused, watches him go. He is about to run after him, but he stops before he reaches the door, thinks, then slowly goes back to his books.

The etude is over.

Both performers, happy, a little embarrassed, interrupting each other, explain to the director where and why they lost it, and where they felt it went well.

Now to the play! We urgently need the text so that we can check what we have done. What fun it is doing the check-up! We can't wait to have another go at the etude as soon as possible!ii

Now let us take Scene 6 of Nikolai Pogodin's play *Kremlin Chimes*, and unravel the etude method by working on the scene.

Scene 6. Masha is meeting Rybakov by Gogol's monument on the boulevard.

In this brief summary of the scene, let's try to determine what's going on.

Sailor Rybakov, in love with Masha, is late for their date.

This is not a normal date. Today, Masha is going to take Rybakov home to meet her parents, but she is yet to tell him what may await him there. She has to forewarn him about Zabelin's attitude to Soviet power.

Rybakov explains to Masha the reason that made him late: Lenin entrusted him with the task of finding a clockmaker who could mend the Kremlin chimes.

We must now work out the events that determine the characters' actions, affecting their behaviour.

1. Rybakov is late for his date.
2. Rybakov's meeting with Lenin, their conversation, with Lenin talking to him about Russia's future and charging him with finding a clockmaker capable of mending the Kremlin chimes.

What do these events lead to? What actions do they provoke?

Rybakov's actions are: catch up with Masha, explain and justify being late.

Masha's: make Rybakov feel guilty.

At this point, let's do an etude. By doing these actions ourselves, we get a sense of what we have failed to include in the etude, despite taking the main theme of it on board. We discover that it is not enough to have identified the scene's events. For one thing, we did not take into account the episode of the Old Woman with the baby, when Rybakov quizzes her about Masha's whereabouts.

Nevertheless, the actors' imagination has been stirred, and, straight away, they have lots of questions:

Why is the Old Woman afraid of the sailor? Why is the date so important? Why is Rybakov late, and why does Masha forgive him for being late? Where do Rybakov and Masha go now, and what time is it? There are many more questions regarding the throughline of the action, the period, relationships, etc., etc.

We go back to the text – to the play. We re-read it, specify the events that drive the action of the play as *a whole*, and instantly see that we have missed the two main events: 'the Revolution' and 'the Silence of the Kremlin Chimes'.

This at once explains a lot of things: who the Old Woman must be, and why she is afraid of Rybakov. She must take him for a 'police spy', why the chimes are silent, and why Rybakov is late. If the chimes required no repair, Rybakov would not be searching for a clockmaker, and he would never have been late for such an important date.

Why is the date so important? Because the sailor Rybakov is about to visit Engineer Zabelin's home for the first time, and he does not know what to expect there.

Masha's plan for the date was to tell Rybakov about the idiosyncratic and complicated character of her father.

Having done a detailed dissection of the scene, we specify the events. Now our list looks like this:

1.   The Revolution
2.   The Silence of the Kremlin Chimes
3.   Rybakov is late
4.   Rybakov's meeting with Lenin
5.   The task with which Lenin charged Rybakov
6.   The forthcoming encounter between Rybakov and Zabelin

Based on this we specify the actions:
For Rybakov:

1.   He has to find out from the Old Woman where Masha has gone; he has to catch up with Masha and explain to her his reasons for being late
2.   Tell Masha about Lenin

For Masha:

1.   Make Rybakov realise he is in the wrong, to be so late for their date
2.   Having learnt Rybakov's reasons for being late, make up with him, and find out if he managed to carry out Lenin's task
3.   Prepare Rybakov for a meeting with her father

For the Old Woman:

1.   Save herself from this dreadful sailor, who must be a 'police spy'.

After we have specified the events, defined the actions, and taken on board all the themes within the scene, we go back to the etude. Now we will conduct ourselves in a much more organic way, our relationships and our actions will be more truthful, and we will find the correct physical sense of self, as well as being much more specific in our inner monologues.

In addition, other questions may arise that will lead us to familiarise ourselves with the specifics of the period, as well as the nature of the relationships, etc. We then will re-read the scene again to find out if we have skipped something in our etude, checking the given circumstances once again.

We will get to know the literary descriptions of the period, research its visual representations, immerse ourselves more deeply in the atmosphere of the contemporary events, soak up a new sense of the time and place of action during the first years after the Revolution.

That's when we do another etude which – thanks to everything we have stored up internally – is now made concrete and tangible and is now close to the author's intention. This is what it looks like now:

On a spring day, full of the apprehension of the first post-revolutionary years, on a deserted boulevard, an Old Woman, a former aristocrat, is sitting on a bench with a baby, the offspring of a once noble family. The Revolution has turned everything upside down in the Russian Empire. There is no longer any certainty, every day you must be on your guard just to survive. Suddenly this huge sailor rushes in. She hopes he won't notice her. He is after information and asks her questions. She pretends not to hear him, busying herself with the baby. But the sailor is insistent, he won't leave her alone, what's more he grabs her hand, he wants to find something out about a girl. How dreadful! He must be a police spy! She'll be murdered! After all, the Revolution is all around us! To get rid of the terrifying sailor, the Old Woman 'betrays' the girl he is looking for, and tells him which way the girl has gone. He leaves. The Old Woman, shaken, grabs the pram with her grandchild, and flees, terrified the 'spy' may be back.

As it turns out, the 'spy' is the girl's boyfriend, and the two of them do come back to the boulevard. They are trying to sort things out. The sailor is late for their date and wants to explain what has happened. But the girl won't listen, reproaching him for being late today of all days, when he is coming over to her house to meet her parents for the first time. He is in the wrong, and must accept it. The sailor tries to explain why he was delayed, but with little success. Masha insists that he has no idea of the kind of person her father is, that he does not take today's meeting seriously.

But he does take it seriously! Rybakov had to go and find a clockmaker to repair the Kremlin chimes. The task was given to him by Lenin himself. And that's what made him late.

But this is terribly important! Why didn't he say so straight away? Did he manage to get the clockmaker?

Then Rybakov tells Masha about his meeting with Lenin, of Lenin's greatness and yet true simplicity, and of his faith in the future. Captivated, Masha listens to his story. The quarrel and the doubt have all gone. Everything is clear and simple. And more importantly – all is well!

Together they go off to the Zabelins, filled with joy and happiness.

The etude is over. Now all is clear to the actors. We can move over to the precise text of the play itself.

Appendix D to pages 67, 72 and 144

Mother by Maxim Gorky

To corroborate this, let's look at a literary example. Let's take Gorky's well-known novel *The Mother*.

After Pavel had been sentenced and sent into exile, Nilovna[1] tried to focus fully on carrying out a serious and important task she took upon herself: to circulate her son's speech.

Gorky describes the mother's intense joy in preparing herself for this important event. He describes how she, sitting at the station, happy and energised, held on to the suitcase which had been entrusted to her. Her train was not yet ready. She had no choice but to wait. She looked around at the people, then she got up and walked over to another bench, nearer the exit to the platform. Suddenly she felt the gaze of a man, who seemed to be familiar to her.

> His watchful eye stung her, a shudder passed through her arm, in which she held the suitcase and the load suddenly grew heavy.
>
> 'I've seen him somewhere', she thought, and with the thought suppressed the vague unpleasant feeling in her breast. She would not allow any other words define the cold sensation that has quietly but powerfully clutched her heart. It grew and rose up in her throat, filling her mouth with a dry, bitter taste, compelling her to turn around and take another look. She did so – the man, cautiously shifting from foot to foot, remained on the same spot; it seemed as if he wanted something but could not bring himself to do it ... Steadily, she walked up to the bench and sat down, carefully, slowly, as if afraid she might tear something up inside herself. Her memory, stirred by a piercing premonition of a disaster, twice brought the man up to her mind's eye – once in a field, in the countryside after Rybin's escape, and the second time – in court ....
>
> They knew who she was, she was being followed – that was clear.
>
> 'Have I been trapped?' she asked herself. And instantly answered, with a shudder:
>
> 'Perhaps, not yet ...'
>
> Then immediately, pulling herself together, said severely:

1 'Nilovna' is the patronymic of Pelageya Nilovna Vlasova, the mother of Pavel Vlasov.

DOI: 10.4324/9780203125205-37

'You are trapped!'

Looking around, blindly, with thoughts sparking, flashing and going out in her brain one after another. 'Leave the suitcase, – get out?' But a brighter spark flashed by, 'Abandon my son's words? Leave it in those hands ...' She pulled the suitcase closer to herself. 'But – leave with it ...? Run away ...'

These thoughts seemed alien to her, as if some outside force jabbed them into her mind. They burnt her, and their burns painfully pierced her brain, lashed her heart like fiery whipcords ...

Then with one great and abrupt effort of her heart that seemed to shake her entire being, she quenched all these cunning, petty, feeble little lights, saying sternly to herself: 'Shame on you!'

She felt better at once, and she grew even stronger as she added:

'Don't disgrace your son! There's nothing to fear ...'

A few more seconds of hesitation seemed to fortify her. Her heartbeat slowed down.

'What will happen now?' she thought as she watched him.

The spy called over the station guard, whispered something in his ear, pointing at her with his eyes ...

She sat further back on the bench.

'If only they don't beat me up ...'

He (the station guard) stopped by her, paused and then asked her quietly and severely: 'What are you looking at?'

'Nothing.'

'Well, there you are, you thief! So old, and still at it!'

'She felt as if his words struck her across the face, once, twice; hoarse and rough, they hurt her, as if tearing apart her cheeks, lashing out her eyes ...

'Me? I am not a thief, you liar!' she shouted from the fullness of her heart, everything in front of her caught up in the whirlwind of her indignation, her heart inebriated with the bitterness of the insult.

The false accusation of being a thief stirred a storm of protest in her, the old grey-haired mother, loyal to her son and his work. She wanted to tell everyone, every person who has not yet found the righteous way, to tell them about her son and his struggle. Proud and with the strength that comes with fighting for truth, she no longer thought of what was going to happen to her later. She burnt with desire to hurry up and tell people the truth about her son's speech.

... She wanted to, she was in a hurry to tell people everything she knew, share all the thoughts whose power she felt.[iii]

The pages, in which Gorky describes the mother's passionate faith in the power of truth, convey the great power of words. It is a wonderful example of 'revealing the life of the human spirit'. With tremendous power Gorky describes Nilovna's unspoken thoughts, her inner battle with herself. That is why her passionate words, which burst from the bottom of her heart, affect us so deeply.

Appendix E to pages 74 and 121

Juliet's soliloquy from *Romeo and Juliet*

Let's take another example – Juliet's monologue from Act 4, scene 3. It's the night before Juliet's wedding to Paris. Friar Laurence, having secretly married Romeo and Juliet, comes up with a plan that should help Juliet escape the hateful wedding, and join exiled Romeo in Mantua. She must drink a sleeping potion that will make her seem dead to her family, rather than asleep. She will then be taken to the Capulet family vault in an open coffin. In the meantime the Friar will send a message to Romeo to come back to Verona and take her away.

The action in the monologue seems to be quite straightforward: Juliet has to drink the potion. But to make the audience feel how hard it is for the young girl to follow the Friar's advice, the actress must mentally go through the character's inner struggle as she induces herself to drink it. Shakespeare reveals the depth of Juliet's feelings with staggering power. She is firm in her decision to follow the Friar's advice, has promised him to find strength and courage in her love for Romeo. But when the moment comes for her to drink the potion, she is so terrified that she is on the verge of giving up her plan and calling back her mother and her nurse, having just sent them away. Juliet pictures what would happen to her if she gives in to her fear and fails to drink the potion: eternal separation from Romeo and a hateful marriage to Paris. She makes the decision. 'Come, vial', she exclaims. Suddenly a terrifying thought stops her:

> What if this mixture do not work at all?
> Shall I be married then tomorrow morning?

The very thought of that marriage so disgusts Juliet, seems so impossible that she prefers to die, even if the potion fails to work. It occurs to her that she should have a weapon ready. She hides a dagger under her pillow, and imagines how, once the effect of the potion has warn off, she will see Romeo again, and how happy they will be seeing each other after all their suffering. Discarding all her doubts, she brings up the vial to her lips, then suddenly stops again:

> What if it be poison which the Friar
> Subtly have ministered to have me dead,

DOI: 10.4324/9780203125205-38

    Lest in this marriage he should be dishonoured
    Because he married me before to Romeo?

A new terrifying picture arises in her mind: Friar Laurence, scared of being exposed, has decided to kill her and save himself. But then she instantly recalls all she knows about him, how respected he is by everyone, his holy life, and how eager he has been to help her. The Friar that she recalls now could never betray her so. 'All will happen as the Friar promised me: I will just sleep, I won't die.' But her imagination conjures up yet another danger:

    How if, when I am laid into the tomb,
    I wake before the time that Romeo
    Come to redeem me? There's a fearful point!

In horror, she imagines a hideous picture of waking: night, the cold, the foul stench in the vault 'where for this many hundred years the bones of all my bur-ied ancestors are packed', Tybalt's bloodied corpse, and the ghosts, who they say wander around at night. A thought suddenly strikes her, 'O, if I wake, shall I not be distraught, environed with all these hideous fears …?' She is imagining horrendous pictures of her own madness, when something comes to her mind's eye that makes her forget her fear. She sees Tybalt rising from his tomb, rushing out in search of Romeo. Romeo is in danger! And Juliet, with only Romeo's image now in her mind, swallows the potion.

Appendix F to pages 106, 116 and 123

Chatski's monologue from Act I of *Woe from Wit*

Let's take as an example Chatski's monologue from Act 1 of *Woe from Wit*. Excited by being back in Moscow after a long time away, excited by seeing again the girl he loves, Chatski wants to hear all about the people he used to know, but although he asks Sofya about them, he does not wait for her answer. His mind is jam-packed, literally jam-packed, with memories, and he draws a typically sharp-witted and sarcastic series of ruthless character-sketches of them, just as he remembers them. He wants to know whether anything has changed in his absence or are things 'now' 'just as they've ever been'. He wonders if Famusov's affinities have changed, or if he still remains

> – a loyal member of the English Club
> For ever – till he breathes his last?

He is curious to know if Sofya's uncle 'has reached the end of his cavorting in this life'; and whether someone else, whose name escapes him – 'a swarthy type, with legs like a crane's', 'he might've been a Turk, or was he Greek?' – who used to flash by 'in the dining-rooms and salons', is he about? He wants to know about the three 'idle fops, who tried for fifty years to hide their age'. At this moment another memory comes to mind:

> But what of our sunshine? our treasure?
> Whose looks scream out:
> Theatre and Masquerade …

That man, who is himself obese', while 'his actors are all as thin as rakes', provokes a jolly memory. Once at a winter ball in that man's house, Chatski and Sofya discovered 'in a secret room' someone 'who made the sounds of a nightingale'.

But that memory is overtaken by yet another one. And what about 'the consumptive', a relative of Sofya's:

> … the enemy to books,
> He on the Science Board got himself a place,

DOI: 10.4324/9780203125205-39

And loudly demanded everyone to vow
That literacy and education were to be banned!

Sick to death of these people, Chatski ran away from them. But now that he is destined to see them again, he keeps chatting about them with his childhood friend, since

– having been away, when you get back,
The smoke of Fatherland is so sweet and pleasant!
Hence all my never-ending questions.

He wants know of an old auntie, the spinster, 'with a house full of fostered girls and pugs', and about the state of education in Russia, has it stayed the same?

They make such fuss of hiring a horde of tutors
In numbers, great; in price – the cheapest ...
Think of our own tutor, his cap and gown,
His raised forefinger, all the signs of learning? ...

Then a new memory flares up – the dancing master –

And Guiollment, the wind-swept Frenchman?
Has he not taken the plunge yet?
Is he not married yet to a princess,
Pulkheria Andreievna, perchance?

Nemirovich-Danchenko, who directed *Woe from Wit* many times, believed that this speech was the most challenging part for anyone performing the role of Chatski.

How can an actor deliver the speech properly unless he conceives his own picture of a 'swarthy type, with legs like a crane's', his own 'Guiollment', or his own 'Pulkheria Andreievna', etc, inspired by Griboyedov's extraordinary text?

The actor must see them in his mind's eye. This is a complex process that requires a lot of work. Often the actor is satisfied with mental images that naturally come up in the mind of anyone who reads Griboyedov's text. But these images – be they vague, or vivid – unfortunately vanish rather quickly. The actor's mental image of these people must be such that his memory of them turns into a part and parcel of his personal recollections, and in this conversation he shares only a fraction of whatever he knows about them.

Stanislavski said that if we looked at Chatski as a person rather than as a stage character, then we could understand that in delivering his first act speech, and enquiring about Famusov, or the 'swarthy type, with legs like a crane's' and all of his other 'old acquaintances', he sees them in his mind's eye as they used to be, when he saw them last time three years earlier.

Frequently, when the actor sees nothing behind the lines, he hams up an interest in those people, while being totally indifferent to them, since none of his 'old acquaintances' exist in his imagination.

We often refer to musicians or dancers, who have special exercises that allow them to practise and develop their craft on a daily basis. However, the actors do not seem to know what they should be doing at home, outside rehearsals.

Developing your character's mental images is the training for your imagination that will produce enormous results, second to none.

Appendix G to page 118

Vladimir Mayakovsky describes the process of writing the poem 'Sergei Yesenin'[1]

I start to select words.

You've passed on, Seryozha, into the world beyond …
You've passed on irrevocably into the world beyond …
You've passed on, Esenin, into the world beyond …

Which is a better line?

They are all rubbish! But why?

The first line is fake because of the word 'Seryozha'. I never addressed Yesenin with such familiarity. The word would be just as unacceptable now since in its wake it will bring scores of other fake words, that I would never have used, inappropriate to the relationship that we had, such as, 'dear chum', 'brother', etc.

The second line is bad since there is no need for the word 'irrevocably', it is there by accident, inserted for the sake of the metre. It is useless, explains nothing, in fact it is a hindrance. What does this 'irrevocably' actually mean? Has anyone ever died 'revocably'? Is there such a thing as death with an express return?

The third line is of no use due to its solemnity (the overall purpose has gradually convinced me: this is what's wrong with all three lines). Why is such solemnity inadmissible? Because, firstly, it provides an excuse for attributing evangelical beliefs in life after death to me – which I don't have – and secondly, such solemnity makes the verse quite funereal, rather than tendentious and obscures the overall purpose. As a result, I introduce the words 'as they say', instead.

'You have passed on, as they say, into the world beyond.' The line is now done. 'As they say', without being a direct jibe, subtly lowers the pathos of

---

1 This refers to Mayakovsky's poem written after the poet Sergei Yesenin committed suicide in 1925 (ed. note).

DOI: 10.4324/9780203125205-40

the verse, and simultaneously removes any suspicion regarding the author's belief in any nonsense beyond the grave. The line is done, and instantly becomes the basis defining the whole of the four-line verse: it must have a duality, with no skipping around on account of grief, but on the other hand, no need for tearful whining. The four lines must be split half-way through: two solemn lines, and two using mundane, everyday speech, making each pair stand out by contrast ...

Then Mayakovsky writes:

Now, with no further commentary, I shall cite a step-by-step process of working on another line:

1. our days for fun are ill equipped
2. our days for joy are ill equipped
3. our days for happiness are ill equipped
4. our life for fun is ill equipped
5. our life for joy is ill equipped
6. our life for happiness is ill equipped
7. for jubilation is our planet ill equipped
8. for merriment is our planet ill equipped
9. not all that well is our planet equipped for jubilation
10. not all that well is our planet equipped for fun
11. our little planet for pleasure is not that well equipped; and, finally, the last one:
12. for fun is our planet ill equipped

I could make a whole speech in defence of the final line, but now I shall limit myself to simply copying the lines from my draft copy, to demonstrate how much work goes into refining just a few words.[iv]

Appendix H to page 144

Examples from Alexei Tolstoy's *The Way of Sorrows* and Mikhail Sholokhov's *Virgin Soil Upturned*[v]

Let's take another example. This time from Alexei Tolstoy's novel *The Way of Sorrows*.

Vadim Roshchin is on the side of the Whites.[1]

'The task that had tormented him like a mental illness ever since he left Moscow – to take revenge on the Bolsheviks for the humiliation they inflicted – was carried out. He took his revenge.'[2]

Everything seems to be going just as he had hoped it would. But the thought that he may have been wrong torments him. One day, on a Sunday, Roshchin finds himself in an old churchyard. The sound of a children's choir, and 'the deacon's deep bass' comes from the church. He is burnt, stung by his thoughts.

'My Motherland', thought Vadim … 'That's Russia … That's what used to be Russia … None of it exists any more, and will never come back … The boy in a satinette shirt has turned into a killer.'

Roshchin wants to get rid of these painful thoughts. Tolstoy describes how he 'got up, and started pacing up and down on the grass, with his hands behind his back, cracking his knuckles'.

But his thoughts took him to a place 'to which he seemed to have slammed the door forcefully shut'.

He had thought that he was going to be killed, but it ended up differently. 'So what?' he thought. 'It is easy to die, but hard to live … It's to the credit of each and every one of us that we are ready to give up, for our Motherland, as it is perishing, not merely a living bag of flesh and bones, but all of the thirty-five years of our life, all our attachments, hopes … and all our purity …'

---

1 'The Russian Civil War was a multi-party civil war in the former Russian Empire immediately after the two Russian revolutions of 1917, as many factions vied to determine Russia's political future. The two largest combatant groups were the Red Army, fighting for the Bolshevik form of socialism led by Vladimir Lenin, and the loosely allied forces known as the White Army, which included diverse interests favouring political monarchism, capitalism and social democracy, each with democratic and anti-democratic variants.' Wikipedia, 'Russian Civil War', viewed 18 December 2020, https://en.wikipedia.org/wiki/Russian_Civil_War (trans. note).

2 *The Way of Sorrows* by Alexei Tolstoy. Book 3, chapter 5 (ed. note).

DOI: 10.4324/9780203125205-41

These thoughts were so painful that he let out a loud groan. Only the groan escaped him. The thoughts that whizzed around his head were heard by no one. But the inner intensity caused by his thoughts was reflected in his behaviour. Not only did he fail to join in a conversation with Teplov about 'the Bolsheviks fleeing from Moscow with their suitcases via Archangel', and 'the whole of Moscow being heavily mined',[3] etc., etc., he was barely able to stop himself from slapping Teplov's face.

In one of the most amazing and powerful moments in the novel Roshchin runs into Teleghin, the person Roshchin used to think of as a brother, his closest friend. But now, after the Revolution, they have found themselves in opposing camps: Roshchin with the Whites, Teleghin with the Reds.

At a railway station, while waiting for his train to Yekaterinoslav, Roshchin sat down on a hard wooden bench with a high back, 'he covered his eyes with his hand – and stayed seated like that for many hours, motionless …'.

Tolstoy describes other people, who sat down by him then got up and left, then suddenly, and 'apparently, planning to stay awhile', someone else sat down next to him. 'He started shaking his leg, his thigh, – the whole of the bench. He would not go away, nor would he stop.' Roshchin without moving, asked the uninvited guest to stop it.

'Forgive me. Bad habit.'

The sound of the man's voice seemed deeply familiar to him, stirring in his mind some vague but dear memories.

'Roshchin, without taking away his hand, pulled the fingers apart and squinted sideways at the person next to him. It was Teleghin.'

Roshchin instantly understood that the only reason for Teleghin to be there was as a Bolshevik counter-intelligence agent. Roshchin's duty was to report him to the Station Commandant straight away. But there was a bitter struggle in his heart. Tolstoy writes that 'he was choked with terror', pushing himself into the back of the seat, rooted to the spot.

'… If I turn him in, within an hour Dasha's husband, mine and Katia's brother, would be chucked out dead, with no boots, on a pile of rubbish under a fence … What's to be done? Get up and go? But then Teleghin might recognise me, and in confusion, call after me. Can I save him?'

His thoughts are at boiling point. But neither of them speak. Not a sound. On the outside, seemingly, nothing's going on. 'Stock still, as if asleep, Roshchin and Teleghin sat there next to each other on the oak seat. The station was quite deserted by now. The night watchman shut the doors to the platforms. Then Teleghin said under his breath, without opening his eyes: "Thank you, Vadim".'[4]

---

3 *The Way of Sorrows* by Alexei Tolstoy. Book 3, chapter 5 (ed. note).
4 *The Way of Sorrows* by Alexei Tolstoy. Book 3, chapter 10 (ed. note).

Then Tolstoy describes Teleghin calmly getting up and walking away, without looking back, and Roshchin rushing after him. With only one thought on his mind, 'Give him a hug, just one hug.'

Here's another example, from Mikhail Sholokhov's *Virgin Soil Upturned*.

On his way to join Dubtsov's team, Granddad Shchukar, exhausted by the midday heat, spread out his old coat in the shade.

Here again, externally, nothing much seems to be happening. The old man, dazed by the heat, settles under a thornbush and dozes off in its cool shade.

But Sholokhov penetrates the realm hidden from our eyes. He unveils to us Shchukar's thoughts, as he ponders things, one-to-one with himself. The living truth of the character does not fail to delight us since Sholokhov, as he is writing of his Shchukar, knows everything there is to know about him. What he does, how he speaks or moves, and what he thinks about, at various points of his life.

'Well, you couldn't prick me out with a needle from a snug spot like this till the evening. I'll have a glorious snooze and warm my old bones in the sunshine, then pay Dubtsov a visit and have some porridge there. I'll say I didn't have time to have any breakfast at home, and they'll feed me, they sure will!'

Shchukar moves in his dreams from porridge to meat that he hasn't had for ages ....

'Ah, to gobble up a nice chunk of lamb, about four pounds of it, say, for dinner! Particularly, if it's roasted with a nice bit of fat. Or if it comes to that, bacon and eggs wouldn't be bad either, only plenty of 'em ...'

And then on to his favourite dish – dumplings.

'... And then there's dumplings and sour cream, that's a holy dish, better than any sacrament, particularly when they put the little darlings on your plate and then add some more till they make a big pile, then shake the plate gentle-like to let the trickle down to the bottom and cover every dumpling from head to foot. And it's even better when them dumplings aren't on a plate but in a nice deep bowl so that there's more room for them and for the spoon.'

Famished, forever famished Shchukar, how can we understand who he is without his food fantasies, or his dreams where he is 'hurriedly, burning his lips, gulping down ... hot rich noodle soup with goose giblets ...'. And on waking, says to himself, 'what a lot of rubbish you dream about sometimes, for no reason at all! Life's just a mockery! In your sleep you sit there tucking into a lovely plate of noodles as if you could never stop, and when you wake up, all your old woman shoves at you is black bread and water with a bit of onion, damn the nasty stuff.'[5]

---

5 *Virgin Soil Upturned* by Mikhail Sholokhov. Book 2, chapter 18 (ed. note).

Appendix I to page 165

More Sinned Against than Sinning by Alexander Ostrovsky

Let's take an example from Alexander Ostrovsky's play *More Sinned Against than Sinning* and examine the law of perspective through the monologue of one of its characters, Nil Dudukin.

A famous actress, Elena Kruchinina, is in town. She has heard of a public row that happened the night before, which is blamed on Neznamov, one of the actors in the company. He is now in big trouble. The Governor is threatening to have him banished from the town. Neznamov is defiant, but 'to make matters worse, his residence permit papers are not quite right'. Kruchinina takes it upon herself to interfere on behalf of the young actor and approaches the Governor, asking him to help Neznamov. The Governor assures her he will. Kruchinina returns to her hotel after her meeting with the Governor, and finds Dudukin waiting for her. She asks him to tell her about Neznamov, and the kind of person he is. Dudukin begins his story:

I'll give you a brief account of his biography, as he himself related it to me. [Here Ostrovsky puts the first full-stop, apparently indicating a short pause, while Dudukin tries to remember everything Neznamov told him.]

He doesn't remember or know his father, or his mother, having been brought up somewhere a long way away, practically near the Siberian border, in the house of a childless but well-to-do couple, from the civil servant class, who for a long time he considered to be his parents. [The second full-stop. According to the 'laws of gradation', the intonation of a full-stop depends on the position of a sentence within the whole extract performed. We realise that Neznamov's story has only just started, and Dudukin wants to relate to Kruchinina, Neznamov's earliest childhood memories. Consequently, the full-stop is put here to give a slight emphasis to the fact that in those far-off days Neznamov's life was good, since he believed then that he had both a father and mother.]

He was loved, they treated him well, but not without an occasional rebuke, in a fit of temper, for being illegitimate. [Here the full-stop is extremely soft, since the next sentence is to give this one an explanation.]

DOI: 10.4324/9780203125205-42

Of course, he did not understand what that word meant, and only later worked out its meaning. [Here the full-stop is a little longer, since the very word 'later' conjures up for Dudukin the image of the would-be Neznamov, which he is set to reveal gradually and in great detail to Kruchinina.]

He was even given some tuition, he went to some kind of cheap private school, and, for a provincial actor, got quite a decent education. [This full-stop is even more substantial, despite the fact that the above phrase is only an add-on to the previous remark that Neznamov did not live badly. But most importantly it lays the ground for the following crucial point.]

He lived like this until the age of fifteen or so, but after that he went through a time of such tribulation that he cannot recall it without terror. [This full-stop is perhaps more like a colon, since at this point Dudukin embarks on recounting a bitter tale of Neznamov's trials and tribulations.]

The civil servant died, and his widow married a retired land-surveyor, bringing about a life of constant drinking, violent quarrels and brawls, with Neznamov being on the receiving end of it all. [Light, a very light full-stop that allows Dudukin in the next sentence to expand on what he meant by saying that Neznamov was 'on the receiving end of it all'.]

He was banished to the kitchen and was to eat with the servants; often he was kicked out of the house at night, and had to sleep in the open air. [Here the full-stop is still light but more substantial than the one before, since Dudukin's next sentence concerns Neznamov's response to the injustice and the injuries.]

Sometimes he would run away after all the verbal abuse and beatings, vanishing for a week at a time, staying somewhere with journeymen, beggars and down-and-outs of all sorts, and from then on all he got from other people was a barrage of ignominious verbal abuse. [The full-stop is needed here to underscore the crucial sentence that characterises Neznamov's inner world.]

That life made him angry, embittered, and so feral that he started to bite back like a wild beast. [Quite a lengthy full-stop, as it marks the end of a certain period in Neznamov's life, nevertheless it also contains the continuation of the narrative, as if Dudukin is getting ready to approach the essential point of his story.]

Finally, one fine day he was thrown out of the house for good; he then joined the troupe of itinerant players, moving with them to another town. [The full-stop here sounds like an ellipsis, like an unfinished phrase. As if it aims to stir the curiosity about how Neznamov's life has gone on for him in his new career: the theatre. And here's the answer.]

With no legal documents, he was deported from that town under guard, back to his place of residence. [The full-stop highlights the main event in Neznamov's life. He has no 'legal documents', he is not an equal member of society, he is subject to the whims of the police. Yet it is not the final full-stop, as the story continues. In the sentence above, Dudukin only mentions the first blow, the beginning of Neznamov's multiple 'journeys of deportation'. It is only in the next sentence that he completes his tale.]

It turned out that all his documents had been lost; he was dragged from one department to the next, until finally they gave him a copy of his court summons, with which he has been touring with commercial companies from town to town, forever terrified that at any point the police can send him back to his original place of residence. [Here it is, at long last, the final full-stop to his story, after which neither his partner nor the audience should expect anything else to be said. It is done. As far as its inflection is concerned, it has 'landed at the bottom'.]

Appendix J to page 185

Philistines by Maxim Gorky: Bessemenov's throughline

Let's analyse the throughline of Bessemenov's behaviour in the Act 2 scene.

They are about to have dinner at the Bessemenov's household. Nil is impatient and approaches Polia, no longer able to wait till she is alone. He is expecting her to give him the answer to his proposal of marriage.

Bessemenov, suspicious, is straining to catch what they are saying, then intervenes in their conversation and demands an explanation of what's going on. What kind of secret can either of them possibly have that they cannot share with him? Polia gets so flustered by Bessemenov's blunt interference, that she is lost for words. But Nil calmly declares to him that he has proposed to Polia, and has been asking her just now if she has an answer for him.

The intensive inner tempo-rhythm of suspense while Bessemenov persists in getting an answer from them, changes abruptly as soon as he gets it.

Gorky's extensive stage direction describes how Nil's words affect all those present.

> Bessemenov looks at him and Polia in amazement, with his spoon up in mid-air. Akulina Ivanovna is rooted to the spot. Teterev looks straight ahead, blinking heavily. The wrist of his hand on his knee, twitching. Polia has lowered her head.

As we see, the playwright imagines that this event, i.e., Nil's proposal to Polia has so shaken the Bessemenovs and Teterev that, for a while, outwardly they become virtually paralysed. Bessemenov does not even notice that he is holding his spoon in mid-air. He is totally engrossed by the news, which he has been utterly unprepared for, and it takes him some time to recover in the new overwhelming circumstances.

Is there a way of mastering the true internal and external tempo-rhythm of the scene?

The external tempo-rhythm is dictated by the author. Bessemenov is frozen in the position he was in when Nil spoke.

But his inner tempo-rhythm is jam-packed. A hurricane of thoughts sweeps through his brain: 'I've failed to spot it! How come? What about Tatiana? She is drawn to Nil. How could he have chosen poverty-stricken

DOI: 10.4324/9780203125205-43

Polia over my daughter? And there I was, thinking I'd do him a great favour by letting him marry my daughter. How dare he? How dare they? Ungrateful wretches! All my life, I've given them food and drink …', etc., etc., etc.

Each actor playing Bessemenov will create his own 'inner monologue' in his own way, otherwise, he would not understand what it means to be so transfixed by an event, that for a while he could hardly move.

'So-o-o', utters Bessemenov finally, and then like an automaton he repeats after Teterev, 'Actually … it's all very simple!'

Bessemenov has not yet recovered from the news that has shaken him to the core, he does not know as yet how to react to it, and as if to gain time, he resorts to putting on his usual act of an aggrieved martyr.

He will be silent, he won't say a word. If they don't need his advice, he is not going to force it on anyone.

But sticking to his vow of silence is beyond Bessemenov. With every passing second, the resentment and anger he has tried to supress are becoming more and more intense, until he can no longer hold back from reproaching them.

'… You're far from generous in your gratitude for my food and lodgings … Yours is an underhand way of living …', says he.

When Nil answers him by saying that there is nothing Bessemenov could reproach him for, since he has always paid back Bessemenov for his food and lodgings by working hard, and will continue to pay him back in the same way, that he has never lived 'in an underhand way', has always lived and will continue to live openly, that he has loved Polia for a long time, and never tried to hide it from anyone, Bessemenov, with a huge effort to control himself, still reserved, still – according to Gorky's stage direction – restraining himself, says: 'So, so! Very well … Go ahead then. Get married. We won't hinder you.' But then instantly, unable to contain himself, poses the main, as it seems to him, and most crucial question:

'But have you got any capital to live on? If it's not a secret – do tell.'

'We shall work', answers Nil. 'I am getting a transfer to the depot … And she … she will also get a job … And you will continue to get thirty roubles a month from me as usual.'

'Let's see. Promises are easy to make …', responds Bessemenov, still with a reserved, or even more reserved, manner.

The conflict between his desire to contain himself and his ever increasing rage is torture.

'Let me give you an IOU', suggests Nil suddenly, wishing to show Bessemenov that he understands that the only form of guarantee that can reassure him is a promissory note. Nil has realised that Bessemenov is incapable of a normal human relationship, which implies that the word of honour from the person who Bessemenov considers to be his adoptive son carries a certain value.

The thought of a promissory note makes Teterev ecstatic. 'You petty bourgeois!', he exclaims. 'Take his IOU note! Take it!'

Bessemenov tries to stop Teterev, but the latter, excited by the prospect of fully revealing Bessemenov's petty bourgeois nature, continues: 'Do, do take it. You wouldn't dare, would you? Your conscience will pull you up short, you wouldn't dare ... Nil, give him a receipt: I promise to pay, let's say, monthly ...'

Bessemenov understands all too well that by offering him a promissory note, Nil is contemptuously attacking him from the position of his new, hateful world-view, that is kicking aside Bessemenov and his whole world as useless old rags, blocking the way to the formation of the new man.

'Why not take your IOU? ... ' he says, still with restraint, 'it has been earned, I believe. I have provided for you – food and drink, clothes and shoes – since you were ten years old ... until twenty-seven ... Well ...'

Nil is trying to prevent the burgeoning row, sensing that a violent storm is bubbling up behind Bessemenov's outward restraint.

'Wouldn't it be better to settle our accounts later, not now?' he suggests.

'We could do it later', responds Bessemenov, still with self-restraint, but suddenly, 'he boils over' as Gorky puts in his stage direction, and loses all control: 'Only remember, Nil, from now on you are my – and I am your – enemy! I'll never forgive you this insult, I cannot! Get that!'

And then, like a burst dam, forgetting himself, as he gives vent to the long-checked feeling of hatred and helpless anger, Bessemenov, as Gorky puts it, 'screams without listening': 'Remember! Treating contemptuously the person who fed you, clothed you ... doing all this ... without asking permission ... or advice ... in secret ... And you! So meek! So quiet! Why so crestfallen? Eh? Nothing to say? Do you know what I can ...'

The torrent of long suppressed feelings of the proprietorial and hurt vanity of the man, whose brain rejects the idea of another person's right to be free and independent, even in their private life, is cut short by Nil: 'You cannot do anything! Stop this racket! I am also a master in this house. I have worked here for ten years and given you all my wages. Here, right here *(he stamps his foot, and points around with his hand – in a wide gesture)* I have invested quite a bit into all this! He who toils is the master ...'

At this climactic point, Gorky brings the new man, a representative of the emerging proletariat, who feels, with every fibre of his soul, that he has the right to live and to have a future, into collision with a narrow-minded man of property, who in his helpless anger against the new life that is sweeping him out of the way, is trying to stop the course of history.

Having heard, from his point of view, this most shocking statement, 'He who toils is the master ...', Bessemenov, as Gorky puts it, 'stares at Nil, astounded'. His only mainstay that he has believed solid – his property and money that have given him unlimited power over people – is being pulled like a rug from under his feet. Confused, he asks:

'Wha-at? You? A master? You?'

And after Nil's response: 'Yes, he who toils is the master ... Remember that!' These words fill Bessemenov with terror, because thousands just like Nil are rising up behind him, and he, Bessemenov, has nothing but threats with which to oppose them; that he is completely alone in his battle against them, this terrifying new force that he wants but cannot stop. He gives in to his wife and lets himself be taken away to his room, with a passing aside:

'Well, good! You stay then … the master! Let's see … who really is the master. We'll see!'

The evolution of the scene's tempo-rhythm is complex and diverse.

Having analysed the Act 2 scene, we move on. As we define Bessemenov's tempo-rhythm, we can see that the fundamental challenge for the actor playing him lies in the conflict between the character's inner shock at the news of Nil's marriage and his external restraint that requires such enormous will-power to sustain.

The evolution of Bessemenov's tempo-rhythm in the scene is built around the breakdown of his restraint, under the growing pressure of the seething torrent of anger and irritation.

Bessemenov's external and internal tempo-rhythms are both organically linked to his assessment of the events that occur before him, as well as his inherent nature, the subtext and his 'inner monologue'.

If we follow the throughline of Bessemenov's behaviour throughout his role, if we uncover – as Stanislavski urges us to do – the internal and external tempo-rhythms of each scene, of each section in the roles of all the other characters, we will realise that this impassioned struggle permeates the whole play; that the play's main theme, its central conflict, is the clash of everything that Bessemenov stands for, the clash of the materialist narrow-minded bourgeois world, with the new young people, who are full of life and high ideals. So the play's tempo-rhythm emerges out of this impassioned struggle between the old and the new, and, despite being varied, is fully connected to the throughline of the play's action.

This clearly demonstrates that tempo-rhythm is organically linked with the given circumstances, tasks, actions of the play, and its overall internal conceptual contents.

Appendix K to page 174

Ilya Repin's *Ivan the Terrible and his Son Ivan*

Figure A.2[vi]

Ivan the Terrible and his Son Ivan on 16 November 1581 is a painting by Russian realist artist Ilya Repin made between 1883 and 1885. The work is variously referred to as *Ivan the Terrible and his Son Ivan*, with or without the date, or *Ivan the Terrible Killing his Son*. On display at the Tretyakov Gallery in Moscow.

DOI: 10.4324/9780203125205-44

Notes

i V. Surikov, *Boyarynya Morozova*, 1887, viewed 18 December 2020, https://commons. wikimedia.org/wiki/File:Vasily_Surikov_-_<start_Cyr>Боярыня_Морозова<end_ Cyr>_-_Google_Art_Project.jpg and https://en.wikipedia.org/wiki/Vasily_Surikov.

ii The notation taken by S.G. Sokolov during the rehearsals of Viktor Rozov's play *Pages of a Life* at the Central Children's Theatre.

iii M. Gorky, *Mother*. London, D. Appleton & Company, 1906.

iv Vladimir Mayakovsky, *Polnoye Sobranie Sochinenij*. Moscow, GIKHL, 1959, vol.XII, pp.103–104, p.111.

v M. Sholokhov, *Virgin Soil Upturned* (Penguin Modern Classics). London, Penguin, 1977.

vi I. Repin, *Ivan the Terrible and his Son Ivan*, 1885, viewed 18 December 2020, https:// en.wikipedia.org/wiki/Ivan_the_Terrible_and_His_Son_Ivan.

Index

accents 136, 155, 157, 177; and correct
pronunciation 152; regional 152;
students attempt to get rid of superfluous
'accentuation' 155
active analysis 17–18, 20, 22, 38, 42–3,
46, 48, 52, 54–80, 82–4, 108–10, 113;
general principles 27–36; methodology
of 8, 13, 17–18, 20, 22, 26, 48, 56,
77, 82; period of 76; process of 35, 77;
students of 78; use of 59
actors 13–22, 26–36, 38–44, 52–6, 61–5,
67–84, 91–5, 97–111, 113–28, 134–8,
140–4, 151–5, 157–8, 160–2, 165–79,
182–6, 188–91, 200–4, 219–26, 233–5;
Alexander Lensky 91, 124, 168n3, 168,
241–2; Alexander Yuzhin 33; Amtman-
Briedit 219; Bolduman 219; Chekhov,
Mikhail Aleksandrovich "Michael"
194n1, 195, 201; craftsmanship 174; and
directors 36, 116, 125, 188; figurative
thinking onstage 117; I.M. Kudryavtsev
196; imagination 29, 38, 41, 69–70,
75, 93, 99, 101, 207; Ivan Dmitrevsky
91, 91n2; Ivan Moskvin 81, 100, 176;
Konstantin Varlamov 91, 169; Leonid
Leonidov 75, 80, 169–71, 176, 186;
liberating 9, 18, 101; Livanov 219;
Maria Yermolova 91, 124–5; Mikhail
Shchepkin 32, 35, 67, 91–2, 97, 178;
Mochalov 91; Nikolai Khmelev 13n15,
13, 13n14, 13–16, 73, 75, 80, 114,
114n2, 176; Olga Sadovskaya 91; onstage
19, 65, 149; performance 28, 32, 65, 69,
79–80, 83–4, 89, 92, 138–9, 149, 152,
167–8, 177–8; Prov Sadovsky 91, 91n1,
91, 178, 178n3, 178n3; Salvini 103,
139, 171; Tarkhanov 80, 219; Vladlen
Davydov 91; young 79–80, 185, 241
actors preparatory work 33, 69–70, 143

*An Actor's Work on Himself in the Creative
Process of Embodiment* 34, 43, 88, 90, 95,
106, 111, 112, 116, 151n2, 159, 176n1,
182n5
adaptations 3, 28, 75, 124, 137, 149,
161, 172–5, 202, 207; audacious 174;
comedic 174; independent 175; linear
137; spontaneous 174; unexpected 224
Aleksandrinski Theatre, St Petersburg
45n3, 169n4
Alexei Mikhailovich (Tsar) 213
Anna Karenina 61, 66n3, 75n3, 75n3,
143–4, 144n4, 145n5
Arbuzov, Alexei 3
The Ardent Heart 169
art 1–6, 62–3, 77–9, 81, 89, 91–4, 96–7,
115–17, 127–8, 139–40, 148–9, 151–2,
155–7, 160–2, 172, 186, 188–9, 197–8,
202–3; collections and collectors 4;
figurative 172; forms 125, 172; high 125;
historians 6n1, 172, 172n4; plastic 151
artistic directors 3n4, 9n11, 16n22, 19,
19n26, 23
'artistic recitation' 9, 89, 127–39
artists 17–18, 21, 93–4, 99, 114,
116, 124–5, 151, 173, 179, 202;
conveying depth of the actual scene
(third dimension) 156; creative 48;
genuine 161; great 79; lawlessness and
humiliations suffered by 12
atmosphere 7, 54, 78–81, 134, 184, 200,
228; backstage 79–80; creative 78–81;
good working 79
audiences 18–19, 26, 29, 62, 68–9, 80,
96–7, 116–17, 122, 124, 135, 146,
168–70, 177, 179; affected through
living mental images 122; complaining
about the actors not being heard 184;
perceiving the actor as a living human